MARINADES

MARGARET MORGAN
and
MARY MORGAN PEDLOW

Memorial

RIVERSIDE PUBLIC LIBRARY

ALSO BY LUCY VASERFIRER

Flavored Butters

Seared to Perfection

MARINADES

THE QUICK-FIX WAY TO TURN EVERYDAY FOOD INTO EXCEPTIONAL FARE, WITH 400 RECIPES

LUCY VASERFIRER

THE HARVARD COMMON PRESS • BOSTON, MASSACHUSETTS

The Harvard Common Press
www.harvardcommonpress.com

Printed in the United States of America
Printed on acid-free paper

Library of Congress Cataloging-in-Publication Data
Vaserfirer, Lucy.
   Marinades : the quick-fix way to turn everyday food into exceptional fare, with 400 recipes / Lucy Vaserfirer.
        pages cm.
   Includes index.
    ISBN 978-1-55832-827-3 (pbk.)
1. Marinades. I. Title.
    TX819.M26V37 2014
    641.7--dc23   2013036547

Cover recipes—Front: Grilled Baby Back Ribs in Asian Plum Marinade, page 211; back: Grilled Chicken Breasts in All-Purpose Tex-Mex Marinade, page 168; spine: Grilled Lamb Rib Chops in Curry Marinade, page 245

BOOK DESIGN BY DEBORAH KERNER
PHOTOGRAPHY, FOOD STYLING, AND PROP STYLING BY LUCY VASERFIRER

10 9 8 7 6 5 4 3 2 1

DEDICATED TO
EVERY HOME COOK
WHO NEEDS A LITTLE
INSPIRATION SOMETIMES

Contents

MAKING
MARINADES

MARINADES MAKE THE MEAL

Wouldn't you love knowing at the end of a busy day that something delicious and homemade is already started for dinner?

Well, with the investment of just the few minutes it takes to blend a handful of ingredients into a marinade, you can have just that. While you're out making the most of your day, doing absolutely anything but worrying about what's for dinner, your chicken breasts, steaks, or chops are hard at work absorbing tons of delicious flavor. Dinner practically cooks itself; you just have to move it to the grill. It's that easy. It's that quick. It's that delicious, and there's that much variety.

Could this be real? Wouldn't it be easier to just have takeout? Trust me when I say that marinades are the ultimate in convenience cooking. And yet the flavors are bold and vibrant, as if you slaved all day. Just give it a go for one dinner, and you'll find yourself making marinated meals night after night and feeling very clever doing it.

Commercially prepared marinated meats are mushy and unappealing and ultimately leave you in the dark about what you're feeding your family. Overpriced bottled marinades taste tired and bland and are loaded with preservatives and unpronounceable ingredients. So how do you get started making your own amazing marinades from scratch? Read on.

MARINADE DEFINED

A marinade is a flavorful liquid in which food is soaked in order to flavor it or, sometimes, to tenderize it—or both. Marinades can be thin and runny, they can be thick and have a paste-like consistency, or they can be somewhere in between.

There's some confusion between the words *marinade* and *marinate*, so let me take a moment to clarify the difference:

Marinade is a noun. It refers to the flavorful liquid.

Marinate is a verb. It's what you do with the food when you put it in the marinade.

THE PURPOSE OF MARINADES

FLAVOR

Plain and simple, marinades make food taste fantastic! They add flavor, giving variety and interest to a wide range of foods. This is their primary purpose.

TENDERIZATION

Much has been made of the ability of marinades to tenderize tough meat. Some marinades do have some tenderizing properties, but only when certain ingredients (such as tropical fruit or dairy products) are used, and these properties are quite limited in usefulness. So when it comes to tenderness, you are better off relying on matching the right cut of meat with the right cooking method rather than on marinades.

THE ELEMENTS OF MARINADES

SALTY

The salty element is the main seasoning in the marinade. It heightens and enhances and brings out flavors. Examples include soy sauce, miso, and fish sauce. And of course, plain old salt counts, too.

SOUR

Chefs refer to the sour element as the acid. Acid adds zip to a marinade and has a way of perking up the flavors. Examples include vinegar, verjus, wine, fruit puree and juice (especially citrus), tamarind, buttermilk, sour cream, and yogurt.

Acid can also affect the texture of the marinated food. It's a commonly held belief that acid in a marinade functions as a tenderizer. Generally, however, the reverse is true. Acid denatures or "cooks" raw protein—you can actually see this happening when the surface of a marinating protein begins to go from translucent to opaque, and the result is tougher rather than more tender. The exception is dairy products such as buttermilk, sour cream, and yogurt, which are relatively mild acids and do in fact tenderize proteins.

Personally, I don't worry much when I'm marinating such dense, tight-textured foods as chicken, beef, and pork because the acid affects only the surface. Seafood, on the other hand, is much more delicate and has an open texture that allows marinades to penetrate deeply; if left in an acidic marinade for too long, fish and shellfish will become tough, dry, and unpalatable.

SWEET

The sweet element balances the salt and acid and facilitates caramelization and browning during cooking. High proportions of sweeteners also make a marinade thick and sticky and tend to act as a glaze. Examples include sugar, brown sugar, honey, maple syrup, molasses, fruit preserves, and soda.

FAT

Fat adds richness and flavor and is a carrier of fat-soluble flavors. It also facilitates cooking and helps prevent marinated foods from sticking to the grill. Examples include olive oil, canola oil, sesame oil, and even coconut milk.

ALCOHOL

Alcohol adds flavor and is a carrier of both water-soluble and fat-soluble flavors. Just a little bit in a marinade will do a lot to amp up flavor. Examples include beer, wine, and spirits.

FLAVORINGS

As the name suggest, this element's only function is to add flavor to the party. Examples include herbs, spices, chiles, fruits, vegetables, onions, shallots, garlic, ginger, mustard, horseradish, coffee, soda . . . the list goes on and on.

UMAMI

After salty, sour, sweet, and bitter, umami is the fifth taste. Though it's difficult to articulate, the umami element adds savoriness, richness, meatiness, heartiness, brothiness, mouth-fillingness, and just plain deliciousness to a marinade. And interestingly, combining two or more umami ingredients together seems to increase the umami taste exponentially.

Examples include garlic, anchovies, cheese, ketchup and other tomato products, mushrooms, and seaweed. Fermented and aged ingredients such as soy sauce, miso, fish sauce, and Worcestershire sauce are particularly rich in umami.

PROPORTIONS

Every marinade doesn't necessarily include every one of these elements, and many ingredients play the role of several elements at once. For example, soy sauce adds salt, flavor, and umami; wine brings acidity and flavor; sour cream introduces acidity, fat, and flavor; and soda offers sweetness, acidity, and flavor to a marinade.

There is no hard and fast rule or formula to follow for how much of each element to use in a marinade—it's more a question of balance and desired flavor profile. But a good jumping-off point for a well-balanced marinade is equal amounts of salty, sour, and sweet ingredients with a glug of oil and the desired flavorings.

For instance, for a classic Asian-style marinade for steak or salmon, I might start with 2 tablespoons each soy sauce, rice vinegar, and honey and 1 or 2 tablespoons canola oil. To that I might add, say, some sake, ginger, and garlic. Then I'd taste the mixture, carefully evaluating the balance and flavor to determine if it's what I was going for. I'd make any necessary adjustments and then taste again before using it.

NOTES ON INGREDIENTS

When it comes to ingredients, learn how each one behaves and be discriminating with your selections. Your finished dish can be only as good as the ingredients that go into it.

SALT AND PEPPER

Use kosher salt for marinades. It's readily available and cheap, and it has a clean, crisp flavor. Do not use expensive sea salt, as its nuances are lost once it dissolves, and avoid using iodized salt, which has a harsh, metallic flavor.

Use freshly ground black pepper.

SPICES

If at all possible, toast and grind whole spices yourself rather than using purchased preground spices. The dry heat of toasting brings out the essential oils in spices, heightening their aroma and flavor.

TOASTING and grinding spices is quick and easy. Heat a small, heavy uncoated sauté pan over medium heat until very hot but not smoking. Add whole spices and toast, stirring or shaking the pan constantly, until the spices are very fragrant and a shade or two darker, 1 to 2 minutes. Watch them closely so that they don't burn. Transfer to a small bowl immediately and let cool to room temperature. Grind the spices using a mortar and pestle, spice mill, or a coffee grinder that you use only for spices.

HERBS

Fresh herbs offer vibrant, lively flavor, so they are preferable in most marinades. Both stems and leaves can be used for tender herbs such as parsley and cilantro; use only the leaves of herbs with tough or woody stems, such as basil, thyme, oregano, rosemary, and sage.

Dried herbs have a different character from their fresh counterparts, but they have their place, too. Dried oregano, for example, has a unique flavor that's desirable in some recipes. And I can't get enough of herbes de Provence, a traditional French dried herb blend (see page 188).

WINE

You should always cook with wine that is good enough to drink on its own, which rules out those inferior products marketed as "cooking wine." Don't break the bank on a fancy bottle, though—you can find some terrific wines for under ten dollars.

PAPAYA AND PINEAPPLE

Exercise extreme caution when using fresh papaya or pineapple in a marinade. These fruits may taste great, but they contain fast-acting enzymes that break down proteins, turning your meat into an unpalatable mush if left in contact for too long. Having said that, you can get good results if you use only a small quantity of these fruits and their juices in a marinade, or if the food is in contact with the marinade for only a short time. High temperatures kill the protein-eating enzymes in papaya and pineapple, so pasteurized juices and canned or preserved fruit can be used without the threat of mushy meat.

DAIRY PRODUCTS

As mentioned previously, dairy products are the only tenderizers that reliably yield pleasing results and desirable texture. Always be gentle when handling foods marinated in buttermilk, sour cream, yogurt, and whey, and oil your grill grate thoroughly to avoid sticking and tearing.

NOTES ON TOOLS AND EQUIPMENT

Using the right tool for the job not only ensures success but also makes any cooking task easier and more enjoyable.

POTS AND PANS

Quality pots and pans are a kitchen essential. A pot or pan should be heavy enough that it retains its heat when food is added, but not so heavy that it's difficult to maneuver or doesn't respond when the heat is adjusted. Its core should be made of a highly conductive material such as aluminum, copper, or cast iron for even heat distribution, as hot spots will cause scorching. Preferably it should have a durable nonreactive finish such as stainless steel or enamel so that it doesn't react with acidic ingredients and is easy to clean (pans finished with stainless steel have the extra advantage of being dishwasher safe, which I love). Handles should be oven safe as well as comfortable. Sloped sides on sauté pans allow flipping and tossing and facilitate easy access for turning food with a spatula. Except when you are cooking very delicate foods such as eggs and fish, avoid nonstick finishes because they are degraded by high heat and inhibit browning. My favorite brand of cookware is All-Clad, which combines all of these features.

Pots and pans should be large enough to accommodate ingredients without over-crowding.

- An 8- to 10-inch (small to medium-size) sauté pan is useful for such tasks as toasting spices and chiles, and a 12-inch or larger pan is a must for everything from sautéing to searing to pan-frying.

- A 2-quart saucepan is a convenient size for making most sauces, marinades, infused oils, syrups, and caramel.

- An 8-quart pot with a tight-fitting lid is just right for braising and deep-frying.

FINE-MESH SIEVE

This is my tool of choice for so many different tasks, from draining ingredients, to making berry or chile purees, to smoothing pâté, to straining infusions. A fine-mesh sieve will hold back undesirable bits like seeds and fibers, but unlike a double-mesh sieve or chinois, it will allow fruit and vegetable solids and pulp to pass through. Larger sieves made of stainless steel are the most practical because they're efficient, nonreactive, and sturdy—and can go in the dishwasher.

MORTAR AND PESTLE

When I need to grind a small quantity of spice, I always reach for my mortar and pestle over my electric spice grinder. With a heavy, generously sized marble mortar and pestle, small amounts of spices are quickly reduced to powder, while they seem to fly around and around inside the electric appliance without ever breaking down sufficiently. This low-tech option also happens to be easier to clean and much more gratifying to use, especially if you had any frustrations in your day. (I do, however, prefer my electric grinder for making larger batches of spice blends such as Chinese five-spice powder and curry powder.) The mortar and pestle is also fantastic for mashing herbs and sliced garlic, ginger, chiles, and other flavorings to a paste.

I find it helpful to start with a pounding motion (there go those frustrations!) and then, as the ingredients are crushed, switch to a circular motion to continue breaking them down to the desired degree.

BRINGING MARINADE INGREDIENTS TOGETHER

Making marinades couldn't be simpler! It's often as easy as stirring a few ingredients together. But sometimes ingredients must be cooked together in order to melt them, soften them, infuse them, or bring about flavor changes. For both quality and safety purposes, cooked marinades must be cooled completely before use—you don't want to start prematurely cooking your meat in a hot marinade, and you certainly don't want raw meat or seafood hanging out in a warm environment.

When large amounts of fruits, vegetables, herbs, or other solid ingredients are used, the ingredients can be pureed together in a mortar and pestle, blender, or food processor.

SEASONING TO TASTE

Overall, marinades should be boldly seasoned—after all, the amount of salt and pepper in the marinade must be enough to season the food that's marinated in it.

But what does "season to taste" mean? Salt is added to food to bring out its inherent flavors and make it taste better, not to make it taste salty. Food that doesn't have enough salt tastes flat and uninteresting, so it's important to know how to season correctly. Add salt a little at a time, and always taste as you go. When the flavors pop, and you can taste each individual component, the dish is seasoned perfectly. If you are unsure, simply remove a small amount of the marinade to a bowl, and season it. Once you think it's perfect, add a little more salt and taste again. Does it taste better now, or is it just too salty? Now you have trained your palate, and you know exactly how it should taste. Return this small amount to the rest of the marinade and season the entire quantity. Keep in mind that you can always add more salt to a marinade (or to the finished dish), but you cannot take it out once you've added too much.

Adding pepper to taste isn't so technical; it's more a matter of personal preference. So just go ahead and add as little or as much as you'd like!

HOW MUCH MARINADE TO USE

As a rule of thumb, each serving of chicken, meat, or fish requires 2 to 3 tablespoons of a liquid or paste-type marinade. It's a good idea to lean toward the high side of the range and use 3 tablespoons per serving for foods with more surface area—like shrimp, scallops, meat for kabobs, and cut vegetables. On the other hand, roasts and other large foods may require less marinade per serving because they have less surface area. And you will need a greater volume of chunky marinades made of diced or sliced vegetables.

THE HANDY-DANDY ZIP-TOP BAG

MARINATING inside a zip-top bag—the 1-gallon size works best—allows you to minimize the amount of marinade necessary for any food. When you press all the air out of the bag as you seal it, the marinade is drawn up and around the food, maximizing contact between the two. That means you can use less marinade than with any other vessel.

Another benefit of using zip-top bags is that it makes the whole process more convenient—no bowls or whisks required, and nothing to wash afterward. The bag will stay open by itself if you open it wide and cuff the top, allowing you to measure the marinade ingredients right into it. Then you simply shake the bag to blend everything together, or sort of squeeze and massage the bag when the marinade includes sticky ingredients like honey. Once it's well combined, just pop the food into the bag and turn it in the marinade to coat. Seal the bag, pressing out all the air as you do, and refrigerate the whole thing until it's time to cook—you don't even have to flip it. And at the end, the bag goes straight into the trash, so cleanup is a snap. Did I say handy-dandy? The zip-top bag acts as your sous chef and dishwasher all in one!

Still, if you prefer to marinate in a dish or bowl, choose one made of glass or other nonreactive material. In terms of size, the food should just fit snugly in a single layer so that the level of the marinade is as deep as possible and the food is submerged as much as possible. You'll have to flip the food periodically for it to marinate evenly.

When you're trying to decide how much marinade to make, it's helpful to remember that 1 cup is equal to 16 tablespoons, so in general, ½ cup of marinade is enough for 4 chicken breasts, pork chops, steaks, fish fillets, or thick slabs of tofu, and ¾ cup is about right for 4 servings of lamb chops, shrimp, sea scallops, kabob meat, or cut vegetables. If the marinating food is generously surrounded, that's plenty—it doesn't have to be floating or swimming (or drowning) in marinade. Using large quantities of marinade for small amounts of meat is just wasteful.

WHEN A FRUIT is marinated, the flavorful liquid is usually some type of syrup or sweetened spirit, and the term used is *macerate* rather than *marinate*. It takes approximately 1/3 cup of syrup to macerate 3 pounds of fruit. Soaking time is relatively short—just 30 to 45 minutes should do the trick.

STORING MARINADES

Marinades can be made in quantity and kept refrigerated for several days or frozen for as long as a month. Store portions of ready-made marinade right in 1-gallon zip-top bags, and then when it comes time to think about dinner, all you have to do is thaw it if necessary, drop in some meat, and breathe a sigh of relief knowing that the next meal's taken care of!

WHAT TO MARINATE

Pretty much any animal protein, including cuts large and small of chicken, pork, beef, lamb, veal, fish, shrimp, scallops, squid, duck, and game can benefit from a soak in a marinade. The flavors of tofu and vegetables can also be improved with marination. Mushrooms, zucchini and summer squash, eggplant, bell peppers, onions, oven-dried tomatoes, and cooked artichoke hearts work particularly well. Olives, certain cheeses such as fresh mozzarella and feta, and even hard-cooked eggs are sometimes flavored with marinades.

MAXIMIZING FLAVOR PENETRATION

Marinades penetrate only the surface layer of foods, and this is deep enough to have a huge impact on flavor. But it's possible to speed and increase absorption of a marinade by making slashes in the food with a knife, puncturing it all over with a fork or Jaccard meat tenderizer (a tool that pokes holes into meat with rows of needle-like blades), or cutting it into smaller pieces to increase the surface area. You can also inject marinade directly into food using a syringe-like tool specially made for the purpose. Be aware that techniques involving cutting or piercing will alter the texture of the food.

MARINATION TIME

Chicken, pork, beef, and other meats should be marinated for at least 2 hours and as long as 24 hours, and a few meat dishes such as sauerbraten require several days of soaking. Personally, I like to marinate most meats overnight for both convenience and intensity of flavor.

Seafood is more delicate and has an open texture, so marinades penetrate relatively quickly. As a rule, fish, shrimp, sea scallops, and squid should be marinated for no longer than 20 to 45 minutes. Beyond that, the acid in the marinade will "cook" the seafood, making it tough and dry. However, if the marinade doesn't contain any acid, seafood can be left to soak much longer.

Raw vegetables tend to soak up flavors quickly, so marination times of 30 minutes to 1 hour are sufficient, but longer won't hurt. Cooked vegetables, olives, and cheeses (to be served as snacks and appetizers) should be allowed to marinate at least overnight, but 2 to 3 days is often better.

In addition to the type of food, it's also useful to consider the *size* of the food when determining how long to marinate it. For example, a whole chicken could use more time in contact with the marinade than boneless, skinless chicken breasts, and those chicken breasts could use more time than chunks of chicken cut for kabobs. The more surface area a food has, the faster it can soak up flavors.

Luckily, marination time windows are fairly wide, which allows plenty of flexibility when it comes to planning.

MARINATION TEMPERATURE

If marination time is less than 1 hour, you can leave foods at room temperature to marinate. To ensure food safety, always refrigerate any foods that must marinate for more than 1 hour.

ANDREW VASERFIRER, head butcher, charcutier, and master of all things meat at Houston's popular Revival Market (he also happens to be my little brother), explains that marinating foods in a bag sealed by a clamp-style vacuum sealer such as a FoodSaver does two things: it requires a smaller quantity of marinade and it allows for better marinade contact (much like a zip-top bag). But he says that the oft-touted idea that these machines can create enough of a vacuum to open the "pores" of the meat so that it soaks up more marinade more quickly is a myth. These machines remove air but do not actually create a vacuum in the bag. However, Andrew points out that commercial producers of premarinated meats use vacuum tumblers (which look like small cement mixers) because the physical agitation combined with a real decrease in pressure does increase marinade absorption and also tenderization of meat.

For speeding the marination process at home, Andrew says the best tool for the job is a Jaccard meat tenderizer.

COOKING MARINATED FOODS

Most often they're grilled, but marinated foods may be cooked using any method at all, including searing, sautéing, stir-frying, pan-frying, deep-frying, oven-frying, broiling, roasting, braising, barbecuing, and smoking. (Two notable exceptions are Japanese *tataki*, in which the meat or fish is marinated after it's cooked, and ceviche or Hawaiian *poke*, in which the fish is never exposed to heat at all, but rather "cooked" in the marinade.)

Regardless of the way in which the food is to be cooked, it should be removed from the refrigerator and allowed to rest at room temperature for about half an hour. You will find that taking the chill off of food will allow it to cook more evenly. Another step you should take to ensure the quality of your finished dish is to pick off any large bits of spices or other flavorings clinging to the food so that they don't burn. Finally, pat the food dry with paper towels, since excess surface moisture will inhibit caramelization and browning.

MARINADES AS GLAZES, BASTES, AND SAUCES

If you're not inclined to throw out the yummy stuff that's left in the bag once the marinated food is removed, you can use it as a glaze, baste, or sauce. However, the marinade must be cooked to be rendered safe from any potentially harmful bacteria that may have hitched a ride on the raw meat or seafood.

- You can use a marinade that has had raw poultry, meat, or seafood in it as a *glaze or baste* provided that the marinade is heated all the way up to a sizzle during cooking. (Fruity marinades make particularly good glazes and bastes.)

- You can use a marinade that has had raw poultry, meat, or seafood in it as a *sauce* provided that you bring it to a boil first.

Having said that, using the minimal amount of marinade usually means that there's little left to use as a sauce, so I often make a double or triple batch and set part of it aside before adding the raw meat.

ABOUT THE RECIPES

This book contains a wide variety of marinade ideas that will take you through every shelf of your pantry, up and down every aisle at the market, and then all the way around the world.

The recipes are organized according to the main flavoring or ethnic influence. So, while Dill-Lemon Marinade could fit in the chapter on Citrus Marinades, I chose to include it with the Herb Marinades since the dill flavor is more pronounced. Similarly, the Herbed Gyro Marinade is inspired by the foods of Greece, so I included it in European Marinades rather than in Herb Marinades.

Within each recipe, the tool section tells you at a glance if a recipe can be mixed right in a zip-top bag or if it requires the use of a blender, food processor, or mortar and pestle, and if it entails any cooking. This is intended to give you a sense of how involved that particular marinade is. To use a chef term, it's there to help you do your *mise en place*.

THICKNESS VERSUS WEIGHT |||||||

THE RECIPES call for cuts of meat, chicken, and seafood according to how you would order them from your butcher or fishmonger.

For example, chicken breasts, many types of fish fillets, and certain steaks (like flatiron and flank) are called for by weight. Steaks and chops from the rib and loin, on the other hand, are called for by thickness rather than by weight because they are marketed by thickness, and it's the thickness that's important in terms of the cooking time.

AS A GENERAL GUIDE:

- 1-inch-thick boneless pork loin and rib chops weigh about 6 ounces each.
- 1- to 1¼-inch-thick rib-eye and strip steaks weigh about 12 ounces each.
- 1- to 1¼-inch-thick beef sirloin steaks weigh 1¼ to 1½ pounds each.
- 1¼- to 1½-inch-thick beef tenderloin steaks weigh about 8 ounces each.
- 1-inch-thick frenched lamb rib chops weigh about 3 ounces each.
- 1- to 1¼-inch-thick lamb leg steaks weigh about 1 pound each.
- 1- to 1¼-inch-thick veal rib chops weigh about 8 ounces each.

The yield section gives an approximation of how much marinade the recipe makes in cups and quarts. It also gives an estimation of the number of main-course servings that the marinade will cover by applying the 2 to 3 tablespoons per serving rule (see page 16) to the various foods listed in the Suggested Uses. You may notice some variance in the estimated number of servings depending on the surface area of the foods to be marinated. Note that you can always use less of the marinade for a smaller number of servings, or double or triple the recipe for a larger number.

Ingredients in the recipes are listed in an order that reflects my own personal workflow. My habit is usually to measure out liquid ingredients, then do any dirty work including dicing and mincing, and then measure out sugar and other dry ingredients, dry herbs, and finally spices. I always zest citrus fruits before juicing them. I like to chop ingredients in the order that will keep my cutting board the neatest, so I always start with fruits and vegetables. Garlic is sticky, chiles contain capsaicin (and the more it spreads on your cutting board, the more likely it is to get on your skin and irritate it), and herbs are especially messy, so I always mince them last. Adding minced and diced ingredients such as garlic to the liquid ingredients as soon as they are cut up seems to cut down on oxidation. I hope you find this workflow to be as practical and efficient as I do.

The recipe procedures are designed to be as easy to follow as possible. Recipes requiring unusual knife cuts or prepared ingredients such as julienned onions or roasted bell peppers include links to step-by-step tutorials on my blog, Hungry Cravings.

The Suggested Uses section lists foods that are particularly well suited to the given marinade, along with recommended marination times and cooking techniques.

For each marinade, I've given you a recipe intended to fit into the most hectic lifestyles and satisfy the pickiest, most demanding eaters. Both the food to be marinated and the marination time are highlighted with color for quick reference at a glance. This will give you an idea of how long in advance to get started. I've also included serving suggestions that are easy and accessible as well as fun and creative to inspire outstanding dinners every night of the week.

In many cases, I've given you more than one serving suggestion. These are my favorite recipes because they answer not only the question of what's for dinner for one night but also what's for dinner for the next couple of nights. I like to marinate and cook enough food for two or even three meals at once and then repurpose the leftovers into entirely different dishes. For example, marinated chicken breasts are served as fajitas fresh off the grill; leftovers become tortilla soup one night and club sandwiches the next. There's absolutely no easier way to meal-plan, and it keeps my hungry (and one might say spoiled) family satisfied!

Keep in mind that the suggested uses are just that—suggestions. They are my ideas and recommendations for foods and cooking methods that would work best with the particular marinade, but they are not meant to exclude other foods or methods. If a marinade lists only pork and beef in the suggested uses, but you think salmon would be great, then by all means use salmon. If a recipe suggests steaks, but you'd rather serve kabobs, then break out the skewers. And if a recipe suggests that the food be grilled but it's too cold out, then go ahead and use a stovetop grill pan or frying pan, or turn on your broiler.

CREATING YOUR OWN MARINADES

With 200 marinade recipes and even more ideas for how to use them, there's something here for everyone, no matter your taste or your mood, no matter what's in the pantry or fridge, and no matter if it's a weeknight or special occasion.

That being said, one of the joys of cooking is tinkering with a recipe or even inventing your own recipe. After you try just a few of the recipes in this book, you'll notice that many marinades have common ingredients and similar procedures. Once you get the hang of making and using marinades, and once you have a sense of which ingredients are used in what proportions and—maybe most important—what a well-balanced marinade tastes like, you'll be able to improvise.

Start by substituting one herb for another, swapping out the vinegar with fresh lemon or lime juice, or using honey in place of plain sugar. Play around with the recipes and experiment, tweaking the amount of this ingredient or that one, and see how the results change. Then move on to starting from scratch. Blend salty, sour, sweet, fat, alcohol, flavoring, and umami ingredients of your choice, tasting as you go. Think about both the balance and flavor and adjust as necessary until it tastes perfect to you. That's all there is to creating your own signature marinade!

HERB
MARINADES

These marinades are based on the vibrant flavors of fresh (and, to a lesser extent, dry) herbs. You'll find a wide variety of recipes for common herbs like rosemary, basil, mint, and parsley, plus a few for more unusual varieties such as arugula and fresh horseradish. Classics like Rosemary-Garlic Marinade and Dill-Lemon Marinade and more unique flavor combinations like Tarragon-Grapefruit Marinade might just inspire you to plant an herb garden if you don't already have one.

Rosemary-Garlic Marinade

All cooks should know and use this essential recipe. The perfect pairing of rosemary and garlic enhances both large roasts and individual cuts of chicken, pork, beef, lamb, and veal. You'll notice that the lemon juice is optional. Sometimes I use it and sometimes I don't—it just depends on my mood. It's equally delicious either way.

TOOL: 1-gallon zip-top bag

YIELD: about 1/2 cup (enough for 2 to 4 servings)

1/4 CUP EXTRA-VIRGIN OLIVE OIL

2 TABLESPOONS FRESHLY SQUEEZED LEMON JUICE, OPTIONAL

6 GARLIC CLOVES, MINCED

2 TABLESPOONS MINCED FRESH ROSEMARY

KOSHER SALT

FRESHLY GROUND BLACK PEPPER

MEASURE the oil, lemon juice, garlic, and rosemary into a 1-gallon zip-top bag and shake or squeeze until blended. Season to taste with salt and pepper.

SUGGESTED USES: whole chicken or pieces, pork loin or chops, beef tenderloin or steaks, veal rib roast or chops, or lamb leg, rack, or chops (marinated 2 hours to overnight for individual cuts and overnight for roasts), grilled or roasted

GRILLED LAMB RIB CHOPS

FOR 2 SERVINGS, add 6 frenched lamb rib chops (about 1 inch thick) to the Rosemary-Garlic Marinade in the zip-top bag and turn to coat. Seal the bag, letting out all the air. Marinate for at least 2 hours and up to overnight in the refrigerator.

Set the bag aside at room temperature for about half an hour. Remove the chops from the marinade, pat dry with paper towels, then grill over direct high heat until medium-rare, 10 to 12 minutes (or until the desired doneness), turning once. Moisture will just begin to accumulate on the surface of the chops when they are medium-rare. Tent the chops with foil and let rest for 5 to 10 minutes before serving.

These lamb chops will go with just about any starch or seasonal vegetable you'd like, but my family especially enjoys them served with garlicky sautéed greens such as spinach or chard and roasted new potatoes with rosemary.

Rosemary-Balsamic Marinade

Balsamic vinegar lends a rich sweet-and-sour note to the essential rosemary-garlic marinade, and cutting back on the garlic makes for a subtler flavor.

TOOL: 1-gallon zip-top bag

YIELD: about $1/2$ cup (enough for 2 to 4 servings)

1/4 CUP EXTRA-VIRGIN OLIVE OIL

2 TABLESPOONS BALSAMIC VINEGAR

3 GARLIC CLOVES, MINCED

1 TABLESPOON MINCED FRESH ROSEMARY

KOSHER SALT

FRESHLY GROUND BLACK PEPPER

MEASURE the oil, balsamic vinegar, garlic, and rosemary into a 1-gallon zip-top bag and shake or squeeze until blended. Season to taste with salt and pepper.

SUGGESTED USES: pork chops, beef steaks, veal chops, or lamb chops (marinated 2 hours to overnight), grilled

GRILLED RIB-EYE OR STRIP STEAKS

FOR 4 SERVINGS, add 4 boneless rib-eye or strip steaks (1 to $1^1/4$ inches thick) to the Rosemary-Balsamic Marinade in the zip-top bag and turn to coat. Seal the bag, letting out all the air. Marinate for at least 2 hours and up to overnight in the refrigerator.

Set the bag aside at room temperature for about half an hour. Remove the steaks from the marinade, pat dry with paper towels, then grill over direct high heat until medium-rare, 12 to 14 minutes (or until the desired doneness), turning once. Moisture will just begin to accumulate on the surface of the steaks when they are medium-rare. Tent the steaks with foil and let rest for 5 to 10 minutes before carving and serving.

Serve the steaks, thinly sliced, in a sandwich, on a salad, tossed into pasta, or with any starch and seasonal vegetable you'd like.

Rosemary-Mustard Marinade

In another variation on the rosemary-garlic marinade theme, mustard is the acid of choice. This version is especially good with larger cuts, as it forms a bit of a crust while the roast is in the oven.

TOOL: 1-gallon zip-top bag

YIELD: about 2/3 cup (enough for 6 to 8 servings)

1/4 CUP EXTRA-VIRGIN OLIVE OIL

2 TABLESPOONS DIJON MUSTARD

1 TABLESPOON FRESHLY SQUEEZED LEMON JUICE

3 GARLIC CLOVES, MINCED

1 TABLESPOON MINCED FRESH ROSEMARY

KOSHER SALT

FRESHLY GROUND BLACK PEPPER

MEASURE the oil, mustard, lemon juice, garlic, and rosemary into a 1-gallon zip-top bag and shake or squeeze until blended. Season to taste with salt and pepper.

SUGGESTED USES: pork loin, beef tenderloin, or veal rib roast, or lamb leg or rack (marinated overnight), roasted

ROASTED PANCETTA-STUFFED PORK LOIN

FOR 6 TO 8 SERVINGS, butterfly 1 boneless pork loin roast (about 3 pounds), or ask your butcher do it for you, and pound it flat with a meat mallet. Spread the cut surface with a spoonful of the Rosemary-Mustard Marinade and cover it with a single layer of thinly sliced pancetta, then roll and tie the roast before adding it to the rest of the marinade in the zip-top bag. Seal the bag, letting out all the air. Marinate overnight in the refrigerator. (You can also marinate the roast without butterflying or stuffing it.)

Set the bag aside at room temperature for about half an hour. Remove the pork from the marinade and place on a rack in a roasting pan. Roast the pork in a preheated 350°F oven until medium, 65 to 80 minutes (or until the desired doneness). A meat thermometer inserted in the center will register 140°F when the roast is medium. Tent the roast with foil and let rest for 15 to 20 minutes before carving and serving.

This pork roast is particularly delicious with creamy roasted-garlic mashed potatoes, but it will go with just about any starch or seasonal vegetable you're in the mood for.

Rosemary-Maple Marinade

Here the flavors of rosemary and maple come through in equal measure. This marinade shows that maple syrup shouldn't be relegated to the breakfast table. Just be sure to buy pure maple syrup as opposed to "maple-flavored" corn syrup.

TOOL: 1-gallon zip-top bag

YIELD: about $1/3$ cup (enough for about 2 servings)

2 TABLESPOONS SOY SAUCE

2 TABLESPOONS PURE MAPLE SYRUP

1 TABLESPOON EXTRA-VIRGIN OLIVE OIL

1 GARLIC CLOVE, MINCED

1 $1/2$ TEASPOONS MINCED FRESH ROSEMARY

FRESHLY GROUND BLACK PEPPER

MEASURE the soy sauce, maple syrup, oil, garlic, and rosemary into a 1-gallon zip-top bag and shake or squeeze until blended. Season to taste with pepper.

SUGGESTED USES: cubes of boneless, skinless chicken thighs or country-style pork ribs (marinated 2 hours to overnight) or salmon fillets (marinated 20 to 45 minutes), grilled or broiled

GRILLED CHICKEN KABOBS

FOR 4 APPETIZER OR 2 MAIN-COURSE SERVINGS, add 4 boneless, skinless chicken thighs (about 4 ounces each), cut into 1 $1/2$-inch pieces, to the Rosemary-Maple Marinade in the zip-top bag and turn to coat. Seal the bag, letting out all the air. Marinate for at least 2 hours and up to overnight in the refrigerator.

Set the bag aside at room temperature for about half an hour. Remove the chicken from the marinade, pat dry with paper towels, and skewer onto rosemary branches that have been stripped of their leaves and soaked in water. Grill the skewers, covered, on an oiled grill grate over direct medium heat until just cooked through, 10 to 12 minutes, turning once. The chicken will be firm to the touch and the juices will run clear when it is just cooked through. Tent the skewers with foil and let rest for 5 to 10 minutes before serving.

Sweet potato side dishes pair well with the flavor of maple syrup and are therefore a tasty accompaniment to these chicken kabobs.

Basil-Mint Marinade

Fresh and perky, this marinade is perfect to make in the summertime, when basil and mint are both abundant.

TOOLS: blender • 1-gallon zip-top bag

YIELD: about 1 cup (enough for 5 to 8 servings)

1/4 CUP EXTRA-VIRGIN OLIVE OIL

2 TABLESPOONS FRESHLY SQUEEZED LEMON JUICE

3/4 CUP LIGHTLY PACKED FRESH BASIL LEAVES

1/2 CUP LIGHTLY PACKED FRESH MINT LEAVES

1 GARLIC CLOVE, SLICED

KOSHER SALT

FRESHLY GROUND BLACK PEPPER

COMBINE the oil, lemon juice, basil, mint, and garlic in a blender and blend until smooth. Season to taste with salt and pepper.

SUGGESTED USES: boneless, skinless chicken thighs, pork chops, or lamb chops (marinated 2 hours to overnight), grilled or broiled

GRILLED CHICKEN THIGHS

FOR 8 SERVINGS, combine the Basil-Mint Marinade and **16 boneless, skinless chicken thighs (about 4 ounces each)** in a 1-gallon zip-top bag and turn to coat. Seal the bag, letting out all the air. Marinate for **at least 2 hours and up to overnight** in the refrigerator.

Set the bag aside at room temperature for about half an hour. Remove the chicken from the marinade, pat dry with paper towels, then grill, covered, on an oiled grill grate over direct medium heat until just cooked through, 12 to 14 minutes, turning once. The chicken will be firm to the touch and the juices will run clear when it is just cooked through. Tent the chicken with foil and let rest for 5 to 10 minutes before serving.

Serve the chicken thighs with a room-temperature salad of cooked wheat berries and diced heirloom tomatoes and red onions dressed with olive oil and lemon juice.

Basil-Tangerine Marinade

Basil is blended along with a whole tangerine, rind and all, for a bright, zesty marinade.

TOOLS: blender • fine-mesh sieve • 1-gallon zip-top bag

YIELD: about 3/4 cup (enough for 4 to 6 servings)

1/3 CUP EXTRA-VIRGIN OLIVE OIL

1/2 CUP LIGHTLY PACKED FRESH BASIL LEAVES

1 TANGERINE, SCRUBBED AND CUT INTO EIGHTHS

1 SHALLOT, SLICED

KOSHER SALT

FRESHLY GROUND BLACK PEPPER

COMBINE the oil, basil, tangerine, and shallot in a blender and blend until smooth. Force the puree through a fine-mesh sieve to remove the fibers and seeds. Season to taste with salt and pepper.

SUGGESTED USES: chicken breasts or lamb chops (marinated 2 hours to overnight) or fish fillets or shrimp (marinated 20 to 45 minutes), grilled

GRILLED CHICKEN BREASTS

FOR 6 SERVINGS, combine the Basil-Tangerine Marinade and 6 boneless, skinless chicken breasts (about 8 ounces each), pounded to an even thickness of 1/2 to 3/4 inch, in a 1-gallon zip-top bag and turn to coat. Seal the bag, letting out all the air. Marinate for at least 2 hours and up to overnight in the refrigerator.

Set the bag aside at room temperature for about half an hour. Remove the chicken from the marinade, pat dry with paper towels, then grill on an oiled grill grate over direct high heat until just cooked through, 10 to 12 minutes, turning once. The chicken will be firm to the touch and the juices will run clear when it is just cooked through. Tent the chicken with foil and let rest for 5 to 10 minutes before serving.

Couscous with tangerine segments and almonds is my choice for serving with these chicken breasts.

Mint-Parsley Marinade

The fresh flavors of tabbouleh inspired this marinade.

TOOLS: blender • 1-gallon zip-top bag

YIELD: about $1/2$ cup (enough for 2 to 4 servings)

$1/4$ CUP EXTRA-VIRGIN OLIVE OIL

2 TABLESPOONS FRESHLY SQUEEZED LEMON JUICE

$1/3$ CUP LIGHTLY PACKED FRESH MINT LEAVES

$1/3$ CUP LIGHTLY PACKED FRESH FLAT-LEAF PARSLEY LEAVES

$1/4$ CUP DICED RED ONION

2 GARLIC CLOVES, SLICED

KOSHER SALT

FRESHLY GROUND BLACK PEPPER

COMBINE the oil, lemon juice, mint, parsley, onion, and garlic in a blender and blend until smooth. Season to taste with salt and pepper.

SUGGESTED USES: chicken breasts or lamb leg steaks or chops (marinated 2 hours to overnight) or vegetables (marinated 30 minutes to 1 hour), grilled

GRILLED LAMB LEG STEAKS

FOR 4 SERVINGS, combine the Mint-Parsley Marinade and 2 lamb leg steaks (1 to $1 1/4$ inches thick) in a 1-gallon zip-top bag and turn to coat. Seal the bag, letting out all the air. Marinate for at least 2 hours and up to overnight in the refrigerator.

Set the bag aside at room temperature for about half an hour. Remove the steaks from the marinade, pat dry with paper towels, then grill over direct high heat until medium-rare, 10 to 14 minutes (or until the desired doneness), turning once. Moisture will just begin to accumulate on the surface of the steaks when they are medium-rare. Tent the steaks with foil and let rest for 5 to 10 minutes before carving and serving.

Serve the steaks, thinly sliced, over zesty tabbouleh or with an heirloom tomato salad.

Mint-Dill Marinade

Pairing these two light and lively herbs makes for a vibrant marinade.

TOOLS: blender • 1-gallon zip-top bag

YIELD: about 1/2 cup (enough for 2 to 4 servings)

1/4 CUP PLUS 2 TABLESPOONS EXTRA-VIRGIN OLIVE OIL

2 TABLESPOONS FRESHLY SQUEEZED LEMON JUICE

1/4 CUP LIGHTLY PACKED FRESH MINT LEAVES

1/4 CUP LIGHTLY PACKED FRESH DILL FRONDS

3 TABLESPOONS SLICED SCALLIONS

KOSHER SALT

FRESHLY GROUND BLACK PEPPER

COMBINE the oil, lemon juice, mint, dill, and scallions in a blender and blend until smooth. Season to taste with salt and pepper.

SUGGESTED USES: boneless, skinless chicken thighs or lamb chops (marinated 2 hours to overnight) or fish fillets or shrimp (marinated 20 to 45 minutes), grilled or broiled

GRILLED CHICKEN THIGHS

FOR 4 SERVINGS, combine the Mint-Dill Marinade and 8 boneless, skinless chicken thighs (about 4 ounces each) in a 1-gallon zip-top bag and turn to coat. Seal the bag, letting out all the air. Marinate for at least 2 hours and up to overnight in the refrigerator.

Set the bag aside at room temperature for about half an hour. Remove the chicken from the marinade, pat dry with paper towels, then grill, covered, on an oiled grill grate over direct medium heat until just cooked through, 12 to 14 minutes, turning once. The chicken will be firm to the touch and the juices will run clear when it is just cooked through. Tent the chicken with foil and let rest for 5 to 10 minutes before serving.

Serve the chicken thighs with a simple salad of sliced tomatoes, English cucumbers, and red onions.

Parsley-Lemon Marinade

I was thinking of gremolata, the topping that's added to the well-known Italian dish osso buco, when I created this marinade. It has a fresh, sprightly flavor.

TOOLS: blender • 1-gallon zip-top bag

YIELD: about 1/2 cup (enough for 2 to 4 servings)

1/4 CUP EXTRA-VIRGIN OLIVE OIL

2 TEASPOONS GRATED LEMON ZEST

2 TABLESPOONS FRESHLY SQUEEZED LEMON JUICE

1/4 CUP LIGHTLY PACKED FRESH FLAT-LEAF PARSLEY LEAVES

1 SHALLOT, SLICED

1 GARLIC CLOVE, SLICED

KOSHER SALT

FRESHLY GROUND BLACK PEPPER

COMBINE the oil, lemon zest, lemon juice, parsley, shallot, and garlic in a blender and blend until smooth. Season to taste with salt and pepper.

SUGGESTED USES: chicken breasts, pork chops, veal chops, or lamb chops (marinated 2 hours to overnight) or fish fillets (marinated 20 to 45 minutes), grilled

GRILLED VEAL RIB CHOPS

FOR 4 SERVINGS, combine the Parsley-Lemon Marinade and 4 boneless veal rib chops (1 to 1 1/4 inches thick) in a 1-gallon zip-top bag and turn to coat. Seal the bag, letting out all the air. Marinate for at least 2 hours and up to overnight in the refrigerator.

Set the bag aside at room temperature for about half an hour. Remove the chops from the marinade, pat dry with paper towels, then grill over direct high heat until medium-rare, 10 to 14 minutes (or until the desired doneness), turning once. Moisture will just begin to accumulate on the surface of the chops when they are medium-rare. Tent the chops with foil and let rest for 5 to 10 minutes before serving.

These veal chops will go with just about any starch or seasonal vegetable you'd like.

Dill-Lemon Marinade

The combination of lemon and dill is a perfect pairing. It's a classic with seafood, but it also does wonders to perk up chicken and vegetables. This is one marinade that ought to be in every cook's repertoire.

TOOL: 1-gallon zip-top bag

YIELD: about 1/2 cup (enough for 2 to 4 servings)

1/4 CUP EXTRA-VIRGIN OLIVE OIL

1 TABLESPOON PLUS 1 TEASPOON GRATED LEMON ZEST

2 TABLESPOONS FRESHLY SQUEEZED LEMON JUICE

2 GARLIC CLOVES, MINCED

2 TABLESPOONS MINCED FRESH DILL FRONDS

KOSHER SALT

FRESHLY GROUND BLACK PEPPER

MEASURE the oil, lemon zest, lemon juice, garlic, and dill into a 1-gallon zip-top bag and shake or squeeze until blended. Season to taste with salt and pepper.

SUGGESTED USES: chicken breasts (marinated 2 hours to overnight), fish fillets (especially salmon), shrimp, or sea scallops (marinated 20 to 45 minutes), or vegetables (marinated 30 minutes to 1 hour), grilled or broiled

GRILLED SALMON FILLETS

FOR 4 SERVINGS, add 4 skinned, boneless salmon fillets (6 to 8 ounces each) to the Dill-Lemon Marinade in the zip-top bag and turn to coat. Seal the bag, letting out all the air. Marinate for at least 20 minutes and up to 45 minutes at room temperature.

Remove the fillets from the marinade and pat dry with paper towels. Grill the fillets on an oiled grill grate over direct high heat until medium-rare, 8 to 10 minutes (or until the desired doneness), turning once. The fillets will barely begin to flake when they are medium-rare. Tent the fillets with foil and let rest for 5 to 10 minutes before serving.

Serve the salmon fillets over pasta primavera or with any starch and seasonal vegetable you'd like.

Sage-Orange Marinade

This marinade is suited to poultry and pork and is particularly welcome in the fall, when sage is the flavor of the season.

TOOL: 1-gallon zip-top bag

YIELD: about 1/2 cup (enough for about 4 servings)

2 TABLESPOONS EXTRA-VIRGIN OLIVE OIL

1 TEASPOON GRATED ORANGE ZEST

2 TABLESPOONS FRESHLY SQUEEZED ORANGE JUICE

2 TABLESPOONS DIJON MUSTARD

1/4 CUP MINCED FRESH SAGE

KOSHER SALT

FRESHLY GROUND BLACK PEPPER

MEASURE the oil, orange zest, orange juice, mustard, and sage into a 1-gallon zip-top bag and shake or squeeze until blended. Season to taste with salt and pepper.

SUGGESTED USES: chicken breasts, turkey breast cutlets, or pork chops (marinated 2 hours to overnight), grilled or broiled

GRILLED PORK LOIN OR RIB CHOPS

FOR 4 SERVINGS, add 4 boneless pork loin or rib chops (about 1 inch thick) to the Sage-Orange Marinade in the zip-top bag and turn to coat. Seal the bag, letting out all the air. Marinate for at least 2 hours and up to overnight in the refrigerator.

Set the bag aside at room temperature for about half an hour. Remove the chops from the marinade, pat dry with paper towels, then grill over direct high heat until medium, 13 to 15 minutes (or until the desired doneness), turning once. Moisture will just begin to pool on the surface of the chops when they are medium. Tent the chops with foil and let rest for 5 to 10 minutes before serving.

Serve the chops with herbed sourdough or cornbread dressing and steamed green beans.

Tarragon-Grapefruit Marinade

The slight bitterness of grapefruit is the perfect foil for sweet, anise-like tarragon. The herb has a very assertive flavor, so feel free to use more or less as you like.

TOOL: 1-gallon zip-top bag

YIELD: about 1/2 cup (enough for 2 to 4 servings)

---

2 TABLESPOONS EXTRA-VIRGIN OLIVE OIL

2 TEASPOONS GRATED GRAPEFRUIT ZEST

1/4 CUP FRESHLY SQUEEZED GRAPEFRUIT JUICE

1 SHALLOT, MINCED

1 TABLESPOON MINCED FRESH TARRAGON

1 TABLESPOON SUGAR

KOSHER SALT

FRESHLY GROUND BLACK PEPPER

MEASURE the oil, grapefruit zest and juice, shallot, tarragon, and sugar into a 1-gallon zip-top bag and shake or squeeze until blended. Season to taste with salt and pepper.

SUGGESTED USES: white fish fillets, shrimp, or sea scallops (marinated 20 to 45 minutes), grilled or broiled

GRILLED SHRIMP

FOR 2 SERVINGS, add 1/2 to 3/4 pound peeled, deveined large shrimp (21/25 count) to the Tarragon-Grapefruit Marinade in the zip-top bag and turn to coat. Seal the bag, letting out all the air. Marinate for at least 20 minutes and up to 45 minutes at room temperature.

Remove the shrimp from the marinade and pat dry with paper towels. Grill the shrimp on an oiled grill grate over direct high heat until just cooked through, 4 to 5 minutes, turning once. The shrimp will be firm to the touch, opaque and pink, and beginning to curl when they are just cooked through.

Toss the shrimp with diced red onion, celery, and grapefruit segments and dress with mayonnaise, lemon juice, and a touch of Dijon mustard for a light salad. Serve on a split baguette or on a bed of mesclun greens.

Chervil-Verjus Marinade

In this marinade, delicate chervil is paired with verjus, the unfermented juice of unripened grapes. Verjus is a subtle acid with less of a bite than either lemon juice or vinegar; it can be found at many gourmet shops.

TOOL: 1-gallon zip-top bag

YIELD: about ½ cup (enough for 2 to 4 servings)

1/3 CUP WHITE VERJUS

1 TABLESPOON EXTRA-VIRGIN OLIVE OIL

2 TEASPOONS DIJON MUSTARD

1 SHALLOT, MINCED

1 TABLESPOON MINCED FRESH CHERVIL

KOSHER SALT

FRESHLY GROUND BLACK PEPPER

MEASURE the verjus, oil, mustard, shallot, and chervil into a 1-gallon zip-top bag and shake or squeeze until blended. Season to taste with salt and pepper.

SUGGESTED USES: chicken breasts (marinated 2 hours to overnight) or white fish fillets, shrimp, or sea scallops (marinated 20 to 45 minutes), grilled or broiled

GRILLED SEA SCALLOPS

FOR 2 SERVINGS, add 6 jumbo sea scallops (about 2 ounces each), side muscles removed, to the Chervil-Verjus Marinade in the zip-top bag and turn to coat. Seal the bag, letting out all the air. Marinate for at least 20 minutes and up to 45 minutes at room temperature.

Remove the scallops from the marinade and pat dry with paper towels. Grill the scallops on an oiled grill grate over direct high heat until medium-rare, 6 to 7 minutes (or until the desired doneness), turning once. Moisture will just begin to accumulate on the surface of the scallops when they are medium-rare.

These scallops will go with just about anything. Serve them with an herb salad dressed with a light vinaigrette or whatever starch and seasonal vegetable you're in the mood for.

Summer Savory–Red Wine Marinade

Fresh savory tastes like a mix of thyme and oregano with a hint of black pepper—it's like the allspice of fresh herbs. Here's one recipe that makes use of this intriguing flavoring. I like to use a dry red wine that's neither too oaky nor too tannic when cooking—Pinot Noir fits the bill nicely, but other reds can be used as well.

TOOL: 1-gallon zip-top bag

YIELD: about 1/2 cup (enough for 2 to 4 servings)

1/4 CUP PINOT NOIR OR OTHER DRY RED WINE

2 TABLESPOONS EXTRA-VIRGIN OLIVE OIL

1 TEASPOON RED WINE VINEGAR

1 SHALLOT, MINCED

1 GARLIC CLOVE, MINCED

2 TEASPOONS MINCED FRESH SUMMER SAVORY

1 BAY LEAF, CRUMBLED

KOSHER SALT

FRESHLY GROUND BLACK PEPPER

MEASURE the wine, oil, vinegar, shallot, garlic, savory, and bay leaf into a 1-gallon zip-top bag and shake or squeeze until blended. Season to taste with salt and pepper.

SUGGESTED USES: beef steaks, lamb chops, or boneless, skin-on duck breasts (marinated 2 hours to overnight), grilled

GRILLED RIB-EYE OR STRIP STEAKS

FOR 4 SERVINGS, add **4 boneless rib-eye or strip steaks (1 to 1 1/4 inches thick)** to the Summer Savory–Red Wine Marinade in the zip-top bag and turn to coat. Seal the bag, letting out all the air. Marinate for **at least 2 hours and up to overnight** in the refrigerator.

Set the bag aside at room temperature for about half an hour. Remove the steaks from the marinade and pat dry with paper towels, picking off any bits of bay leaf. Grill over direct high heat until medium-rare, 12 to 14 minutes (or until the desired doneness), turning once. Moisture will just begin to accumulate on the surface of the steaks when they are medium-rare. Tent the steaks with foil and let rest for 5 to 10 minutes before serving.

Serve these steaks with roasted potatoes or your favorite starch and a salad or seasonal vegetable.

Fresh Horseradish Marinade

You might think that using freshly grated horseradish would yield a marinade that's too strong, but steak seems to soak up all of the root's flavor and little of its pungency. The result is delicious. Fellow horseradish lovers, let me tell you it's truly worth the effort to peel and grate a fresh root! If, however, the fresh stuff is nowhere to be found, simply use a heaping ¼ cup of prepared horseradish in its place and omit the vinegar.

TOOL: 1-gallon zip-top bag

YIELD: about ½ cup (enough for about 4 servings)

1/4 CUP CANOLA OIL

1 TABLESPOON PLUS 1 TEASPOON WHITE WINE VINEGAR

2 TEASPOONS WORCESTERSHIRE SAUCE

1/4 CUP PACKED GRATED FRESH HORSERADISH (SEE BELOW)

1/2 TEASPOON MINCED FRESH THYME, OPTIONAL

KOSHER SALT

FRESHLY GROUND BLACK PEPPER

MEASURE the oil, vinegar, Worcestershire sauce, horseradish, and thyme into a 1-gallon zip-top bag and shake or squeeze until blended. Season to taste with salt and pepper.

FRESH HORSERADISH	Peel fresh horseradish with either a sharp paring knife or a vegetable peeler and grate the fibrous root using a fine cheese grater. But exercise caution—it's pungent stuff and its fumes can irritate your eyes worse than raw onions. Work with it in a well-ventilated area and try to avoid leaning in.

SUGGESTED USES: beef steaks (marinated 2 hours to overnight), grilled; beef tenderloin or prime rib (marinated overnight), roasted; salmon fillets (marinated 20 to 45 minutes), grilled

GRILLED SIRLOIN STEAKS

FOR 4 SERVINGS, add 2 sirloin steaks (1 to 1^1/$_4$ inches thick) to the Fresh Horseradish Marinade in the zip-top bag and turn to coat. Seal the bag, letting out all the air. Marinate for at least 2 hours and up to overnight in the refrigerator.

Set the bag aside at room temperature for about half an hour. Remove the steaks from the marinade, pat dry with paper towels, then grill over direct high heat until medium-rare, 10 to 14 minutes (or until the desired doneness), turning once. Moisture will just begin to accumulate on the surface of the steaks when they are medium-rare. Tent the steaks with foil and let rest for 5 to 10 minutes before carving and serving.

Serve the steaks, thinly sliced, in a sandwich, on a salad, tossed into pasta, or with potatoes and a seasonal vegetable.

Arugula Marinade

Though arugula is frequently used as a salad green, it can also be treated as an herb. It gives this marinade a nutty, peppery zing.

TOOLS: food processor • 1-gallon zip-top bag

YIELD: about 1/2 cup (enough for about 4 servings)

1/3 CUP EXTRA-VIRGIN OLIVE OIL

1 TABLESPOON FRESHLY SQUEEZED LEMON JUICE

1 CUP PACKED BABY ARUGULA

2 GARLIC CLOVES, SLICED

KOSHER SALT

COMBINE the oil, lemon juice, arugula, and garlic in a food processor and process until smooth. Season to taste with salt.

SUGGESTED USES: chicken breasts or beef steaks (marinated 2 hours to overnight), grilled; halibut fillets (marinated 20 to 45 minutes), baked

BAKED HALIBUT FILLETS

FOR 4 SERVINGS, combine the Arugula Marinade and **4 skinned, boneless halibut fillets (6 to 8 ounces each)** in a 1-gallon zip-top bag and turn to coat. Seal the bag, letting out all the air. Marinate for **at least 20 minutes and up to 45 minutes** at room temperature.

Remove the fillets from the marinade and place on a rimmed baking sheet. Bake the fillets in a preheated 450°F oven until just cooked through, 12 to 13 minutes. The fillets will begin to flake when they are just cooked through.

Serve the halibut fillets on a bed of orzo tossed with halved cherry tomatoes and olive oil and topped with shavings of Parmigiano-Reggiano and toasted pine nuts or walnut pieces.

Scarborough Fair Marinade

The combination of herbs made famous in song is featured in this marinade.

TOOL: 1-gallon zip-top bag

YIELD: about 1/2 cup (enough for 2 to 4 servings)

1/4 CUP EXTRA-VIRGIN OLIVE OIL

2 TABLESPOONS PINOT GRIS OR OTHER DRY WHITE WINE

1 GARLIC CLOVE, MINCED

1 TABLESPOON MINCED FRESH FLAT-LEAF PARSLEY

2 TEASPOONS MINCED FRESH SAGE

2 TEASPOONS MINCED FRESH ROSEMARY

1 1/2 TEASPOONS MINCED FRESH THYME

KOSHER SALT

FRESHLY GROUND BLACK PEPPER

MEASURE the oil, wine, garlic, parsley, sage, rosemary, and thyme into a 1-gallon zip-top bag and shake or squeeze until blended. Season to taste with salt and pepper.

SUGGESTED USES: chicken breasts, turkey breast cutlets, pork chops, veal chops, or lamb chops (marinated 2 hours to overnight), grilled

GRILLED CHICKEN BREASTS

FOR 4 SERVINGS, add 4 boneless, skinless chicken breasts (about 8 ounces each), pounded to an even thickness of 1/2 to 3/4 inch, to the Scarborough Fair Marinade in the zip-top bag and turn to coat. Seal the bag, letting out all the air. Marinate for at least 2 hours and up to overnight in the refrigerator.

Set the bag aside at room temperature for about half an hour. Remove the chicken from the marinade, pat dry with paper towels, then grill on an oiled grill grate over direct high heat until just cooked through, 10 to 12 minutes, turning once. The chicken will be firm to the touch and the juices will run clear when it is just cooked through. Tent the chicken with foil and let rest for 5 to 10 minutes before serving.

Serve the chicken breasts with rice pilaf and green beans or your favorite starch and seasonal vegetable.

Green Goddess Marinade

Chock-full of herbs and inspired by the retro salad dressing, this marinade is a delicious way to flavor chicken and fish.

TOOLS: blender • 1-gallon zip-top bag

YIELD: about 1 1/4 cups (enough for 6 to 10 servings, or 4 servings and a salad)

1/2 CUP BUTTERMILK

1/2 CUP SOUR CREAM

1 TABLESPOON FRESHLY SQUEEZED LEMON JUICE

1 ANCHOVY FILLET

2 TABLESPOONS LOOSELY PACKED FRESH FLAT-LEAF PARSLEY LEAVES

2 TABLESPOONS LOOSELY PACKED FRESH CHERVIL LEAVES

1 TABLESPOON LOOSELY PACKED FRESH TARRAGON LEAVES

1 TABLESPOON MINCED FRESH CHIVES

1 GARLIC CLOVE, SLICED

KOSHER SALT

FRESHLY GROUND BLACK PEPPER

COMBINE the buttermilk, sour cream, lemon juice, anchovy, parsley, chervil, tarragon, chives, and garlic in a blender and blend until smooth. Season to taste with salt and pepper.

SUGGESTED USES: chicken breasts (marinated 2 hours to overnight) or fish fillets or shrimp (marinated 20 to 45 minutes), grilled

SALAD WITH GRILLED CHICKEN BREASTS

FOR 4 SERVINGS, combine about 1/2 cup of the Green Goddess Marinade and 4 boneless, skinless chicken breasts (about 8 ounces each), pounded to an even thickness of 1/2 to 3/4 inch, in a 1-gallon zip-top bag and turn to coat. Seal the bag, letting out all the air. Marinate for at least 2 hours and up to overnight in the refrigerator.

Set the bag aside at room temperature for about half an hour. Remove the chicken from the marinade, pat dry with paper towels, then grill on an oiled grill grate over direct high heat until just cooked through, 10 to 12 minutes, turning once. The chicken will be firm to the touch and the juices will run clear when it is just cooked through. Tent the chicken with foil and let rest for 5 to 10 minutes before carving and serving.

Serve the chicken breasts, thinly sliced, over a salad of butter lettuce or mesclun greens. Use the remaining marinade as the salad dressing.

Marinade for Artichoke Hearts

Why buy a jar of marinated artichoke hearts when you can make your own? Cook and quarter fresh artichokes if they're in season or thaw frozen ones and drain them well before soaking them in the marinade for several days. Marinated artichokes keep for a week or two in a tightly sealed container in the refrigerator. Serve at room temperature.

TOOL: 1-gallon zip-top bag

YIELD: about 1 cup (enough for 6 to 8 servings)

3/4 CUP EXTRA-VIRGIN OLIVE OIL

3 TABLESPOONS FRESHLY SQUEEZED LEMON JUICE

2 TABLESPOONS WHITE WINE VINEGAR

4 GARLIC CLOVES, MINCED

1 TEASPOON DRIED BASIL

1 TEASPOON DRIED OREGANO

1/2 TEASPOON DRIED THYME

1 TEASPOON CRUSHED RED PEPPER

KOSHER SALT

FRESHLY GROUND BLACK PEPPER

MEASURE the oil, lemon juice, vinegar, garlic, basil, oregano, thyme, and crushed red pepper into a 1-gallon zip-top bag and shake or squeeze until blended. Season to taste with salt and black pepper.

MARINATED ARTICHOKE HEARTS

FOR 6 TO 8 SERVINGS, add 1 pound cooked and quartered artichoke hearts to the Marinade for Artichoke Hearts in the zip-top bag and turn to coat. Seal the bag, letting out all the air. Marinate for at least 3 days and up 4 days in the refrigerator.

Serve the marinated artichoke hearts as a part of an antipasto platter, in a sandwich, or tossed into pasta.

Herb-Infused Olive Oil Marinade

Marinated cheese, olives, tomatoes, and peppers make wonderful tidbits to serve when company comes over—that is, if you can resist depleting the supply every time you open the refrigerator door. Packed into jars, they make lovely hostess gifts (note, however, that jars will require quite a bit more marinade than a zip-top bag). A good, fruity olive oil is the key to this marinade. Marinated foods keep for a week or two tightly sealed in the refrigerator. Serve at room temperature.

TOOLS: saucepan • 1-gallon zip-top bag

YIELD: about 1 cup (enough for 6 to 8 servings)

1 CUP EXTRA-VIRGIN OLIVE OIL

3 FRESH ROSEMARY SPRIGS

2 FRESH THYME SPRIGS

2 FRESH OREGANO SPRIGS

2 STRIPS LEMON ZEST

2 GARLIC CLOVES, SLICED

2 BAY LEAVES

1/4 TEASPOON CRUSHED RED PEPPER

GENEROUS PINCH OF FRESHLY GROUND BLACK PEPPER

COMBINE the oil, rosemary, thyme, oregano, lemon zest, garlic, bay leaves, crushed red pepper, and black pepper in a small saucepan and bring to a boil. Remove from the heat and let cool to room temperature.

MARINATED CHEESE, OLIVES, OVEN-DRIED TOMATOES, OR ROASTED BELL PEPPERS

FOR 6 TO 8 SERVINGS, combine the Herb-Infused Olive Oil Marinade and 1 pound fresh mozzarella perlini, bite-size cubes of feta, or slices of chèvre; 10 to 12 ounces kalamata olives; 12 oven-dried plum tomatoes (recipe follows); or 3 or 4 roasted red bell peppers cut into strips in a 1-gallon zip-top bag and turn to coat. Seal the bag, letting out all the air. Marinate for at least 2 days and up 4 days in the refrigerator.

Serve the marinated foods as an hors d'oeuvre or as part of an antipasto platter. Toss into pasta or salad or layer into a sandwich. Be sure there's plenty of bread to sop up all that luscious oil.

Oven-Dried Tomatoes

Oven-dried tomatoes are baked in a low oven for a long period of time until much of their moisture is driven off. They have a meaty texture and concentrated flavor and are ideal for marinating and adding to pastas, salads, and sandwiches.

YIELD: 72 pieces

12 PLUM TOMATOES, CUT INTO SIXTHS
2 TABLESPOONS EXTRA-VIRGIN OLIVE OIL
KOSHER SALT
FRESHLY GROUND BLACK PEPPER

PREHEAT the oven to 225°F. Toss together the tomatoes and olive oil in a small bowl. Arrange the tomatoes, cut sides up, in a single layer on a rimmed baking sheet and season to taste with salt and pepper. Bake until slightly dried but still tender, 2 to 2 1/2 hours. Let cool. Leftovers can be stored, tightly covered in the refrigerator, for several days.

SPICE
MARINADES

PEPPERCORNS, PAPRIKA, SAFFRON, AND JUNIPER BERRIES STAR IN
RECIPES SUCH AS Mixed Peppercorn Marinade, Spicy Cajun
Marinade, AND Saffron–White Wine Marinade. YOU MAY
ALREADY HAVE ALL OF THE INGREDIENTS ON HAND IN YOUR PANTRY,
BUT IT'S WORTH CHECKING THAT YOUR DRY SPICES, WHICH SHOULD
BE KEPT NO MORE THAN A FEW MONTHS FOR THE BEST FLAVOR, ARE
RELATIVELY FRESH AND AROMATIC. PURCHASE SPICES IN BULK AND
GET ONLY AS MUCH AS YOU'LL USE IN A SHORT PERIOD OF TIME, AND
YOU'LL NEVER HAVE TO WORRY ABOUT STALE SPICES AGAIN—AND
YOU'LL SAVE MONEY, TOO.

Mixed Peppercorn Marinade

When peppercorns are coarsely cracked instead of being finely ground, their flavor and texture are elevated from a supporting role to the star of the dish. Crack peppercorns in a mortar and pestle, or seal them in a plastic bag and tap them with a rolling pin, meat mallet, or the bottom of a small, heavy sauté pan.

TOOL: 1-gallon zip-top bag

YIELD: about 1/2 cup (enough for 2 to 4 servings)

1/4 CUP EXTRA-VIRGIN OLIVE OIL

1/4 CUP WHITE WINE VINEGAR

1/2 TEASPOON GRANULATED GARLIC

1/2 TEASPOON FRESHLY CRACKED BLACK PEPPERCORNS

1/2 TEASPOON FRESHLY CRACKED DRIED GREEN PEPPERCORNS

1/2 TEASPOON FRESHLY CRUSHED PINK PEPPERCORNS

1/4 TEASPOON FRESHLY CRACKED WHITE PEPPERCORNS

KOSHER SALT

MEASURE the oil, vinegar, granulated garlic, and black, green, pink, and white peppercorns into a 1-gallon zip-top bag and shake or squeeze until blended. Season to taste with salt.

SUGGESTED USES: chicken breasts, pork chops, or beef steaks (marinated 2 hours to overnight), fish fillets, shrimp, or sea scallops (marinated 20 to 45 minutes), or vegetables (marinated 30 minutes to 1 hour), grilled or broiled

GRILLED RIB-EYE OR STRIP STEAKS

FOR 4 SERVINGS, add 4 boneless rib-eye or strip steaks (1 to 1 1/4 inches thick) to the Mixed Peppercorn Marinade in the zip-top bag and turn to coat. Seal the bag, letting out all the air. Marinate for at least 2 hours and up to overnight in the refrigerator.

Set the bag aside at room temperature for about half an hour. Remove the steaks from the marinade, pat dry with paper towels, then grill over direct high heat until medium-rare, 12 to 14 minutes (or until the desired doneness), turning once. Moisture will just begin to accumulate on the surface of the steaks when they are medium-rare. Tent the steaks with foil and let rest for 5 to 10 minutes before carving and serving.

Serve the steaks, thinly sliced, in a sandwich, on a salad, tossed into pasta—especially fettuccine Alfredo—or with any starch and seasonal vegetable you'd like.

Paprika Marinade

My mother always seasons chicken and pork with plenty of paprika, cayenne, granulated garlic, and copious amounts of black pepper. (Now that I think about it, I can't remember if she uses the granulated garlic or if it's something I added somewhere along the way.) The blend is spicy and delicious, and as an added bonus it gives everything it's applied to a most appetizing burnished red color. It's my idea of comfort food, so I decided to reinterpret the spice mixture in marinade form. The fresh onion and garlic make it all the more intense. I'm pretty sure Mom would approve.

TOOL: 1-gallon zip-top bag

YIELD: about 3/4 cup (enough for 4 to 6 servings)

1/4 CUP PLUS 2 TABLESPOONS CANOLA OIL

1/2 CUP GRATED YELLOW ONION

2 GARLIC CLOVES, MINCED

2 TABLESPOONS PAPRIKA

1 TEASPOON FRESHLY GROUND BLACK PEPPER

1/2 TEASPOON CAYENNE PEPPER

KOSHER SALT

MEASURE the oil, onion, garlic, paprika, black pepper, and cayenne into a 1-gallon zip-top bag and shake or squeeze until blended. Season to taste with salt.

SUGGESTED USES: whole chicken (marinated overnight) or pork loin, tenderloin, or chops (marinated 2 hours to overnight for individual cuts and overnight for roasts), grilled or roasted

ROASTED CHICKEN

FOR 4 TO 6 SERVINGS, add **1 whole chicken (3½ to 4 pounds)** to the Paprika Marinade in the zip-top bag and turn to coat, trying to get some of the marinade into the cavity. Seal the bag, letting out all the air. Marinate **overnight** in the refrigerator.

Set the bag aside at room temperature for about half an hour. Remove the chicken from the marinade and truss. Roast the chicken on a rack in a roasting pan in a preheated 400°F oven until just cooked through, 55 to 65 minutes. The drumsticks will wiggle freely in their joints, the meat of the drumsticks will have noticeably shrunk away from the knuckles, the juices will run clear, and a meat thermometer inserted in the thickest part of the breast will register 160°F when it is just cooked through. Tent the chicken loosely with foil and let rest for 15 to 20 minutes before carving and serving (the internal temperature should rise to 165°F).

Serve the chicken with buttery mashed potatoes and a salad or seasonal vegetable.

Spicy Cajun Marinade

If it's good blackened, it's good in this marinade.

TOOL: 1-gallon zip-top bag

YIELD: about 1/3 cup (enough for about 2 servings)

1/4 CUP CANOLA OIL

1 TEASPOON FRESHLY SQUEEZED LEMON JUICE

2 GARLIC CLOVES, MINCED

1/2 TEASPOON DRIED THYME

1/2 TEASPOON DRIED OREGANO

1 TEASPOON ONION POWDER

1 TEASPOON PAPRIKA

1 TEASPOON FRESHLY GROUND BLACK PEPPER

1/2 TEASPOON FRESHLY GROUND WHITE PEPPER

1/2 TEASPOON CAYENNE PEPPER

KOSHER SALT

MEASURE the oil, lemon juice, garlic, thyme, oregano, onion powder, paprika, black pepper, white pepper, and cayenne into a 1-gallon zip-top bag and shake or squeeze until blended. Season to taste with salt.

SUGGESTED USES: chicken breasts or beef steaks (marinated 2 hours to overnight) or salmon fillets, shrimp, or sea scallops (marinated 20 to 45 minutes), grilled or seared; catfish fillets (marinated 20 to 45 minutes), baked

BAKED CATFISH FILLETS

FOR 2 SERVINGS, add 2 skinned, boneless catfish fillets (6 to 8 ounces each) to the Spicy Cajun Marinade in the zip-top bag and turn to coat. Seal the bag, letting out all the air. Marinate for at least 20 minutes and up to 45 minutes at room temperature.

Remove the fillets from the marinade and place on a rimmed baking sheet. Bake the fillets in a preheated 450°F oven until cooked through, 14 to 16 minutes. The fillets will flake when they are cooked through.

Serve the catfish fillets with dirty rice and a seasonal vegetable; pile them with shredded lettuce, sliced tomato, pickle chips, and Tabasco mayo inside toasted split baguettes like a po'boy sandwich; or serve them with any other accompaniments that would pair well with blackened fish.

Saffron–White Wine Marinade

Saffron gives this marinade a golden hue and deep, earthy flavor. If you don't have a mortar and pestle, you can crumble the saffron threads between your thumb and forefinger to release the flavor.

TOOLS: mortar and pestle • 1-gallon zip-top bag

YIELD: about 1/3 cup (enough for about 2 servings)

3 TABLESPOONS EXTRA-VIRGIN OLIVE OIL

2 TABLESPOONS PINOT GRIS OR OTHER DRY WHITE WINE

1 GARLIC CLOVE, MINCED

GENEROUS PINCH OF SAFFRON, GROUND WITH A MORTAR AND PESTLE

KOSHER SALT

FRESHLY GROUND BLACK PEPPER

MEASURE the oil, wine, garlic, and saffron into a 1-gallon zip-top bag and shake or squeeze until blended. Season to taste with salt and pepper.

SUGGESTED USES: chicken breasts (marinated 2 hours to overnight) or shrimp or sea scallops (marinated 20 to 45 minutes), grilled; halibut fillets (marinated 20 to 45 minutes), baked

BAKED HALIBUT FILLETS

FOR 2 SERVINGS, add 2 skinned, boneless halibut fillets (6 to 8 ounces each) to the Saffron–White Wine Marinade in the zip-top bag and turn to coat. Seal the bag, letting out all the air. Marinate for at least 20 minutes and up to 45 minutes at room temperature.

Remove the fillets from the marinade and pat dry with paper towels. Bake the fillets on a rimmed baking sheet in a preheated 450°F oven until just cooked through, 12 to 13 minutes. The fillets will begin to flake when they are just cooked through.

Serve the halibut fillets with risotto with green peas.

Juniper-Rosemary Marinade

Juniper, which gives gin its distinctive piney aroma and flavor, pairs perfectly with rosemary. Juniper berries are available in the spice section of most gourmet shops.

TOOL: 1-gallon zip-top bag

YIELD: about 1/3 cup (enough for about 2 servings)

1/4 CUP PINOT NOIR OR OTHER DRY RED WINE

1 TABLESPOON EXTRA-VIRGIN OLIVE OIL

1 SHALLOT, MINCED

1 GARLIC CLOVE, MINCED

1 TEASPOON MINCED FRESH ROSEMARY

2 TEASPOONS JUNIPER BERRIES, CRUSHED

KOSHER SALT

FRESHLY GROUND BLACK PEPPER

MEASURE the wine, oil, shallot, garlic, rosemary, and juniper berries into a 1-gallon zip-top bag and shake or squeeze until blended. Season to taste with salt and pepper.

SUGGESTED USES: pork chops, beef steaks, or lamb chops (marinated 2 hours to overnight), grilled

GRILLED PORK LOIN OR RIB CHOPS

FOR 2 SERVINGS, add 2 boneless pork loin or rib chops (about 1 inch thick) to the Juniper-Rosemary Marinade in the zip-top bag and turn to coat. Seal the bag, letting out all the air. Marinate for at least 2 hours and up to overnight in the refrigerator.

Set the bag aside at room temperature for about half an hour. Remove the chops from the marinade, pat dry with paper towels, then grill over direct high heat until medium, 13 to 15 minutes (or until the desired doneness), turning once. Moisture will just begin to pool on the surface of the chops when they are medium. Tent the chops with foil and let rest for 5 to 10 minutes before serving.

Serve the chops with roasted rosemary potatoes and a seasonal vegetable.

AROMATIC VEGETABLE AND TOMATO
MARINADES

SOME VEGETABLES—CARROTS, CELERY, ONIONS, BELL PEPPERS, AND GARLIC, FOR EXAMPLE—ARE SO BOLD THEY'LL LEND THEIR PERFUME TO WHATEVER OTHER FOODS THEY COME IN CONTACT WITH, AND ARE THUS KNOWN AS AROMATICS. THESE VEGETABLES CAN BE USED SINGLY OR IN COMBINATION, AND THEY HAVE DIFFERENT EFFECTS DEPENDING ON WHETHER THEY'RE RAW OR COOKED. SOME OF THE SIMPLEST YET MOST SURPRISING AND TRANSFORMATIVE RECIPES, SUCH AS MIREPOIX MARINADE AND CAJUN TRINITY MARINADE, APPEAR IN THIS CHAPTER.

Mirepoix Marinade

The first vocabulary term any culinary student learns is *mirepoix*. It's a vegetable mixture comprising two parts onion to one part each carrot and celery. This aromatic blend is the foundation of classical French cooking and a critical flavoring for stocks and sauces. It's also often used in marinades for roasted and braised foods. According to my husband, poultry buried overnight in mirepoix marinade and then roasted tastes like chicken soup or Thanksgiving turkey.

TOOL: 1-gallon zip-top bag

YIELD: about 6 cups (enough for 4 to 6 servings)

2 TABLESPOONS EXTRA-VIRGIN OLIVE OIL

1 YELLOW ONION, JULIENNED (SEE PAGE 297)

2 CELERY RIBS, DICED

2 CARROTS, DICED

4 GARLIC CLOVES, MINCED

1/4 TEASPOON DRIED THYME

1 BAY LEAF, CRUMBLED

KOSHER SALT

FRESHLY GROUND BLACK PEPPER

MEASURE the oil, onion, celery, carrots, garlic, thyme, and bay leaf into a 1-gallon zip-top bag and shake or squeeze until blended. Season to taste with salt and pepper.

SUGGESTED USES: whole chicken or turkey (triple the marinade for a 12-pound bird) or pieces, pork loin, or beef prime rib (marinated overnight), roasted

ROASTED CHICKEN

FOR 4 TO 6 SERVINGS, add 1 whole chicken (3^1/$_2$ to 4 pounds) to the Mirepoix Marinade in the zip-top bag and turn to coat, trying to get some of the marinade into the cavity. Seal the bag, letting out all the air. Marinate overnight in the refrigerator.

Set the bag aside at room temperature for about half an hour. Remove the chicken from the marinade, pat dry with paper towels, picking off any vegetables and bits of bay leaf, and truss. Roast the chicken on a rack in a roasting pan in a preheated 400°F oven until just cooked through, 55 to 65 minutes. The drumsticks will wiggle freely in their joints, the meat of the drumsticks will have noticeably shrunk away from the knuckles, the juices will run clear, and a meat thermometer inserted in the thickest part of the breast will register 160°F when it is just cooked through. Tent the chicken with foil and let rest for 15 to 20 minutes before carving and serving (the internal temperature should rise to 165°F).

Serve the chicken with your favorite comfort food side dishes. I like it with buttery mashed potatoes and peas.

Cajun Trinity Marinade

The combination of onion, celery, and green bell pepper, commonly known as the trinity, is to Cajun cooking what onion, celery, and carrot *mirepoix* is to French—the highly aromatic medley forms the flavor base of the cuisine. Though it's usually sautéed, it can lend its flavor in raw form in a marinade. You can find blackening spice in the spice section of most grocery stores.

TOOL: 1-gallon zip-top bag

YIELD: about 2 1/4 cups (enough for about 6 servings)

2 TABLESPOONS CANOLA OIL

1 TABLESPOON FRESHLY SQUEEZED LEMON JUICE

2 TEASPOONS Tabasco SAUCE

1 CUP DICED YELLOW ONION

1/2 CUP DICED CELERY

1/2 CUP DICED GREEN BELL PEPPER

2 GARLIC CLOVES, MINCED

1 BAY LEAF, CRUMBLED

2 TEASPOONS BLACKENING SPICE

KOSHER SALT

FRESHLY GROUND BLACK PEPPER

MEASURE the oil, lemon juice, Tabasco, onion, celery, bell pepper, garlic, bay leaf, and blackening spice into a 1-gallon zip-top bag and shake or squeeze until blended. Season to taste with salt and pepper.

SUGGESTED USES: whole chicken or beef tenderloin (marinated overnight), roasted or smoked

SMOKED CHICKEN

FOR 4 TO 6 SERVINGS, add 1 whole chicken (3¹/₂ to 4 pounds) to the Cajun Trinity Marinade in the zip-top bag and turn to coat, trying to get some of the marinade into the cavity. Seal the bag, letting out all the air. Marinate overnight in the refrigerator.

Set the bag aside at room temperature for about half an hour. Remove the chicken from the marinade, pat dry with paper towels, picking off any vegetables and bits of bay leaf, and truss. Smoke the chicken in a 200° to 225°F smoker until just cooked through, 3 to 4 hours. The drumsticks will wiggle freely in their joints, the meat of the drumsticks will have noticeably shrunk away from the knuckles, the juices will run clear, and a meat thermometer inserted in the thickest part of the breast will register 160°F when it is just cooked through. Tent the chicken with foil and let rest for 15 to 20 minutes before carving and serving (the internal temperature should rise to 165°F).

Serve the chicken with dirty rice or cornbread or shred it to use in gumbo or jambalaya.

Simple Garlic Marinade

There's nothing to distract from the bold, pungent flavor of garlic in this versatile, no-fuss marinade.

TOOL: 1-gallon zip-top bag

YIELD: about $1/2$ cup (enough for 2 to 6 servings)

¼ CUP PLUS 2 TABLESPOONS EXTRA-VIRGIN OLIVE OIL

6 GARLIC CLOVES, MINCED

1 BAY LEAF, CRUMBLED

GENEROUS PINCH OF CRUSHED RED PEPPER

KOSHER SALT

FRESHLY GROUND BLACK PEPPER

MEASURE the oil, garlic, bay leaf, and crushed red pepper into a 1-gallon zip-top bag and shake or squeeze until blended. Season to taste with salt and black pepper.

SUGGESTED USES: chicken breasts, pork chops, beef steaks, veal chops, or lamb chops (marinated 2 hours to overnight), fish fillets, shrimp, sea scallops, or squid (marinated 20 to 45 minutes), or vegetables (marinated 30 minutes to 1 hour), grilled

GRILLED FLANK STEAK

FOR 4 TO 6 SERVINGS, add 2 flank steaks (1 to 1 $1/2$ pounds each) to the Simple Garlic Marinade in the zip-top bag and turn to coat. Seal the bag, letting out all the air. Marinate for at least 2 hours and up to overnight in the refrigerator.

Set the bag aside at room temperature for about half an hour. Remove the steaks from the marinade and pat dry with paper towels, picking off any bits of bay leaf. Grill over direct high heat until medium-rare, 10 to 12 minutes (or until the desired doneness), turning once. Moisture will just begin to accumulate on the surface of the steaks when they are medium-rare. Tent the steaks with foil and let rest for 5 to 10 minutes before carving and serving.

Serve the steaks, thinly sliced, in a sandwich, on a salad, tossed into pasta, or with any starch and seasonal vegetable you'd like.

Roasted Garlic Marinade

Sweet and mellow roasted garlic produces a marinade that has all of the flavor but little of the pungency of Simple Garlic Marinade (page 60).

TOOLS: small baking dish • blender • 1-gallon zip-top bag

YIELD: about 1/2 cup (enough for 2 to 4 servings)

2 HEADS GARLIC

2 FRESH THYME SPRIGS

2 FRESH ROSEMARY SPRIGS

1/4 CUP PLUS 2 TABLESPOONS EXTRA-VIRGIN OLIVE OIL

KOSHER SALT

FRESHLY GROUND BLACK PEPPER

PREHEAT the oven to 350°F. Cut the stem end off the heads of garlic to expose the cloves within. Place the garlic in a small baking dish, add the thyme and rosemary, drizzle with 2 tablespoons of the olive oil, and cover tightly with aluminum foil. Roast until meltingly tender and golden brown, 40 to 45 minutes. Let cool to room temperature, discard the thyme and rosemary sprigs, and peel the garlic. Transfer the roasted garlic and its oil to a blender, add the remaining 1/4 cup olive oil, and blend until smooth. Season to taste with salt and pepper.

SUGGESTED USES: chicken breasts, pork chops, beef steaks, or lamb chops (marinated 2 hours to overnight) or fish fillets, shrimp, or sea scallops (marinated 20 to 45 minutes), grilled or broiled

GRILLED FLATIRON STEAKS

FOR 4 SERVINGS, combine the Roasted Garlic Marinade and 4 flatiron steaks (about 8 ounces each) in a 1-gallon zip-top bag and turn to coat. Seal the bag, letting out all the air. Marinate for at least 2 hours and up to overnight in the refrigerator.

Set the bag aside at room temperature for about half an hour. Remove the steaks from the marinade, pat dry with paper towels, then grill over direct high heat until medium-rare, 10 to 12 minutes (or until the desired doneness), turning once. Moisture will just begin to accumulate on the surface of the steaks when they are medium-rare. Tent the steaks with foil and let rest for 5 to 10 minutes before carving and serving.

These steaks will go with just about anything—serve, thinly sliced, in a sandwich, on a salad, tossed into pasta, or with any starch and seasonal vegetable you feel like having.

Double Garlic Marinade

If you have oil left over from making a large quantity of roasted garlic, this marinade is a good way to use it up. Of course, purchased roasted garlic oil can also be used.

TOOL: 1-gallon zip-top bag

YIELD: about $1/3$ cup (enough for about 2 servings)

3 TABLESPOONS ROASTED GARLIC OIL

2 TABLESPOONS FRESHLY SQUEEZED LEMON JUICE

2 TABLESPOONS SOY SAUCE

$1/2$ TEASPOON WORCESTERSHIRE SAUCE

2 GARLIC CLOVES, MINCED

2 TABLESPOONS PACKED LIGHT BROWN SUGAR

FRESHLY GROUND BLACK PEPPER

MEASURE the roasted garlic oil, lemon juice, soy sauce, Worcestershire, garlic, and brown sugar into a 1-gallon zip-top bag and shake or squeeze until blended.

SUGGESTED USES: chicken breasts, pork chops, beef steaks, or lamb chops (marinated 2 hours to overnight) or fish fillets, shrimp, or sea scallops (marinated 20 to 45 minutes), grilled

GRILLED CHICKEN BREASTS

FOR 2 SERVINGS, add 2 boneless, skinless chicken breasts (about 8 ounces each), pounded to an even thickness of $1/2$ to $3/4$ inch, to the Double Garlic Marinade in the zip-top bag and turn to coat. Seal the bag, letting out all the air. Marinate for at least 2 hours and up to overnight in the refrigerator.

Set the bag aside at room temperature for about half an hour. Remove the chicken from the marinade, pat dry with paper towels, then grill on an oiled grill grate over direct high heat until just cooked through, 10 to 12 minutes, turning once. The chicken will be firm to the touch and the juices will run clear when it is just cooked through. Tent the chicken with foil and let rest for 5 to 10 minutes before carving and serving.

Serve these chicken breasts thinly sliced in a wrap, on a salad, tossed into pasta, or with any starch and seasonal vegetable your family likes.

Vidalia Onion Marinade

This marinade is inspired by the sweet onions that are prized in the South.
If Vidalia onions are unavailable, use Mauis or any other variety of sweet onion.
In keeping with the regional theme, use an American whiskey such as bourbon;
I like Jack Daniel's.

TOOL: 1-gallon zip-top bag

YIELD: about 3/4 cup (enough for about 6 servings)

2 TABLESPOONS CANOLA OIL

1 TABLESPOON CIDER VINEGAR

1 TABLESPOON WHISKEY

1 TABLESPOON SOY SAUCE

1 TEASPOON TABASCO SAUCE

1/2 teaspoon WORCESTERSHIRE SAUCE

1/3 CUP GRATED VIDALIA ONION

1 TABLESPOON SUGAR

KOSHER SALT

FRESHLY GROUND BLACK PEPPER

MEASURE the oil, vinegar, whiskey, soy sauce, Tabasco, Worcestershire, onion, and sugar into a 1-gallon zip-top bag and shake or squeeze until blended. Season to taste with salt and pepper.

SUGGESTED USES: chicken breasts, pork chops, or beef steaks (marinated 2 hours to overnight), grilled or broiled; catfish fillets (marinated 20 to 45 minutes), baked

BAKED CATFISH FILLETS

FOR 6 SERVINGS, add 6 skinned, boneless catfish fillets (6 to 8 ounces each) to the Vidalia Onion Marinade in the zip-top bag and turn to coat. Seal the bag, letting out all the air. Marinate for at least 20 minutes and up to 45 minutes at room temperature.

Remove the fillets from the marinade and pat dry with paper towels. Bake the fillets on a rimmed baking sheet in a preheated 450°F oven until cooked through, 14 to 16 minutes. The fillets will flake when they are cooked through.

Serve the catfish fillets with Southern-style side dishes such as cornbread and collard greens.

AROMATIC VEGETABLE AND TOMATO MARINADES

French Onion Marinade

Here French onion soup—and dip—are reinterpreted in marinade form. Cooking the onions slowly until they are deep brown brings out the sweetness and richness of their natural sugars.

TOOLS: sauté pan • blender • 1-gallon zip-top bag

YIELD: about 1/2 cup (enough for about 4 servings)

1/4 CUP EXTRA-VIRGIN OLIVE OIL

1 MEDIUM YELLOW ONION, JULIENNED (SEE PAGE 297)

1 TABLESPOON BALSAMIC VINEGAR

1/2 TEASPOON FRESH THYME LEAVES

KOSHER SALT

FRESHLY GROUND BLACK PEPPER

HEAT a medium-size, heavy sauté pan over medium-low heat. Add the oil and onion and cook, stirring frequently, for 50 to 55 minutes, or until caramelized. Let cool to room temperature. Combine the caramelized onion along with its oil, the balsamic vinegar, and the thyme in a blender and blend until smooth. Season to taste with salt and pepper.

SUGGESTED USES: chicken breasts or pork tenderloin (marinated overnight), roasted; beef steaks (marinated overnight), grilled

GRILLED SIRLOIN STEAKS

FOR 4 SERVINGS, combine the French Onion Marinade and 2 sirloin steaks (1 to 1 1/4 inches thick) in a 1-gallon zip-top bag and turn to coat. Seal the bag, letting out all the air. Marinate overnight in the refrigerator.

Set the bag aside at room temperature for about half an hour. Remove the steaks from the marinade and pat dry with paper towels, then grill over direct high heat until medium-rare, 10 to 14 minutes (or until the desired doneness), turning once. Moisture will just begin to accumulate on the surface of the steaks when they are medium-rare. Tent the steaks with foil and let rest for 5 to 10 minutes before carving and serving.

For French onion sandwiches, stuff a baguette with the steaks, thinly sliced, additional caramelized onions (if you want to gild the lily), and Gruyère or Emmental cheese. Broil until the cheese is melted.

Roasted Red Pepper Marinade

Roasted red peppers impart a sweetness and subtle campfire flavor to this brightly colored marinade, which also doubles as a salad dressing. Homemade roasted red bell peppers taste much better than the ones that come in jars, and they're not hard to make.

TOOLS: blender • 1-gallon zip-top bag

YIELD: about 3/4 cup (enough for 4 to 6 servings or 2 servings and a salad)

2 TABLESPOONS CANOLA OIL

1 TABLESPOON RED WINE VINEGAR

1 MEDIUM RED BELL PEPPER, ROASTED, PEELED, AND SEEDED (SEE PAGE 297)

1 SMALL SHALLOT, SLICED

1/2 TEASPOON FRESH THYME LEAVES

KOSHER SALT

FRESHLY GROUND BLACK PEPPER

COMBINE the oil, vinegar, roasted bell pepper, shallot, and thyme in a blender and blend until smooth. Season to taste with salt and pepper.

SUGGESTED USES: chicken breasts or beef steaks (especially flank and flatiron) (marinated 2 hours to overnight) or white fish fillets, shrimp, or sea scallops (marinated 20 to 45 minutes), grilled

SALAD WITH GRILLED SHRIMP

FOR 2 SERVINGS, combine about half of the Roasted Red Pepper Marinade with 1/2 to 3/4 pound peeled, deveined large shrimp (21/25 count) in a 1-gallon zip-top bag and turn to coat. Seal the bag, letting out all the air. Marinate for at least 20 minutes and up to 45 minutes at room temperature.

Remove the shrimp from the marinade and pat dry with paper towels. Grill the shrimp on an oiled grill grate over direct high heat until just cooked through, 4 to 5 minutes, turning once. The shrimp will be firm to the touch, opaque and pink, and beginning to curl when they are just cooked through.

Serve the shrimp over mesclun greens or baby arugula. Use the remaining marinade as the salad dressing.

Roasted Red Pepper–Basil Marinade

At the height of summer, roasted red bell peppers and fresh basil are a fantastic combination. Jarred roasted peppers are not desirable here.

TOOLS: blender • 1-gallon zip-top bag

YIELD: about 3/4 cup (enough for 4 to 6 servings)

2 TABLESPOONS EXTRA-VIRGIN OLIVE OIL

1 TABLESPOON BALSAMIC VINEGAR

1/4 CUP LIGHTLY PACKED FRESH BASIL LEAVES

1 MEDIUM RED BELL PEPPER, ROASTED, PEELED, AND SEEDED
   (SEE PAGE 297)

2 GARLIC CLOVES, SLICED

KOSHER SALT

FRESHLY GROUND BLACK PEPPER

COMBINE the oil, balsamic vinegar, basil, roasted bell pepper, and garlic in a blender and blend until smooth. Season to taste with salt and pepper.

SUGGESTED USES: chicken breasts, pork chops, or beef steaks (marinated 2 hours to overnight) or shrimp or sea scallops (marinated 20 to 45 minutes), grilled; halibut fillets (marinated 20 to 45 minutes), grilled or baked

BAKED OR GRILLED HALIBUT FILLETS WITH SUMMER VEGETABLES AND PASTA

FOR 6 SERVINGS, combine the Roasted Red Pepper–Basil Marinade and 6 skinned, boneless halibut fillets (6 to 8 ounces each) in a 1-gallon zip-top bag and turn to coat. Seal the bag, letting out all the air. Marinate for at least 20 minutes and up to 45 minutes at room temperature.

Toss halved cherry tomatoes and diced zucchini and yellow squash with a little olive oil and arrange in a single layer on a rimmed baking sheet. Remove the fillets from the marinade, place them on top of the vegetables, and bake in a preheated 450°F oven until just cooked through, 18 to 20 minutes. The fillets will begin to flake when they are just cooked through.

Serve the halibut fillets and vegetables on a bed of pasta; top with freshly grated Parmigiano-Reggiano.

Alternatively, pat the fillets dry with paper towels, then grill on an oiled grill grate over direct high heat until just cooked through, 8 to 10 minutes, turning once. Serve over a bed of pasta tossed with garlic oil, halved cherry tomatoes, roasted bell pepper strips (red, orange, and yellow, if available), torn basil leaves, and freshly grated Parmigiano-Reggiano.

Fennel-Citrus Marinade

Fennel seems to appear in marinades in seed form far more often than it does in fresh form. However, fennel bulb is highly aromatic and perfectly suited for use in a marinade.

TOOLS: blender • 1-gallon zip-top bag

YIELD: about 1/2 cup (enough for 2 to 4 servings)

3 TABLESPOONS EXTRA-VIRGIN OLIVE OIL

3 TABLESPOONS FRESHLY SQUEEZED ORANGE JUICE

1 TABLESPOON FRESHLY SQUEEZED LEMON JUICE

1/4 CUP DICED FENNEL

2 GARLIC CLOVES, SLICED

1 TABLESPOON SUGAR

KOSHER SALT

FRESHLY GROUND BLACK PEPPER

COMBINE the oil, orange juice, lemon juice, fennel, garlic, and sugar in a blender and blend until smooth. Season to taste with salt and pepper.

SUGGESTED USES: chicken breasts or pork tenderloin medallions (marinated 2 hours to overnight) or fish fillets, shrimp, or sea scallops (marinated 20 to 45 minutes), grilled or broiled

GRILLED PORK TENDERLOIN MEDALLIONS

FOR 2 SERVINGS, combine the Fennel-Citrus Marinade and **1 pork tenderloin (12 to 14 ounces)**, cut on a bias into 1-inch-thick medallions, in a 1-gallon zip-top bag and turn to coat. Seal the bag, letting out all the air. Marinate for **at least 2 hours and up to overnight** in the refrigerator.

Set the bag aside at room temperature for about half an hour. Remove the medallions from the marinade and pat dry with paper towels, then grill over direct high heat until medium, 13 to 15 minutes (or until the desired doneness), turning once. Moisture will just begin to pool on the surface of the medallions when they are medium. Tent the medallions with foil and let rest for 5 to 10 minutes before serving.

Serve the pork medallions over fennel risotto. Garnish with minced fennel fronds, if desired.

Pizza Sauce Marinade

The combination of tomato and dried oregano in this marinade makes me think of pizza. And who wouldn't want to eat chicken that tastes like pizza?

TOOL: 1-gallon zip-top bag

YIELD: about 3/4 cup (enough for 4 to 6 servings)

1/2 CUP TOMATO JUICE

2 TABLESPOONS EXTRA-VIRGIN OLIVE OIL

2 TABLESPOONS RED WINE VINEGAR

1 TABLESPOON TOMATO PASTE

2 GARLIC CLOVES, MINCED

2 TEASPOONS DRIED OREGANO

1/2 TEASPOON ONION POWDER

1/4 TEASPOON CRUSHED RED PEPPER

KOSHER SALT

FRESHLY GROUND BLACK PEPPER

MEASURE the tomato juice, oil, vinegar, tomato paste, garlic, oregano, onion powder, and crushed red pepper into a 1-gallon zip-top bag and shake or squeeze until blended. Season to taste with salt and black pepper.

SUGGESTED USES: chicken breasts (marinated 2 hours to overnight), oven-fried; beef steaks or lamb chops (marinated 2 hours to overnight), grilled or broiled

OVEN-FRIED CHICKEN BREASTS

FOR 6 SERVINGS, add 6 boneless, skinless chicken breasts (about 8 ounces each) to the Pizza Sauce Marinade in the zip-top bag and turn to coat. Seal the bag, letting out all the air. Marinate for at least 2 hours and up to overnight in the refrigerator.

Set the bag aside at room temperature for about half an hour. Shaking off any excess marinade, press each chicken breast into a mixture of half panko bread crumbs and half freshly grated Parmigiano-Reggiano, arrange on a rack on a rimmed baking sheet, and drizzle with canola oil. Bake in a preheated 450°F oven until golden brown and crisp and just cooked through, 28 to 32 minutes. The chicken will be firm to the touch and the juices will run clear when it is just cooked through. Tent the chicken with foil and let rest for 5 to 10 minutes before carving and serving.

Serve these chicken breasts, thinly sliced, atop Caesar salad or fettuccine Alfredo.

Tomato-Coriander Marinade

The pairing of tomato and coriander may be less familiar than that of tomato and basil or tomato and oregano, but as this marinade proves, it's just as successful.

TOOL: 1-gallon zip-top bag

YIELD: about 3/4 cup (enough for about 6 servings)

1/3 CUP TOMATO JUICE

2 TABLESPOONS FRESHLY SQUEEZED LIME JUICE

2 TABLESPOONS SOY SAUCE

1 TABLESPOON CANOLA OIL

1 GARLIC CLOVE, MINCED

2 TABLESPOONS MINCED FRESH CILANTRO

1 1/2 TEASPOONS CORIANDER SEEDS, TOASTED AND GROUND

GENEROUS PINCH OF CAYENNE PEPPER

FRESHLY GROUND BLACK PEPPER

MEASURE the tomato juice, lime juice, soy sauce, oil, garlic, cilantro, coriander, and cayenne into a 1-gallon zip-top bag and shake or squeeze until blended. Season to taste with black pepper.

SUGGESTED USES: chicken breasts (marinated 2 hours to overnight) or fish fillets (marinated 20 to 45 minutes), grilled or broiled

GRILLED SALMON FILLETS

FOR 6 SERVINGS, add 6 skinned, boneless salmon fillets (6 to 8 ounces each) to the Tomato-Coriander Marinade in the zip-top bag and turn to coat. Seal the bag, letting out all the air. Marinate for at least 20 minutes and up to 45 minutes in the refrigerator.

Set the bag aside at room temperature for about half an hour. Remove the fillets from the marinade, pat dry with paper towels, then grill on an oiled grill grate over direct high heat until medium-rare, 8 to 10 minutes (or until the desired doneness), turning once. The fillets will barely begin to flake when they are medium-rare.

Serve the salmon fillets over a salad of garbanzo beans, diced red onions, tomatoes, avocados, and roasted red bell peppers dressed with minced cilantro, lime juice, and olive oil.

Sun-Dried Tomato Marinade

Sun-dried tomatoes impart both sweetness and umami to this rich marinade.

TOOLS: food processor • 1-gallon zip-top bag

YIELD: about 1/2 cup (enough for 2 to 4 servings)

10 SUN-DRIED TOMATO HALVES

2 TABLESPOONS EXTRA-VIRGIN OLIVE OIL

1 TABLESPOON RED WINE VINEGAR

1/4 CUP LIGHTLY PACKED FRESH BASIL LEAVES

2 GARLIC CLOVES, SLICED

KOSHER SALT

FRESHLY GROUND BLACK PEPPER

COMBINE the sun-dried tomatoes and enough boiling water to cover in a bowl and let soak for 10 to 12 minutes, or until rehydrated. Transfer the tomatoes to a paper towel–lined plate and drain for about a minute. Combine the tomatoes, oil, vinegar, basil, and garlic in a food processor and process until smooth. Season to taste with salt and pepper.

SUGGESTED USES: chicken breasts or pork tenderloin or chops (marinated 2 hours to overnight) or white fish fillets or shrimp (marinated 20 to 45 minutes), grilled, baked, or roasted

GRILLED CHICKEN BREASTS

FOR 4 SERVINGS, combine the Sun-Dried Tomato Marinade and 4 boneless, skinless chicken breasts (about 8 ounces each), pounded to an even thickness of 1/2 to 3/4 inch, in a 1-gallon zip-top bag and turn to coat. Seal the bag, letting out all the air. Marinate for at least 2 hours and up to overnight in the refrigerator.

Set the bag aside at room temperature for about half an hour. Remove the chicken from the marinade and pat dry with paper towels, then grill on an oiled grill grate over direct high heat until just cooked through, 10 to 12 minutes, turning once. The chicken will be firm to the touch and the juices will run clear when it is just cooked through. Tent the chicken with foil and let rest for 5 to 10 minutes before carving and serving.

Serve these chicken breasts, thinly sliced, over pasta or salad or use to make panini.

Beet-Horseradish Marinade

Using beets in a marinade may be unusual, but this recipe is sure to delight the eyes as well as the palate. I always make a lot so I can use half of it to make marinated hard-cooked eggs.

TOOLS: small baking dish • blender • 1-gallon zip-top bag

YIELD: about 1⅔ cups (enough for 9 to 12 servings)

1 SMALL BEET

1 CUP WATER

2 TABLESPOONS CANOLA OIL

2 TABLESPOONS WHITE WINE VINEGAR

2 TABLESPOONS GRATED FRESH HORSERADISH (SEE PAGE 40) OR PREPARED HORSERADISH

KOSHER SALT

FRESHLY GROUND BLACK PEPPER

PREHEAT the oven to 350°F. Place the beet in a small baking dish and cover tightly with foil. Roast until cooked through, about 1½ hours. Let cool to room temperature, peel, and quarter. Combine the beet, water, oil, vinegar, and horseradish in a blender and blend until smooth. Season to taste with salt and pepper.

SUGGESTED USES: salmon or halibut fillets or sea scallops (marinated 20 to 45 minutes), baked; hard-cooked eggs (marinated 6 hours to overnight)

BAKED SALMON FILLETS

FOR 6 SERVINGS, combine about half of the Beet-Horseradish Marinade (use the remaining marinade to make the marinated eggs on page 73 or freeze in a 1-gallon zip-top bag for future use) and 6 skinned, boneless salmon fillets (6 to 8 ounces each) in a 1-gallon zip-top bag and turn to coat. Seal the bag, letting out all the air. Marinate for at least 20 minutes and up to 45 minutes at room temperature.

Remove the fillets from the marinade and pat dry with paper towels. Bake the fillets on a rimmed baking sheet in a preheated 450°F oven until medium-rare, 12 to 13 minutes (or until the desired doneness). The fillets will barely begin to flake when they are medium-rare.

Serve the salmon fillets on a bed of mesclun greens tossed with a light vinaigrette and topped with shredded raw beets.

MARINATED EGGS

COMBINE half of the Beet-Horseradish Marinade with **6 peeled hard-cooked eggs** in a 1-gallon zip-top bag and turn to coat. Seal the bag, letting out all the air. Marinate for **at least 6 hours and up to overnight** in the refrigerator.

These fuchsia-colored eggs make for a delicious snack any time of day and are especially pretty served sliced or quartered with a salad or on an open-face sandwich.

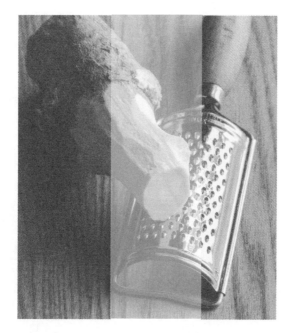

FRUIT
MARINADES

In addition to flavor, fruit offers a balance of sweetness and acidity that is perfectly suited for use in marinades. This chapter features a variety of marinades that utilize fresh fruit, fruit preserves, and fruit juices. For those of you who love sweet and savory combinations, recipes such as Peach-Poblano Marinade, Strawberry-Balsamic Marinade, and Apricot-Rosemary Marinade are sure to become favorites.

Apple-Sage Marinade

Think of this recipe in the fall, when apple and sage are the flavors of the season.

TOOL: 1-gallon zip-top bag

YIELD: about 1/2 cup (enough for 4 to 6 servings)

1/4 CUP APPLE CIDER

1 TABLESPOON CANOLA OIL

1 TABLESPOON CIDER VINEGAR

1 TABLESPOON APPLE BRANDY

1 TABLESPOON HONEY

1 SHALLOT, MINCED

2 TEASPOONS MINCED FRESH SAGE

KOSHER SALT

FRESHLY GROUND BLACK PEPPER

MEASURE the cider, oil, vinegar, brandy, honey, shallot, and sage into a 1-gallon zip-top bag and shake or squeeze until blended. Season to taste with salt and pepper.

SUGGESTED USES: turkey breast cutlets or pork chops (marinated 2 hours to overnight), grilled or broiled; pork loin (marinated overnight), roasted

ROASTED PORK LOIN

FOR 4 TO 6 SERVINGS, add 1 boneless pork loin roast (about 2 pounds) to the Apple-Sage Marinade in the zip-top bag and turn to coat. Seal the bag, letting out all the air. Marinate overnight in the refrigerator.

Set the bag aside at room temperature for about half an hour. Remove the pork from the marinade and place on a rack in a roasting pan. Roast the pork in a preheated 350°F oven until medium, 65 to 80 minutes (or until the desired doneness). A meat thermometer inserted in the center will register 140°F when the roast is medium. Tent the roast with foil and let rest for 15 to 20 minutes before carving and serving.

Serve the pork roast with baked apples.

Peach-Poblano Marinade

This marinade takes advantage of the natural affinity between fruit and chiles.

TOOLS: blender • 1-gallon zip-top bag

YIELD: about ¾ cup (enough for about 6 servings)

⅓ CUP PEACH JAM

2 TABLESPOONS CANOLA OIL

1 TABLESPOON CIDER VINEGAR

1 POBLANO CHILE, ROASTED, PEELED, AND SEEDED (SEE PAGE 297)

1 GARLIC CLOVE, SLICED

KOSHER SALT

FRESHLY GROUND BLACK PEPPER

COMBINE the jam, oil, vinegar, poblano, and garlic in a blender and blend until smooth. Season to taste with salt and pepper.

SUGGESTED USES: chicken breasts, pork chops, or boneless, skin-on duck breasts (marinated 2 hours to overnight), grilled or broiled

GRILLED PORK LOIN OR RIB CHOPS

FOR 6 SERVINGS, combine the Peach-Poblano Marinade and 6 boneless pork loin or rib chops (about 1 inch thick) in a 1-gallon zip-top bag and turn to coat. Seal the bag, letting out all the air. Marinate for at least 2 hours and up to overnight in the refrigerator.

Set the bag aside at room temperature for about half an hour. Remove the chops from the marinade, pat dry with paper towels, then grill over direct high heat until medium, 13 to 15 minutes (or until the desired doneness), turning once. Moisture will just begin to pool on the surface of the chops when they are medium. Tent the chops with foil and let rest for 5 to 10 minutes before serving.

Serve the pork chops with grilled peaches.

Apricot-Rosemary Marinade

This recipe will especially appeal to those who enjoy the interplay of sweet and savory flavors in the same dish.

TOOL: 1-gallon zip-top bag

YIELD: about 1/2 cup (enough for 3 to 4 servings)

1/4 CUP APRICOT JAM

2 TABLESPOONS EXTRA-VIRGIN OLIVE OIL

1 TABLESPOON FRESHLY SQUEEZED LEMON JUICE

1 GARLIC CLOVE, MINCED

2 TEASPOONS MINCED FRESH ROSEMARY

KOSHER SALT

FRESHLY GROUND BLACK PEPPER

MEASURE the jam, oil, lemon juice, garlic, and rosemary into a 1-gallon zip-top bag and shake or squeeze until blended. Season to taste with salt and pepper.

SUGGESTED USES: cubes of boneless, skinless chicken thighs or country-style pork ribs (marinated 2 hours to overnight) or salmon fillets (marinated 20 to 45 minutes), grilled

GRILLED CHICKEN KABOBS

FOR 6 APPETIZER or 3 main-course servings, add 6 boneless, skinless chicken thighs (about 4 ounces each), cut into 1 1/2-inch pieces, to the Apricot-Rosemary Marinade in the zip-top bag and turn to coat. Seal the bag, letting out all the air. Marinate for at least 2 hours and up to overnight in the refrigerator.

Set the bag aside at room temperature for about half an hour. Remove the chicken from the marinade, pat dry with paper towels, and skewer onto rosemary branches that have been stripped of their leaves and soaked in water. Grill the skewers, covered, on an oiled grill grate over direct medium heat until just cooked through, 10 to 12 minutes, turning once. The chicken will be firm to the touch and the juices will run clear when it is just cooked through.

Serve these chicken kabobs with grilled apricots glazed with honey.

Apricot-Ginger-Lime Marinade

Fruity and zingy is what this marinade is.

TOOL: 1-gallon zip-top bag

YIELD: about 1/2 cup (enough for 2 to 4 servings)

1/4 CUP APRICOT JAM

1/2 TEASPOON GRATED LIME ZEST

2 TABLESPOONS FRESHLY SQUEEZED LIME JUICE

1 TABLESPOON CANOLA OIL

1 TABLESPOON SOY SAUCE

1 TEASPOON MINCED FRESH GINGER

1 GARLIC CLOVE, MINCED

KOSHER SALT

FRESHLY GROUND BLACK PEPPER

MEASURE the jam, lime zest, lime juice, oil, soy sauce, ginger, and garlic into a 1-gallon zip-top bag and shake or squeeze until blended. Season to taste with salt and pepper.

SUGGESTED USES: chicken breasts or pork chops (marinated 2 hours to overnight) or shrimp (marinated 20 to 45 minutes), grilled

GRILLED SHRIMP

FOR 2 SERVINGS, add 1/2 to 3/4 pound peeled, deveined large shrimp (21/25 count) to the Apricot-Ginger-Lime Marinade in the zip-top bag and turn to coat. Seal the bag, letting out all the air. Marinate for at least 20 minutes and up to 45 minutes at room temperature.

Remove the shrimp from the marinade, pat dry with paper towels, then grill on an oiled grill grate over direct high heat until just cooked through, 4 to 5 minutes, turning once. The shrimp will be firm to the touch, opaque and pink, and beginning to curl when they are just cooked through.

Serve the shrimp over couscous with dried fruit and almonds. Offer lime wedges on the side.

Strawberry-Balsamic Marinade

I've transformed this combination of flavors—so familiar from the dessert course—into a savory sweet-and-sour marinade.

TOOLS: blender • 1-gallon zip-top bag

YIELD: about $2/3$ cup (enough for about 4 servings)

3 TABLESPOONS STRAWBERRY JAM

2 TABLESPOONS EXTRA-VIRGIN OLIVE OIL

2 TABLESPOONS BALSAMIC VINEGAR

1 $1/4$ OUNCES (ABOUT $1/4$ CUP) STRAWBERRIES

1 GARLIC CLOVE, SLICED

$1/4$ TEASPOON PINK PEPPERCORNS, CRUSHED

KOSHER SALT

FRESHLY GROUND BLACK PEPPER

COMBINE the jam, oil, balsamic vinegar, strawberries, garlic, and pink peppercorns in a blender and blend until smooth. Season to taste with salt and pepper.

SUGGESTED USES: chicken breasts (marinated 2 hours to overnight) or salmon fillets (marinated 20 to 45 minutes), grilled; boneless, skin-on duck breasts (marinated 2 hours to overnight), seared

GRILLED CHICKEN BREASTS

FOR 4 SERVINGS, combine the Strawberry-Balsamic Marinade and 4 boneless, skinless chicken breasts (about 8 ounces each), pounded to an even thickness of $1/2$ to $3/4$ inch, in a 1-gallon zip-top bag and turn to coat. Seal the bag, letting out all the air. Marinate for at least 2 hours and up to overnight in the refrigerator.

Set the bag aside at room temperature for about half an hour. Remove the chicken from the marinade, pat dry with paper towels, then grill on an oiled grill grate over direct high heat until just cooked through, 10 to 12 minutes, turning once. The chicken will be firm to the touch and the juices will run clear when it is just cooked through. Tent the chicken with foil and let rest for 5 to 10 minutes before carving and serving.

Serve the chicken breasts, thinly sliced, over a salad of baby spinach with sliced strawberries and red onions, toasted sliced almonds, and a balsamic vinaigrette.

Raspberry-Chipotle Marinade

At once smoky, sweet, spicy, and fruity, this simple marinade tastes surprisingly like a complex, long-cooked barbecue sauce.

TOOLS: fine-mesh sieve • 1-gallon zip-top bag

YIELD: about 1/2 cup (enough for 2 to 4 servings)

5 TO 6 CANNED CHIPOTLES IN ADOBO SAUCE

1/4 CUP SEEDLESS RASPBERRY JAM

1 TABLESPOON CANOLA OIL

2 TEASPOONS FRESHLY SQUEEZED LIME JUICE

1 GARLIC CLOVE, MINCED

KOSHER SALT

FRESHLY GROUND BLACK PEPPER

FORCE the chipotles through a fine-mesh sieve to remove the skins and seeds. Measure the chipotle puree, raspberry jam, oil, lime juice, and garlic into a 1-gallon zip-top bag and shake or squeeze until blended. Season to taste with salt and pepper.

SUGGESTED USES: chicken pieces or pork chops (marinated 2 hours to overnight), pork ribs (marinated overnight), or salmon fillets (marinated 20 to 45 minutes), grilled

GRILLED BABY BACK RIBS

FOR 2 SERVINGS, add 1 rack pork baby back ribs (2 to 2 1/2 pounds), cut in half, to the Raspberry-Chipotle Marinade in the zip-top bag and turn to coat. Seal the bag, letting out all the air. Marinate overnight in the refrigerator.

Set the bag aside at room temperature for about half an hour. Remove the ribs from the marinade and place them on the grill, meaty side up. Grill the ribs, covered, over indirect medium-low heat until fork-tender, 2 to 2 1/2 hours. The meat will have noticeably shrunk away from the ends of the bones when it is done. Tent the ribs with foil and let rest for 5 to 10 minutes before carving and serving.

Serve the ribs with any side dishes that you might serve at a barbecue, such as cornbread, baked beans, or coleslaw.

Raspberry-Zinfandel Marinade

I thought to combine raspberries, jalapeño, and star anise with Zinfandel in a marinade since the wine is known to have notes of both raspberry and spice.

TOOLS: fine-mesh sieve • 1-gallon zip-top bag

YIELD: about $3/4$ cup (enough for 4 to 6 servings)

2 OUNCES (ABOUT $1/2$ CUP) RASPBERRIES

2 TABLESPOONS ZINFANDEL

2 TABLESPOONS SEEDLESS RASPBERRY JAM

1 TABLESPOON EXTRA-VIRGIN OLIVE OIL

1 SHALLOT, MINCED

1 JALAPEÑO, SEEDED AND MINCED

1 STAR ANISE, BROKEN UP

KOSHER SALT

FRESHLY GROUND BLACK PEPPER

FORCE the raspberries through a fine-mesh sieve. Measure the raspberry puree, wine, jam, oil, shallot, jalapeño, and star anise into a 1-gallon zip-top bag and shake or squeeze until blended. Season to taste with salt and pepper.

SUGGESTED USES: pork tenderloin medallions, boneless, skin-on duck breasts, butterflied Cornish hens, whole quail, venison or boar medallions, or other game (marinated 2 hours to overnight), grilled or seared

GRILLED PORK TENDERLOIN MEDALLIONS

FOR 4 SERVINGS, add 2 pork tenderloins (12 to 14 ounces each), cut on a bias into 1-inch-thick medallions, to the Raspberry-Zinfandel Marinade in the zip-top bag and turn to coat. Seal the bag, letting out all the air. Marinate for at least 2 hours and up to overnight in the refrigerator.

Set the bag aside at room temperature for about half an hour. Remove the medallions from the marinade, pat dry with paper towels, then grill over direct high heat until medium, 13 to 15 minutes (or until the desired doneness), turning once. Moisture will just begin to pool on the surface of the medallions when they are medium. Tent the medallions with foil and let rest for 5 to 10 minutes before serving.

Serve the pork medallions with brown and wild rice pilaf and a seasonal vegetable.

Raspberry-Champagne Marinade

This marinade plays off the notes of berry you taste in Champagne. The combination of jam and infused vinegar makes the raspberry flavor really pop.

TOOL: 1-gallon zip-top bag

YIELD: about 2/3 cup (enough for 4 to 6 servings)

1/3 CUP CHAMPAGNE OR OTHER SPARKLING WINE

3 TABLESPOONS SEEDLESS RASPBERRY JAM

2 TABLESPOONS EXTRA-VIRGIN OLIVE OIL

1 TABLESPOON RASPBERRY VINEGAR

1 GARLIC CLOVE, MINCED

1/4 TEASPOON DRIED BASIL

1/4 TEASPOON DRIED MINT

KOSHER SALT

FRESHLY GROUND BLACK PEPPER

MEASURE the Champagne, jam, oil, vinegar, garlic, basil, and mint into a 1-gallon zip-top bag and shake or squeeze until blended. Season to taste with salt and pepper.

SUGGESTED USES: chicken breasts or boneless, skin-on duck breasts (marinated 2 hours to overnight), grilled or seared; salmon fillets (marinated 20 to 45 minutes), grilled

GRILLED CHICKEN BREASTS

FOR 4 SERVINGS, add 4 boneless, skinless chicken breasts (about 8 ounces each), pounded to an even thickness of 1/2 to 3/4 inch, to the Raspberry-Champagne Marinade in the zip-top bag and turn to coat. Seal the bag, letting out all the air. Marinate for at least 2 hours and up to overnight in the refrigerator.

Set the bag aside at room temperature for about half an hour. Remove the chicken from the marinade, pat dry with paper towels, then grill on an oiled grill grate over direct high heat until just cooked through, 10 to 12 minutes, turning once. The chicken will be firm to the touch and the juices will run clear when it is just cooked through. Tent the chicken with foil and let rest for 5 to 10 minutes before carving and serving.

For a light main-course salad, serve the chicken breasts, thinly sliced, over mesclun greens tossed with raspberries, sliced red onions, and toasted slivered almonds and dressed with a champagne vinegar or lemon vinaigrette.

Blackberry-Syrah Marinade

The hints of blackberry and pepper in Syrah led me to create this marinade.

TOOLS: fine-mesh sieve • 1-gallon zip-top bag

YIELD: about 2/3 cup (enough for 4 to 6 servings)

2 OUNCES (ABOUT 1/2 CUP) BLACKBERRIES

1/4 CUP SYRAH

2 TABLESPOONS SEEDLESS BLACKBERRY JAM

1 TABLESPOON EXTRA-VIRGIN OLIVE OIL

1 GARLIC CLOVE, MINCED

1 BAY LEAF, CRUMBLED

1/4 TEASPOON FRESHLY GROUND BLACK PEPPER

KOSHER SALT

FORCE the blackberries through a fine-mesh sieve. Measure the blackberry puree, wine, jam, oil, garlic, bay leaf, and pepper into a 1-gallon zip-top bag and shake or squeeze until blended. Season to taste with salt.

SUGGESTED USES: pork tenderloin medallions, beef tenderloin steaks, boneless, skin-on duck breasts, butterflied Cornish hens, whole quail, venison or boar medallions, or other game (marinated 2 hours to overnight), grilled or seared

SEARED BEEF TENDERLOIN STEAKS

FOR 4 SERVINGS, add 4 beef tenderloin steaks (1 1/4 to 1 1/2 inches thick) to the Blackberry-Syrah Marinade in the zip-top bag and turn to coat. Seal the bag, letting out all the air. Marinate for at least 2 hours and up to overnight in the refrigerator.

Set the bag aside at room temperature for about half an hour. Remove the steaks from the marinade and pat dry with paper towels. Heat a large, heavy sauté pan over high heat until a few water droplets dance and look like ball bearings rolling around when flicked into the pan. Add 2 tablespoons canola oil and sear the steaks until medium-rare, 7 to 9 minutes (or until the desired doneness), turning once. Moisture will just begin to accumulate on the surface of the steaks when they are medium-rare. Tent the steaks with foil and let rest for 5 to 10 minutes before serving.

Serve the steaks with a potato gratin and a seasonal vegetable.

Huckleberry–Pinot Noir Marinade

The sweet-tart flavor of huckleberries, which are closely related to blueberries, pairs well with a lighter wine. Huckleberries can be difficult to find, as they are usually gathered in the wild and rarely cultivated. If huckleberries are unavailable, substitute blueberries.

TOOLS: fine-mesh sieve • 1-gallon zip-top bag

YIELD: about 3/4 cup (enough for 4 to 6 servings)

3 OUNCES (ABOUT 2/3 CUP) HUCKLEBERRIES

1/4 CUP PINOT NOIR

1 TABLESPOON EXTRA-VIRGIN OLIVE OIL

1 SHALLOT, MINCED

1 TEASPOON MINCED FRESH THYME

1 TABLESPOON SUGAR

KOSHER SALT

FRESHLY GROUND BLACK PEPPER

FORCE the huckleberries through a fine-mesh sieve. Measure the huckleberry puree, wine, oil, shallot, thyme, and sugar into a 1-gallon zip-top bag and shake or squeeze until blended. Season to taste with salt and pepper.

SUGGESTED USES: pork tenderloin medallions, boneless, skin-on duck breasts, butterflied Cornish hens, whole quail, venison or boar medallions, or other game (marinated 2 hours to overnight), grilled or seared

SEARED DUCK BREASTS

FOR 6 SERVINGS, add 6 boneless, skin-on duck breasts (about 8 ounces each), skin scored with a diamond pattern, to the Huckleberry–Pinot Noir Marinade in the zip-top bag and turn to coat. Seal the bag, letting out all the air. Marinate for at least 2 hours and up to overnight in the refrigerator.

Set the bag aside at room temperature for about half an hour. Remove the duck from the marinade and pat dry with paper towels. Heat a large, heavy sauté pan over medium heat until a few water droplets dance and look like ball bearings rolling around when flicked into the pan. Sear the duck, starting with the skin side down, until medium-rare, 10 to 12 minutes (or until the desired doneness), turning once. The duck will just begin to feel firm to the touch when it is medium-rare, and the temperature will register 130°F when an instant-read thermometer is inserted sideways into the center of the breast. Tent the duck with foil and let rest for 5 to 10 minutes before carving and serving.

Serve the duck breasts with potatoes fried or roasted in duck fat and a seasonal vegetable.

Black Currant–Merlot Marinade

Notes of black currant can often be found in merlot, so naturally the two marry well in a marinade. I included rosemary to pick up on the distinct woodsy flavor found in black currants.

TOOL: 1-gallon zip-top bag

YIELD: about ¾ cup (enough for 4 to 6 servings)

¼ CUP MERLOT

¼ CUP BLACK CURRANT PRESERVES

1 TABLESPOON EXTRA-VIRGIN OLIVE OIL

1 SHALLOT, MINCED

¾ TEASPOON MINCED FRESH ROSEMARY

KOSHER SALT

FRESHLY GROUND BLACK PEPPER

MEASURE the wine, preserves, oil, shallot, and rosemary into a 1-gallon zip-top bag and shake or squeeze until blended. Season to taste with salt and pepper.

SUGGESTED USES: pork tenderloin medallions, boneless, skin-on duck breasts, butterflied Cornish hens, whole quail, venison or boar medallions, or other game (marinated 2 hours to overnight), grilled or seared

GRILLED PORK TENDERLOIN MEDALLIONS

FOR 4 SERVINGS, add 2 pork tenderloins (12 to 14 ounces each), cut on a bias into 1-inch-thick medallions, to the Black Currant–Merlot Marinade in the zip-top bag and turn to coat. Seal the bag, letting out all the air. Marinate for at least 2 hours and up to overnight in the refrigerator.

Set the bag aside at room temperature for about half an hour. Remove the medallions from the marinade, pat dry with paper towels, then grill over direct high heat until medium, 13 to 15 minutes (or until the desired doneness), turning once. Moisture will just begin to pool on the surface of the medallions when they are medium. Tent the medallions with foil and let rest for 5 to 10 minutes before serving.

Serve the pork medallions with roasted rosemary potatoes and a seasonal vegetable.

Minted Red Currant Marinade

Tart, sweet red currants are wonderful in marinades (as well as other savory preparations), but since they have a very short season, I opted for jelly rather than the fresh fruit for this recipe.

TOOL: 1-gallon zip-top bag

YIELD: about 2/3 cup (enough for 4 to 6 servings)

1/4 CUP RED CURRANT JELLY

2 TABLESPOONS CANOLA OIL

2 TABLESPOONS FRESHLY SQUEEZED ORANGE JUICE

1 TABLESPOON CHAMPAGNE VINEGAR

1 GARLIC CLOVE, MINCED

1 TABLESPOON MINCED FRESH MINT LEAVES

KOSHER SALT

FRESHLY GROUND BLACK PEPPER

MEASURE the jelly, oil, orange juice, vinegar, garlic, and mint into a 1-gallon zip-top bag and shake or squeeze until blended. Season to taste with salt and pepper.

SUGGESTED USES: pork tenderloin medallions, lamb chops, or boneless, skin-on duck breasts (marinated 2 hours to overnight), grilled or seared

GRILLED LAMB RIB CHOPS

FOR 4 SERVINGS, add 12 frenched lamb rib chops (about 1 inch thick) to the Minted Red Currant Marinade in the zip-top bag and turn to coat. Seal the bag, letting out all the air. Marinate for at least 2 hours and up to overnight in the refrigerator.

Set the bag aside at room temperature for about half an hour. Remove the chops from the marinade, pat dry with paper towels, then grill over direct high heat until medium-rare, 10 to 12 minutes (or until the desired doneness), turning once. Moisture will just begin to accumulate on the surface of the chops when they are medium-rare. Tent the chops with foil and let rest for 5 to 10 minutes before serving.

Serve the lamb chops with brown and wild rice pilaf and a seasonal vegetable.

Cherry-Port Marinade

Cherries are often paired with port in pork and duck dishes. A combination of fresh sweet cherries and sour cherry preserves gives great depth of flavor to this marinade.

TOOLS: saucepan • blender • 1-gallon zip-top bag

YIELD: about 1 cup (enough for 5 to 10 servings)

3/4 CUP RUBY PORT

3 OUNCES (ABOUT 1/2 CUP) CHERRIES, PITTED AND QUARTERED

1 SHALLOT, SLICED

1/2 TEASPOON FRESH THYME LEAVES

1/4 CUP SOUR CHERRY PRESERVES

2 TABLESPOONS EXTRA-VIRGIN OLIVE OIL

KOSHER SALT

FRESHLY GROUND BLACK PEPPER

COMBINE the port, cherries, shallot, and thyme in a small saucepan. Bring to a boil and simmer until the cherries are tender, 2 to 3 minutes. Remove from the heat and let cool to room temperature. Combine the cherry mixture, cherry preserves, and oil in a blender and blend until smooth. Season to taste with salt and pepper.

SUGGESTED USES: pork loin (marinated overnight), roasted; pork tenderloin medallions, boneless, skin-on duck breasts, butterflied Cornish hens, whole quail, venison or boar medallions, or other game (marinated 2 hours to overnight), grilled or seared

ROASTED PORK LOIN

FOR 8 TO 10 SERVINGS, combine the Cherry-Port Marinade and 1 boneless pork loin roast (about 4 pounds) in a 1-gallon zip-top bag and turn to coat. Seal the bag, letting out all the air. Marinate overnight in the refrigerator.

Set the bag aside at room temperature for about half an hour. Remove the pork from the marinade and place on a rack in a roasting pan. Roast the pork in a preheated 350°F oven until medium (or until the desired doneness), 65 to 80 minutes. A meat thermometer inserted in the center will register 140°F when the roast is medium. Tent the roast with foil and let rest for 15 to 20 minutes before carving and serving.

Serve the pork roast with brown and wild rice pilaf and a seasonal vegetable.

Cranberry-Orange Marinade

Try this marinade in the fall for a twist on the typical flavors of the season.

TOOL: 1-gallon zip-top bag

YIELD: about 1 cup (enough for about 8 servings)

1/3 CUP UNSWEETENED CRANBERRY JUICE

1/4 CUP SWEET ORANGE MARMALADE

2 TABLESPOONS FRESHLY SQUEEZED ORANGE JUICE

1 TABLESPOON CANOLA OIL

1 SHALLOT, MINCED

1 GARLIC CLOVE, MINCED

GENEROUS PINCH OF GROUND CINNAMON

GENEROUS PINCH OF GROUND CLOVES

KOSHER SALT

FRESHLY GROUND BLACK PEPPER

MEASURE the cranberry juice, marmalade, orange juice, oil, shallot, garlic, cinnamon, and cloves into a 1-gallon zip-top bag and shake or squeeze until blended. Season to taste with salt and pepper.

SUGGESTED USES: chicken breasts, turkey breast cutlets, or pork chops (marinated 2 hours to overnight), grilled

GRILLED TURKEY BREAST CUTLETS

FOR 8 SERVINGS, add 8 turkey breast cutlets (about 4 ounces each and 1/2 inch thick) to the Cranberry-Orange Marinade in the zip-top bag and turn to coat. Seal the bag, letting out all the air. Marinate for **at least 2 hours and up to overnight** in the refrigerator.

Set the bag aside at room temperature for about half an hour. Remove the turkey from the marinade, pat dry with paper towels, then grill on an oiled grill grate over direct high heat until just cooked through, 8 to 10 minutes, turning once. The turkey will be firm to the touch and the juices will run clear when it is just cooked through. Tent the turkey with foil and let rest for 5 to 10 minutes before serving.

Serve these turkey cutlets with any side dishes you might offer during the Thanksgiving season. Accompany with cranberry sauce if desired.

Cranberry-Cider Marinade

This marinade, with notes of cranberry and apple, will be welcome in the fall.

TOOL: 1-gallon zip-top bag

YIELD: about 1 cup (enough for about 8 servings)

1/3 CUP UNSWEETENED CRANBERRY JUICE

1/3 CUP HARD CIDER

3 TABLESPOONS PURE MAPLE SYRUP

2 TABLESPOONS CANOLA OIL

2 GARLIC CLOVES, MINCED

KOSHER SALT

FRESHLY GROUND BLACK PEPPER

MEASURE the cranberry juice, cider, maple syrup, oil, and garlic into a 1-gallon zip-top bag and shake or squeeze until blended. Season to taste with salt and pepper.

SUGGESTED USES: chicken breasts, turkey breast cutlets, or pork chops (marinated 2 hours to overnight), grilled

GRILLED PORK LOIN OR RIB CHOPS

FOR 8 SERVINGS, add 8 boneless pork loin or rib chops (about 1 inch thick) to the Cranberry-Cider Marinade in the zip-top bag and turn to coat. Seal the bag, letting out all the air. Marinate for at least 2 hours and up to overnight in the refrigerator.

Set the bag aside at room temperature for about half an hour. Remove the chops from the marinade, pat dry with paper towels, then grill over direct high heat until medium, 13 to 15 minutes (or until the desired doneness), turning once. Moisture will just begin to pool on the surface of the chops when they are medium. Tent the chops with foil and let rest for 5 to 10 minutes before serving.

Serve the pork chops with any side dishes you might offer during the Thanksgiving season. Accompany with cranberry sauce or applesauce if desired.

CITRUS
MARINADES

There are so many tasty and creative marinades based on citrus fruits that they deserve a chapter all their own. I often blend whole oranges, grapefruits, lemons, and limes, skin and all—the juice has the necessary acidity, the zest brings the flavor, and though many cooks discard it, the white pith offers just a hint of balancing bitterness. Citrus fruits shine in such recipes as Lemon-Pepper Marinade, Charred Lemon Marinade, and Blood Orange–Rosemary Marinade.

Lemon-Pepper Marinade

If lemon pepper is a staple in your pantry, you should give this simple and versatile marinade a try. The flavor from fresh lemons is so much brighter and more intense, you might never go back to the jarred stuff.

TOOL: 1-gallon zip-top bag

YIELD: about 1/2 cup (enough for 2 to 4 servings)

1/4 CUP EXTRA-VIRGIN OLIVE OIL

2 TABLESPOONS GRATED LEMON ZEST

1/4 CUP FRESHLY SQUEEZED LEMON JUICE

2 TEASPOONS SUGAR

2 TEASPOONS FRESHLY CRACKED BLACK PEPPERCORNS

1/2 TEASPOON GRANULATED GARLIC

1/2 TEASPOON ONION POWDER

KOSHER SALT

MEASURE the oil, lemon zest, lemon juice, sugar, peppercorns, granulated garlic, and onion powder into a 1-gallon zip-top bag and shake or squeeze until blended. Season to taste with salt.

SUGGESTED USES: chicken breasts, pork chops, or beef steaks (marinated 2 hours to overnight), fish fillets, shrimp, or sea scallops (marinated 20 to 45 minutes), or vegetables (marinated 30 minutes to 1 hour), grilled

GRILLED HALIBUT FILLETS

FOR 4 SERVINGS, add 4 skinned, boneless halibut fillets (6 to 8 ounces each) to the Lemon-Pepper Marinade in the zip-top bag and turn to coat. Seal the bag, letting out all the air. Marinate for at least 20 minutes and up to 45 minutes at room temperature.

Remove the fillets from the marinade and pat dry with paper towels. Grill the fillets on an oiled grill grate over direct high heat until just cooked through, 8 to 10 minutes, turning once. The fillets will begin to flake when they are just cooked through.

These halibut fillets will go with just about anything—serve with any starch and seasonal vegetable you'd like.

Charred Lemon Marinade

The caramelized flavor of charred lemon slices makes for a unique marinade. If it's more convenient, feel free to sear the lemon slices in a pan or on the grill until caramelized.

TOOLS: rimmed baking sheet • blender • fine-mesh sieve • 1-gallon zip-top bag

YIELD: about 3/4 cup (enough for 4 to 6 servings)

1 LARGE LEMON, SCRUBBED AND CUT INTO 1/2-INCH SLICES

2/3 CUP PLUS 1 TEASPOON EXTRA-VIRGIN OLIVE OIL

2 GARLIC CLOVES, SLICED

1 TABLESPOON SUGAR

KOSHER SALT

FRESHLY GROUND BLACK PEPPER

PREHEAT the broiler. Toss together the lemon slices and 1 teaspoon of the oil on a rimmed baking sheet, then arrange the lemon slices in a single layer. Broil until golden brown, 10 to 12 minutes. Turn the lemon slices and broil until golden brown, another 7 to 8 minutes. Combine the lemon slices with the remaining 2/3 cup oil, garlic, and sugar in a blender and blend until smooth. Force the puree through a fine-mesh sieve to remove the fibers and seeds. Season to taste with salt and pepper.

SUGGESTED USES: chicken breasts or pork chops (marinated 2 hours to overnight) or fish fillets, shrimp, or sea scallops (marinated 20 to 45 minutes), grilled

GRILLED SEA SCALLOPS

FOR 4 SERVINGS, combine the Charred Lemon Marinade and **12 jumbo sea scallops (about 2 ounces each)**, side muscles removed, in a 1-gallon zip-top bag and turn to coat. Seal the bag, letting out all the air. Marinate for **at least 20 minutes and up to 45 minutes** at room temperature.

Remove the scallops from the marinade, pat dry with paper towels, then grill on an oiled grill grate over direct high heat until medium-rare, 6 to 7 minutes (or until the desired doneness), turning once. Moisture will just begin to accumulate on the surface of the scallops when they are medium-rare.

Serve the scallops with quinoa and steamed asparagus.

Meyer Lemon Marinade

Throwing a lemon—skin and all—into the blender may sound strange, but it gets the most mileage out of the intoxicatingly fragrant and relatively expensive Meyer lemon. The whole-lemon puree has the intensity of flavor of every bit of zest and also the perfect balance of acidity and bitterness. During their short winter season, Meyer lemons are available at many gourmet shops and some supermarkets.

TOOLS: blender • fine-mesh sieve • 1-gallon zip-top bag

YIELD: about 1/2 cup (enough for 2 to 4 servings)

1/3 CUP EXTRA-VIRGIN OLIVE OIL

1 MEYER LEMON, SCRUBBED AND CUT INTO EIGHTHS

2 GARLIC CLOVES, SLICED

2 TABLESPOONS SUGAR

KOSHER SALT

FRESHLY GROUND BLACK PEPPER

COMBINE the oil, lemon, garlic, and sugar in a blender and blend until smooth. Force the puree through a fine-mesh sieve to remove the fibers and seeds. Season to taste with salt and pepper.

SUGGESTED USES: chicken breasts (marinated 2 hours to overnight) or fish fillets, shrimp, or sea scallops (marinated 20 to 45 minutes), grilled

GRILLED CHICKEN BREASTS

FOR 4 SERVINGS, combine the Meyer Lemon Marinade and 4 boneless, skinless chicken breasts (about 8 ounces each), pounded to an even thickness of 1/2 to 3/4 inch, in a 1-gallon zip-top bag and turn to coat. Seal the bag, letting out all the air. Marinate for at least 2 hours and up to overnight in the refrigerator.

Set the bag aside at room temperature for about half an hour. Remove the chicken from the marinade and pat dry with paper towels, then grill on an oiled grill grate over direct high heat until just cooked through, 10 to 12 minutes, turning once. The chicken will be firm to the touch and the juices will run clear when it is just cooked through. Tent the chicken with foil and let rest for 5 to 10 minutes before carving and serving.

For a light main-course salad, serve the chicken breasts thinly sliced over baby spinach or mesclun greens dressed with a lemon-herb vinaigrette. Or serve accompanied by garlicky wilted spinach or chard.

Orange-Coriander Marinade

Coriander is often described as having a citrus-like flavor, so it makes sense that coriander and orange have a particular affinity for one another. Feel free to experiment with lemon and lime as well.

TOOL: 1-gallon zip-top bag

YIELD: about 1/2 cup (enough for 2 to 4 servings)

2 TABLESPOONS EXTRA-VIRGIN OLIVE OIL

2 TEASPOONS GRATED ORANGE ZEST

2 TABLESPOONS FRESHLY SQUEEZED ORANGE JUICE

1/4 CUP GRATED RED ONION

1 TEASPOON CORIANDER SEEDS, TOASTED AND GROUND (SEE PAGE 297)

KOSHER SALT

FRESHLY GROUND BLACK PEPPER

MEASURE the oil, orange zest, orange juice, onion, and coriander into a 1-gallon zip-top bag and shake or squeeze until blended. Season to taste with salt and pepper.

SUGGESTED USES: chicken breasts (marinated 2 hours to overnight) or fish fillets or shrimp (marinated 20 to 45 minutes), grilled or broiled

GRILLED SALMON FILLETS

FOR 4 SERVINGS, add 4 skinned, boneless salmon fillets (6 to 8 ounces each) to the Orange-Coriander Marinade in the zip-top bag and turn to coat. Seal the bag, letting out all the air. Marinate for at least 20 minutes and up to 45 minutes at room temperature.

Remove the fillets from the marinade, pat dry with paper towels, then grill on an oiled grill grate over direct high heat until medium-rare, 8 to 10 minutes (or until the desired doneness), turning once. The fillets will barely begin to flake when they are medium-rare.

Serve the salmon fillets with couscous and a salad of orange segments, red onions, and fresh flat-leaf parsley leaves.

Spicy Orange Marinade

The marmalade that's blended into this spicy marinade gives it an extra orange punch.

TOOL: 1-gallon zip-top bag

YIELD: about 3/4 cup (enough for 4 to 6 servings)

1/4 CUP FRESHLY SQUEEZED ORANGE JUICE

3 TABLESPOONS SWEET ORANGE MARMALADE

2 TABLESPOONS CANOLA OIL

1 TABLESPOON SOY SAUCE

1 JALAPEÑO, SEEDED AND MINCED

1 FRESNO CHILE, SEEDED AND MINCED

GENEROUS PINCH OF CAYENNE PEPPER

KOSHER SALT

FRESHLY GROUND BLACK PEPPER

MEASURE the orange juice, marmalade, oil, soy sauce, jalapeño, Fresno chile, and cayenne into a 1-gallon zip-top bag and shake or squeeze until blended. Season to taste with salt and black pepper.

SUGGESTED USES: chicken breasts, pork chops, or beef steaks (marinated 2 hours to overnight) or fish fillets, shrimp, or sea scallops (marinated 20 to 45 minutes), grilled

GRILLED PORK LOIN OR RIB CHOPS

FOR 6 SERVINGS, add **6 boneless pork loin or rib chops (about 1 inch thick)** to the Spicy Orange Marinade in the zip-top bag and turn to coat. Seal the bag, letting out all the air. Marinate for **at least 2 hours and up to overnight** in the refrigerator.

Set the bag aside at room temperature for about half an hour. Remove the chops from the marinade, pat dry with paper towels, then grill over direct high heat until medium, 13 to 15 minutes (or until the desired doneness), turning once. Moisture will just begin to pool on the surface of the chops when they are medium. Tent the chops with foil and let rest for 5 to 10 minutes before carving and serving.

Serve the pork chops, thinly sliced, over sesame noodles, with some orange segments and zest thrown in if desired.

Blood Orange–Rosemary Marinade

With hints of berries and red wine, blood oranges are so complex that their juice could be used as a marinade all by itself. I've added little to this simple recipe to allow the orange flavor to take center stage.

TOOL: 1-gallon zip-top bag

YIELD: about 1/3 cup (enough for about 2 servings)

1/4 CUP FRESHLY SQUEEZED BLOOD ORANGE JUICE

2 TABLESPOONS EXTRA-VIRGIN OLIVE OIL

1 GARLIC CLOVE, MINCED

1 1/2 TEASPOONS MINCED FRESH ROSEMARY

KOSHER SALT

FRESHLY GROUND BLACK PEPPER

MEASURE the orange juice, oil, garlic, and rosemary into a 1-gallon zip-top bag and shake or squeeze until blended. Season to taste with salt and pepper.

SUGGESTED USES: chicken breasts, pork tenderloin medallions, lamb chops, or boneless, skin-on duck breasts (marinated 2 hours to overnight), grilled

GRILLED PORK TENDERLOIN MEDALLIONS

FOR 2 SERVINGS, add 1 pork tenderloin (12 to 14 ounces), cut on a bias into 1-inch-thick medallions, to the Blood Orange–Rosemary Marinade in the zip-top bag and turn to coat. Seal the bag, letting out all the air. Marinate for at least 2 hours and up to overnight in the refrigerator.

Set the bag aside at room temperature for about half an hour. Remove the medallions from the marinade, pat dry with paper towels, then grill over direct high heat until medium, 13 to 15 minutes (or until the desired doneness), turning once. Moisture will just begin to pool on the surface of the medallions when they are medium. Tent the medallions with foil and let rest for 5 to 10 minutes before serving.

Serve the pork medallions over a mesclun green salad with orange segments, sliced red onions, candied pecans, and a citrus vinaigrette or with new potatoes roasted with rosemary and a seasonal vegetable.

Grapefruit-Champagne Marinade

I often pick up grapefruit notes when I drink Champagne, so I was inspired to use the two flavors together in a marinade.

TOOL: 1-gallon zip-top bag

YIELD: about 3/4 cup (enough for 4 to 6 servings)

1/4 CUP CHAMPAGNE OR OTHER SPARKLING WINE

1 1/2 TEASPOONS GRATED GRAPEFRUIT ZEST

1/4 CUP FRESHLY SQUEEZED GRAPEFRUIT JUICE

2 TABLESPOONS EXTRA-VIRGIN OLIVE OIL

2 TABLESPOONS HONEY

1 SHALLOT, MINCED

KOSHER SALT

FRESHLY GROUND BLACK PEPPER

MEASURE the Champagne, grapefruit zest, grapefruit juice, oil, honey, and shallot into a 1-gallon zip-top bag and shake or squeeze until blended. Season to taste with salt and pepper.

SUGGESTED USES: chicken breasts (marinated 2 hours to overnight) or white fish fillets, shrimp, or sea scallops (marinated 20 to 45 minutes), grilled or broiled

GRILLED SEA SCALLOPS

FOR 4 SERVINGS, add 12 jumbo sea scallops (about 2 ounces each), side muscles removed, to the Grapefruit-Champagne Marinade in the zip-top bag and turn to coat. Seal the bag, letting out all the air. Marinate for at least 20 minutes and up to 45 minutes at room temperature.

Remove the scallops from the marinade, pat dry with paper towels, then grill on an oiled grill grate over direct high heat until medium-rare, 6 to 7 minutes (or until the desired doneness), turning once. Moisture will just begin to accumulate on the surface of the scallops when they are medium-rare.

Serve the scallops over mesclun greens tossed with grapefruit segments, sliced red onions, and wedges of avocado dressed with a citrus vinaigrette.

Four-Citrus Marinade

Orange, grapefruit, lemon, and lime flavors harmonize for a light, zippy marinade.

TOOL: 1-gallon zip-top bag

YIELD: about 3/4 cup (enough for 4 to 6 servings)

1/4 CUP EXTRA-VIRGIN OLIVE OIL

1 TEASPOON GRATED ORANGE ZEST

1 TEASPOON GRATED GRAPEFRUIT ZEST

1 TEASPOON GRATED LEMON ZEST

1 TEASPOON GRATED LIME ZEST

2 TABLESPOONS FRESHLY SQUEEZED ORANGE JUICE

2 TABLESPOONS FRESHLY SQUEEZED GRAPEFRUIT JUICE

1 1/2 TEASPOONS FRESHLY SQUEEZED LEMON JUICE

1 1/2 TEASPOONS FRESHLY SQUEEZED LIME JUICE

2 TABLESPOONS HONEY

2 GARLIC CLOVES, MINCED

KOSHER SALT

FRESHLY GROUND BLACK PEPPER

MEASURE the oil, orange zest, grapefruit zest, lemon zest, lime zest, orange juice, grapefruit juice, lemon juice, lime juice, honey, and garlic into a 1-gallon zip-top bag and shake or squeeze until blended. Season to taste with salt and pepper.

SUGGESTED USES: chicken breasts (marinated 2 hours to overnight) or fish fillets, shrimp, or sea scallops (marinated 20 to 45 minutes), grilled

RECIPE CONTINUES →

FOR 6 SERVINGS, add 6 boneless, skinless chicken breasts (about 8 ounces each), pounded to an even thickness of $1/2$ to $3/4$ inch, to the Four-Citrus Marinade in the zip-top bag and turn to coat. Seal the bag, letting out all the air. Marinate for at least 2 hours and up to overnight in the refrigerator.

Set the bag aside at room temperature for about half an hour. Remove the chicken from the marinade, pat dry with paper towels, then grill on an oiled grill grate over direct high heat until just cooked through, 10 to 12 minutes, turning once. The chicken will be firm to the touch and the juices will run clear when it is just cooked through. Tent the chicken with foil and let rest for 5 to 10 minutes before carving and serving.

Serve these chicken breasts, thinly sliced, in a wrap, on a salad, tossed into pasta, or with any starch and seasonal vegetable your family likes.

CONDIMENT
MARINADES

With little work and few additional ingredients, condiments—from mustard and prepared horseradish to barbecue sauce and pepper jelly and even pickle juice—can be transformed into delicious, boldly flavored marinades. Recipes like Yellow Mustard Marinade, Buffalo Wing Marinade, and Pepper Jelly Marinade give you yet another use for all those little bottles and jars in the back of the pantry and in the refrigerator door.

Balsamic Marinade

If I were pressed to pick a favorite marinade, this one would definitely be in the running. It's easy and delicious and makes almost everything, including chicken, meat, and seafood, taste better. And of note, it makes the best antipasto vegetables ever.

TOOL: 1-gallon zip-top bag

YIELD: about 1 cup (enough for 5 to 8 servings)

1/4 CUP PLUS 2 TABLESPOONS EXTRA-VIRGIN OLIVE OIL

1/4 CUP PLUS 2 TABLESPOONS BALSAMIC VINEGAR

6 GARLIC CLOVES, MINCED

1/4 CUP PLUS 2 TABLESPOONS MIXED MINCED FRESH HERBS
(SUCH AS BASIL, FLAT-LEAF PARSLEY, OREGANO, MARJORAM,
ROSEMARY, AND/OR THYME)

KOSHER SALT

FRESHLY GROUND BLACK PEPPER

MEASURE the oil, balsamic vinegar, garlic, and herbs into a 1-gallon zip-top bag and shake or squeeze until blended. Season to taste with salt and pepper.

SUGGESTED USES: chicken breasts, pork chops, beef steaks, or lamb chops (marinated 2 hours to overnight), fish fillets, shrimp, or sea scallops (marinated 20 to 45 minutes), raw vegetables (marinated 30 minutes to 1 hour), grilled or broiled; roasted vegetables (marinated overnight)

ANTIPASTO VEGETABLES

FOR 6 TO 8 APPETIZER SERVINGS, cut 2 small zucchini, 2 small yellow squash, 1 small globe eggplant, 1 portobello mushroom cap, and 1 small red onion into $1/2$- to $3/4$-inch-thick slices. Arrange in a single layer on rimmed baking sheets, brush with olive oil, and sprinkle with salt and pepper, then roast in a preheated 450°F oven until tender, 16 to 20 minutes, turning once. Cool to room temperature. Add the roasted vegetables and 2 oven-dried plum tomatoes (12 pieces; see page 47) and 1 roasted red bell pepper (see page 297), cut into strips, to the Balsamic Marinade in the zip-top bag and turn gently to coat. Seal the bag, letting out all the air. Marinate overnight in the refrigerator. Alternatively, you can grill the vegetables rather than roast them.

Serve the marinated vegetables as part of an antipasto spread—I'd include a selection of salami, cheeses, and olives and offer either crackers or Italian bread to go with it. These vegetables are also delicious tossed into pasta or salad or stuffed inside panini with plenty of sharp provolone.

Balsamic-Soy Marinade

This was the first marinade I ever learned to make, back in my college days when I moved into my own apartment and started to cook for myself, and it's still a winner after all this time. I especially like it for grilled portobello mushroom caps—it makes them taste like steak.

TOOL: 1-gallon zip-top bag

YIELD: about 1/3 cup (enough for about 2 servings)

2 TABLESPOONS CANOLA OIL

2 TABLESPOONS BALSAMIC VINEGAR

2 TABLESPOONS SOY SAUCE

1/4 TEASPOON TOASTED SESAME OIL

2 GARLIC CLOVES, MINCED

GENEROUS PINCH OF CRUSHED RED PEPPER

FRESHLY GROUND BLACK PEPPER

MEASURE the canola oil, balsamic vinegar, soy sauce, sesame oil, garlic, and crushed red pepper into a 1-gallon zip-top bag and shake or squeeze until blended. Season to taste with black pepper.

SUGGESTED USES: chicken breasts, pork chops, or beef steaks (marinated 2 hours to overnight) or vegetables (marinated 30 minutes to 1 hour), grilled or broiled

GRILLED PORTOBELLOS

FOR 2 SERVINGS, add 2 portobello mushroom caps to the Balsamic-Soy Marinade in the zip-top bag and turn to coat. Seal the bag, letting out all the air. Marinate for **at least 30 minutes and up to 1 hour** at room temperature.

Remove the mushrooms from the marinade and pat dry with paper towels. Grill over direct high heat until tender, 7 to 9 minutes, turning once.

Serve the mushrooms over sticky rice topped with a sprinkling of sliced scallions, with a side of garlicky Chinese greens.

Barbecue Marinade

The easiest and most satisfying marinade of all, and one I rely on all the time, is simply barbecue sauce—either purchased or homemade—and a bit of oil.

TOOL: 1-gallon zip-top bag

YIELD: about $1/2$ cup (enough for 2 to 4 servings)

$1/2$ CUP BARBECUE SAUCE

2 TABLESPOONS CANOLA OIL

MEASURE the barbecue sauce and oil into a 1-gallon zip-top bag and shake or squeeze until blended.

SUGGESTED USES: chicken pieces, pork ribs or chops, or beef ribs or steaks (marinated overnight) or salmon fillets or shrimp (marinated 20 to 45 minutes), grilled

GRILLED BABY BACK RIBS

FOR 2 SERVINGS, add 1 rack pork baby back ribs (2 to $2^1/2$ pounds), cut in half, to the Barbecue Marinade in the zip-top bag and turn to coat. Seal the bag, letting out all the air. Marinate overnight in the refrigerator.

Set the bag aside at room temperature for about half an hour. Remove the ribs from the marinade and place them on the grill, meaty side up. Grill the ribs, covered, over indirect medium-low heat until fork-tender, 2 to $2^1/2$ hours. The meat will have noticeably shrunk away from the ends of the bones when it is done. Tent the ribs with foil and let rest for 5 to 10 minutes before carving and serving.

Serve the ribs with any side dishes that you might serve at a barbecue, such as coleslaw and corn on the cob.

Honey-Mustard Marinade

The combination of honey and mustard works as well in a marinade as it does in a dressing.

TOOL: 1-gallon zip-top bag

YIELD: about 1/2 cup (enough for 2 to 4 servings)

1/4 CUP CANOLA OIL

2 TABLESPOONS HONEY

2 TABLESPOONS DIJON MUSTARD

2 TEASPOONS FRESHLY SQUEEZED LEMON JUICE

2 TABLESPOONS MINCED FRESH FLAT-LEAF PARSLEY

KOSHER SALT

FRESHLY GROUND BLACK PEPPER

MEASURE the oil, honey, mustard, lemon juice, and parsley into a 1-gallon zip-top bag and shake or squeeze until blended. Season to taste with salt and pepper.

SUGGESTED USES: chicken breasts or pork chops (marinated 2 hours to overnight) or salmon fillets or shrimp (marinated 20 to 45 minutes), grilled

GRILLED CHICKEN BREASTS

FOR 4 SERVINGS, add 4 boneless, skinless chicken breasts (about 8 ounces each), pounded to an even thickness of 1/2 to 3/4 inch, to the Honey-Mustard Marinade in the zip-top bag and turn to coat. Seal the bag, letting out all the air. Marinate for at least 2 hours and up to overnight in the refrigerator.

Set the bag aside at room temperature for about half an hour. Remove the chicken from the marinade, pat dry with paper towels, then grill on an oiled grill grate over direct high heat until just cooked through, 10 to 12 minutes, turning once. The chicken will be firm to the touch and the juices will run clear when it is just cooked through. Tent the chicken with foil and let rest for 5 to 10 minutes before carving and serving.

These chicken breasts are perfect in a Cobb salad or other chopped salad.

Maple-Mustard Marinade

Maple syrup replaces honey in this variation on the popular flavor combination.

TOOL: 1-gallon zip-top bag

YIELD: about 3/4 cup (enough for about 6 servings)

1/4 CUP PURE MAPLE SYRUP

1/4 CUP COARSE-GRAIN MUSTARD

2 TABLESPOONS EXTRA-VIRGIN OLIVE OIL

2 TABLESPOONS BALSAMIC VINEGAR

KOSHER SALT

FRESHLY GROUND BLACK PEPPER

MEASURE the maple syrup, mustard, oil, and balsamic vinegar into a 1-gallon zip-top bag until blended. Season to taste with salt and pepper.

SUGGESTED USES: chicken breasts, turkey breast cutlets, pork chops, or beef steaks (marinated 2 hours to overnight) or salmon fillets (marinated 20 to 45 minutes), grilled or broiled

GRILLED PORK LOIN OR RIB CHOPS

FOR 6 SERVINGS, add 6 boneless pork loin or rib chops (about 1 inch thick) to the Maple-Mustard Marinade in the zip-top bag and turn to coat. Seal the bag, letting out all the air. Marinate for **at least 2 hours and up to overnight** in the refrigerator.

Set the bag aside at room temperature for about half an hour. Remove the chops from the marinade, pat dry with paper towels, then grill over direct high heat until medium, 13 to 15 minutes (or until the desired doneness), turning once. Moisture will just begin to pool on the surface of the chops when they are medium. Tent the chops with foil and let rest for 5 to 10 minutes before serving.

Serve the chops with brown rice and snap peas or whatever starch and seasonal vegetable your family prefers.

Yellow Mustard Marinade

This marinade is zesty, quick, and easy. It uses nothing but pantry staples and takes mere moments to whip up—no dicing or chopping required. For an even speedier take on this recipe, simply combine yellow mustard with $1/2$ cup good-quality bottled Italian salad dressing.

TOOL: 1-gallon zip-top bag

YIELD: about $2/3$ cup (enough for 4 to 6 servings)

3 TABLESPOONS EXTRA-VIRGIN OLIVE OIL

3 TABLESPOONS CANOLA OIL

2 TABLESPOONS WHITE WINE VINEGAR

2 TABLESPOONS YELLOW MUSTARD

$1/2$ TEASPOON DRIED BASIL

$1/2$ TEASPOON DRIED OREGANO

$1/2$ TEASPOON DRIED MARJORAM

$1/4$ TEASPOON DRIED THYME

$3/4$ TEASPOON GRANULATED GARLIC

$1/2$ TEASPOON ONION POWDER

$1/4$ TEASPOON CRUSHED RED PEPPER

KOSHER SALT

FRESHLY GROUND BLACK PEPPER

MEASURE the olive oil, canola oil, vinegar, mustard, basil, oregano, marjoram, thyme, granulated garlic, onion powder, and crushed red pepper into a 1-gallon zip-top bag and shake or squeeze until blended. Season to taste with salt and black pepper.

SUGGESTED USES: chicken breasts, pork chops, or beef steaks (marinated 2 hours to overnight), grilled

GRILLED CHICKEN BREASTS

FOR 4 SERVINGS, add 4 boneless, skinless chicken breasts (about 8 ounces each), pounded to an even thickness of $1/2$ to $3/4$ inch, to the Yellow Mustard Marinade in the zip-top bag and turn to coat. Seal the bag, letting out all the air. Marinate for **at least 2 hours and up to overnight** in the refrigerator.

Set the bag aside at room temperature for about half an hour. Remove the chicken from the marinade, pat dry with paper towels, then grill on an oiled grill grate over direct high heat until just cooked through 10 to 12 minutes, turning once. The chicken will be firm to the touch and the juices will run clear when it is just cooked through. Tent the chicken with foil and let rest for 5 to 10 minutes before carving and serving.

These chicken breasts will go with just about anything—serve them over a salad or with any starch and seasonal vegetable you'd like.

Buffalo Wing Marinade

This spicy marinade makes it possible for you to serve irresistible Buffalo wings without a deep fryer or butter-based sauce. Feel free to use your favorite hot sauce in place of the Tabasco.

TOOL: 1-gallon zip-top bag

YIELD: about 1/2 cup (enough for 2 to 4 servings)

1/4 CUP TABASCO SAUCE

2 TABLESPOONS CANOLA OIL

2 GARLIC CLOVES, MINCED

1 TABLESPOON PAPRIKA

KOSHER SALT

MEASURE the Tabasco, oil, garlic, and paprika into a 1-gallon zip-top bag and shake or squeeze until blended. Season to taste with salt.

SUGGESTED USES: chicken breasts (marinated 2 hours to overnight), chicken wings (marinated overnight), or shrimp (marinated 20 to 45 minutes), grilled

GRILLED BUFFALO WINGS

FOR 2 SERVINGS, add 1 1/2 pounds chicken wing flats and drumettes to the Buffalo Wing Marinade in the zip-top bag and turn to coat. Seal the bag, letting out all the air. Marinate overnight in the refrigerator.

Set the bag aside at room temperature for about half an hour. Remove the chicken from the marinade, pat dry with paper towels, then grill, covered, over direct medium heat until just cooked through, 15 to 20 minutes, turning occasionally. The chicken will be firm to the touch, and the meat will have noticeably shrunk away from the knuckles of the drumettes.

Serve the chicken wings with the usual fixings of celery sticks and blue cheese dressing.

Horseradish-Mustard Marinade

Horseradish and mustard are often blended together to make a sauce to serve with beef. It turns out that the combination is just as satisfying, if not more so, in marinade form, as the flavors permeate every morsel.

TOOL: 1-gallon zip-top bag

YIELD: about 1/2 cup (enough for about 4 servings)

2 TABLESPOONS CANOLA OIL

2 TABLESPOONS SOY SAUCE

2 TABLESPOONS COARSE-GRAIN MUSTARD

2 TABLESPOONS PREPARED HORSERADISH

MEASURE the oil, soy sauce, mustard, and horseradish into a 1-gallon zip-top bag and shake or squeeze until blended.

SUGGESTED USES: beef tenderloin or prime rib (marinated overnight), roasted; beef steaks (marinated 2 hours to overnight), grilled

GRILLED SIRLOIN STEAKS

FOR 4 SERVINGS, add 2 sirloin steaks (1 to 1 1/4 inches thick) to the Horseradish-Mustard Marinade in the zip-top bag and turn to coat. Seal the bag, letting out all the air. Marinate for at least 2 hours and up to overnight in the refrigerator.

Set the bag aside at room temperature for about half an hour. Remove the steaks from the marinade, pat dry with paper towels, then grill over direct high heat until medium-rare, 10 to 14 minutes (or until the desired doneness), turning once. Moisture will just begin to accumulate on the surface of the steaks when they are medium-rare. Tent the steaks with foil and let rest for 5 to 10 minutes before carving and serving.

Serve the steaks with creamy horseradish mashed potatoes and a seasonal vegetable.

Horseradish-Tomato Marinade

The sweetness of tomato contrasts nicely with the sharpness of horseradish.

TOOL: 1-gallon zip-top bag

YIELD: about 3/4 cup (enough for about 6 servings)

1/3 CUP TOMATO JUICE

2 TABLESPOONS CANOLA OIL

2 TABLESPOONS RED WINE VINEGAR

1 TABLESPOON TOMATO PASTE

1 TABLESPOON PREPARED HORSERADISH

2 TEASPOONS SUGAR

KOSHER SALT

FRESHLY GROUND BLACK PEPPER

MEASURE the tomato juice, oil, vinegar, tomato paste, horseradish, and sugar into a 1-gallon zip-top bag and shake or squeeze until blended. Season to taste with salt and pepper.

SUGGESTED USES: chicken breasts or beef steaks (marinated 2 hours to overnight) or salmon fillets (marinated 20 to 45 minutes), grilled

GRILLED SALMON FILLETS

FOR 6 SERVINGS, add 6 skinned, boneless salmon fillets (6 to 8 ounces each) to the Horseradish-Tomato Marinade in the zip-top bag and turn to coat. Seal the bag, letting out all the air. Marinate for at least 20 minutes and up to 45 minutes at room temperature.

Remove the fillets from the marinade, pat dry with paper towels, then grill on an oiled grill grate over direct high heat until medium-rare, 8 to 10 minutes (or until the desired doneness), turning once. The fillets will barely begin to flake when they are medium-rare.

Serve the salmon fillets with any tomato side dish. A tomato salad, tomatoes stuffed with bread crumbs and herbs, or a tomato gratin would all be nice choices, especially if they're spiked with a bit of horseradish.

Pepper Jelly Marinade

Pepper jelly is a great ingredient to keep on hand—it packs a lot of flavor but lets you shortcut any dicing or chopping. A generous scoop of pepper jelly and this marinade practically makes itself.

TOOL: 1-gallon zip-top bag

YIELD: about 1 cup (enough for about 8 servings)

1/2 CUP PEPPER JELLY

3 TABLESPOONS CIDER VINEGAR

3 TABLESPOONS SOY SAUCE

2 TABLESPOONS CANOLA OIL

MEASURE the jelly, vinegar, soy sauce, and oil into a 1-gallon zip-top bag and shake or squeeze until blended.

SUGGESTED USES: chicken breasts, pork chops, or beef steaks (marinated 2 hours to overnight), grilled

GRILLED PORK LOIN OR RIB CHOPS

FOR 8 SERVINGS, add 8 boneless pork loin or rib chops (about 1 inch thick) to the Pepper Jelly Marinade in the zip-top bag and turn to coat. Seal the bag, letting out all the air. Marinate for at least 2 hours and up to overnight in the refrigerator.

Set the bag aside at room temperature for about half an hour. Remove the chops from the marinade, pat dry with paper towels, then grill over direct high heat until medium, 13 to 15 minutes (or until the desired doneness), turning once. Moisture will just begin to pool on the surface of the chops when they are medium. Tent the chops with foil and let rest for 5 to 10 minutes before serving.

Serve the chops with any starch at all and a seasonal vegetable.

Smoky Bacon Marinade

If you can wrap it in bacon, why not marinate it in bacon? Save the flavorful fat that renders off from frying bacon and use it as the base for a marinade. The bacon fat must be warm and fluid to blend well with the other ingredients (just make sure it's not hot or it'll melt through the zip-top bag). Canola oil keeps the marinade from solidifying in the refrigerator.

TOOL: 1-gallon zip-top bag

YIELD: about 1 cup (enough for 5 to 8 servings)

1/2 CUP CANOLA OIL

1/4 CUP WARM RENDERED BACON FAT

1 TABLESPOON RED WINE VINEGAR

1/4 CUP DICED YELLOW ONION

1 GARLIC CLOVE, MINCED

1/2 TEASPOON MINCED FRESH THYME

GENEROUS PINCH OF CAYENNE PEPPER

KOSHER SALT

FRESHLY GROUND BLACK PEPPER

MEASURE the oil, bacon fat, vinegar, onion, garlic, thyme, and cayenne into a 1-gallon zip-top bag and shake or squeeze until blended. Season to taste with salt and black pepper.

SUGGESTED USES: chicken breasts (marinated overnight) or fish fillets, shrimp, or sea scallops (marinated 20 to 45 minutes), grilled

GRILLED CHICKEN BREASTS

FOR 8 SERVINGS, add 8 boneless, skinless chicken breasts (about 8 ounces each), pounded to an even thickness of $1/2$ to $3/4$ inch, to the Smoky Bacon Marinade in the zip-top bag and turn to coat. Seal the bag, letting out all the air. Marinate overnight in the refrigerator.

Set the bag aside at room temperature for about half an hour. Remove the chicken from the marinade, pat dry with paper towels, then grill on an oiled grill grate over direct high heat until just cooked through, 10 to 12 minutes, turning once. The chicken will be firm to the touch and the juices will run clear when it is just cooked through. Tent the chicken with foil and let rest for 5 to 10 minutes before carving and serving.

These subtly smoky chicken breasts are delicious served with a rice or barley pilaf made with onions, mushrooms, crumbled bacon, bay leaf, and fresh thyme. They're also wonderful in a sandwich with lettuce, tomato, red onion, and guacamole on ciabatta or diced and used in a Cobb salad.

Pickle Juice Marinade

One of my favorite restaurants offers a "Chicken Little Sandwich" on their happy hour menu. It's nothing but battered and fried chicken and pickle slices on a soft roll, but it's absolutely irresistible. Now, I'm usually not one to eat pickle slices on my sandwiches, but there's something special about the combination of perfectly crisp fried chicken and tangy pickles. The flavors go so well together that it made me dream up this marinade, to be used for—what else—fried chicken.

TOOL: 1-gallon zip-top bag

YIELD: about 1/2 cup (enough for 2 to 3 servings)

1/3 CUP PICKLE JUICE

2 TABLESPOONS CANOLA OIL

MEASURE the pickle juice and oil into a 1-gallon zip-top bag and shake until blended.

SUGGESTED USES: chicken tenders (marinated 2 hours to overnight) or halibut fillet strips or shrimp (marinated 20 to 45 minutes), deep-fried

FRIED CHICKEN TENDERS

FOR 2 TO 3 SERVINGS, add 12 ounces chicken breast tenders to the Pickle Juice Marinade in the zip-top bag and turn to coat. Seal the bag, letting out all the air. Marinate for at least 2 hours and up to overnight in the refrigerator.

Set the bag aside at room temperature for about half an hour. Shaking off any excess marinade, dip each chicken tender into all-purpose flour to coat and shake off any excess. Deep-fry the chicken in batches in 375°F canola oil until golden brown and crisp and just cooked through, 4 to 6 minutes. The chicken will float at the top of the oil and the bubbles will begin to subside when it is just cooked through. Transfer the chicken to a paper towel–lined baking sheet and season to taste with salt.

Serve the chicken tenders with pickle slices and your choice of condiments on split biscuits or soft rolls.

DAIRY
MARINADES

BUTTERMILK, SOUR CREAM, YOGURT, AND WHEY NOT ONLY ADD FLAVOR TO MARINADES BUT ALSO ACT AS MEAT TENDERIZERS; PUNGENT CHEESES SUCH AS BLUE AND FETA SIMPLY IMPART FLAVOR. MANY OF THE RECIPES IN THIS CHAPTER, INCLUDING THE BUTTERMILK RANCH MARINADE AND THE SOUR CREAM AND CHIVE MARINADE, WERE INSPIRED BY THE SOUTHERN TRADITION OF SOAKING CHICKEN IN A SPICY BUTTERMILK MIXTURE BEFORE FRYING. HANDLE FOODS MARINATED IN BUTTERMILK, SOUR CREAM, YOGURT, AND WHEY GENTLY, AND IF GRILLING, OIL THE GRILL GRATE THOROUGHLY TO AVOID STICKING AND TEARING.

Spicy Buttermilk Marinade

This is the most common style of marinade used in the South for fried chicken.

TOOLS: mortar and pestle • 1-gallon zip-top bag

YIELD: about 1/2 cup (enough for about 4 servings)

1/2 CUP BUTTERMILK

1 TEASPOON GRANULATED GARLIC

1 TEASPOON ONION POWDER

1 TEASPOON PAPRIKA

1/4 TEASPOON CELERY SEEDS, GROUND WITH A MORTAR AND PESTLE (SEE BELOW)

1/4 TEASPOON CAYENNE PEPPER

1/4 TEASPOON FRESHLY GROUND BLACK PEPPER

KOSHER SALT

MEASURE the buttermilk, granulated garlic, onion powder, paprika, ground celery seeds, cayenne, and black pepper into a 1-gallon zip-top bag and shake or squeeze until blended. Season to taste with salt.

CELERY SEEDS	I find that whole celery seeds can be somewhat bitter, so I grind them to a powder with a mortar and pestle. If you don't have a mortar and pestle, you can crush them with a small, heavy sauté pan.

SUGGESTED USES: chicken pieces or pork chops (marinated 2 hours to overnight) or beef cube steaks (marinated 2 to 4 hours), deep-fried or pan-fried

FRIED CHICKEN

FOR 4 SERVINGS, add 8 chicken drumsticks and/or thighs to the Spicy Buttermilk Marinade in the zip-top bag and turn to coat. Seal the bag, letting out all the air. Marinate for **at least 2 hours and up to overnight** in the refrigerator.

Set the bag aside at room temperature for about half an hour. Shaking off any excess marinade, dip each chicken piece into all-purpose flour to coat and shake off any excess. Deep-fry the chicken in batches in 350°F canola oil until golden brown and crisp and just cooked through, 13 to 15 minutes. The chicken will float at the top of the oil and the bubbles will begin to subside when it is just cooked through. Transfer the chicken to a paper towel–lined baking sheet and season to taste with salt.

Serve with your favorite comfort food side dishes, such as coleslaw and corn on the cob.

Buttermilk Ranch Marinade

Here I've reinvented the popular salad dressing and veggie dip flavor as a marinade.

TOOL: 1-gallon zip-top bag

YIELD: about ⅔ cup (enough for about 4 servings)

½ CUP BUTTERMILK

1 GARLIC CLOVE, MINCED

1 ½ TABLESPOONS MINCED FRESH FLAT-LEAF PARSLEY

1 ½ TABLESPOONS MINCED FRESH CHIVES

1 TEASPOON MINCED FRESH THYME

¼ TEASPOON FRESHLY GROUND BLACK PEPPER

KOSHER SALT

MEASURE the buttermilk, garlic, parsley, chives, thyme, and pepper into a 1-gallon zip-top bag and shake or squeeze until blended. Season to taste with salt.

SUGGESTED USES: chicken pieces or pork chops (marinated 2 hours to overnight) or beef cube steaks (marinated 2 to 4 hours), deep-fried or pan-fried

CHICKEN-FRIED STEAK WITH GRAVY

FOR 4 SERVINGS, add 4 beef cube steaks (about 6 ounces each) to the Buttermilk Ranch Marinade in the zip-top bag and turn to coat. Seal the bag, letting out all the air. Marinate for at least 2 hours and up to 4 hours in the refrigerator.

Set the bag aside at room temperature for about half an hour. Shaking off any excess marinade, dip each cube steak into all-purpose flour to coat and shake off any excess. Then dip each steak into an egg wash (1 egg beaten with $1/4$ cup milk) and finally back into the all-purpose flour to coat. Heat about $1/4$ inch of canola oil in a large, heavy sauté pan over medium heat until a pinch of flour sizzles immediately when added. Add the steaks and pan-fry until golden brown and crisp and just cooked through, 6 to 8 minutes, turning once. The cube steaks will be firm to the touch when they are just cooked through. Transfer the cube steaks to a paper towel–lined baking sheet and season to taste with salt. Tent the cube steaks with foil to keep warm.

For country-style white gravy, pour all but about 2 tablespoons oil out of the pan. Return the pan to medium heat and stir in 3 tablespoons all-purpose flour. Whisk in $1\,1/2$ cups milk. Bring to a boil, stirring constantly and scraping up the brown bits from the bottom of the pan with a heatproof spatula. Simmer until thickened and saucy, 2 to 3 minutes. Season to taste with salt and lots of black pepper. Serve the cube steaks with the gravy immediately.

Buttermilk mashed potatoes and a garden salad dressed with ranch dressing would go with these cube steaks perfectly, as would any other comfort food sides.

Buttermilk-Lemon-Herb Marinade

Any mixture of finely minced herbs will work in this marinade.

TOOL: 1-gallon zip-top bag

YIELD: about 1/2 cup (enough for about 4 servings)

1/2 CUP BUTTERMILK

1/2 TEASPOON GRATED LEMON ZEST

1 GARLIC CLOVE, MINCED

1 TEASPOON MINCED FRESH ROSEMARY

1 TEASPOON MINCED FRESH OREGANO

1/2 TEASPOON MINCED FRESH THYME

KOSHER SALT

FRESHLY GROUND BLACK PEPPER

MEASURE the buttermilk, lemon zest, garlic, rosemary, oregano, and thyme into a 1-gallon zip-top bag and shake or squeeze until blended. Season to taste with salt and pepper.

SUGGESTED USES: chicken pieces or pork chops (marinated 2 hours to overnight) or beef cube steaks (marinated 2 to 4 hours), deep-fried or pan-fried

FRIED CHICKEN

FOR 4 SERVINGS, add 8 chicken drumsticks and/or thighs to the Buttermilk-Lemon-Herb Marinade in the zip-top bag and turn to coat. Seal the bag, letting out all the air. Marinate for at least 2 hours and up to overnight in the refrigerator.

Set the bag aside at room temperature for about half an hour. Shaking off any excess marinade, dip each chicken piece into all-purpose flour to coat and shake off any excess. Deep-fry the chicken in batches in 350°F canola oil until golden brown and crisp and just cooked through, 13 to 15 minutes. The chicken will float at the top of the oil and the bubbles will begin to subside when it is just cooked through. Transfer the chicken to a paper towel–lined baking sheet and season to taste with salt.

Serve with your favorite comfort food side dishes, such as buttermilk mashed potatoes and coleslaw.

Sour Cream and Chive Marinade

One of the most popular snack food flavor combinations inspired this recipe, which is sure to become a favorite of kids of all ages.

TOOL: 1-gallon zip-top bag

YIELD: about 3/4 cup (enough for about 6 servings)

1/3 CUP BUTTERMILK

1/3 CUP SOUR CREAM

1/2 TEASPOON WORCESTERSHIRE SAUCE

3 TABLESPOONS MINCED FRESH CHIVES

2 GARLIC CLOVES, MINCED

1 TEASPOON ONION POWDER

KOSHER SALT

FRESHLY GROUND BLACK PEPPER

MEASURE the buttermilk, sour cream, Worcestershire, chives, garlic, and onion powder into a 1-gallon zip-top bag and shake or squeeze until blended. Season to taste with salt and pepper.

SUGGESTED USES: chicken pieces or pork chops (marinated 2 hours to overnight) or beef cube steaks (marinated 2 to 4 hours), oven-fried, deep-fried, or pan-fried

OVEN-FRIED PORK LOIN OR RIB CHOPS

FOR 6 SERVINGS, add 6 boneless pork loin or rib chops (about 1 inch thick) to the Sour Cream and Chive Marinade in the zip-top bag and turn to coat. Seal the bag, letting out all the air. Marinate for at least 2 hours and up to overnight in the refrigerator.

Set the bag aside at room temperature for about half an hour. Shaking off any excess marinade, press each chop into panko bread crumbs, arrange on a rack on a rimmed baking sheet, and drizzle with canola oil. Bake the chops in a preheated 450°F oven until golden brown and crisp and cooked to medium (or until the desired doneness), 18 to 20 minutes. When you press on them, the chops will have a slight bit of give when they are medium. Tent the chops with foil and let rest for 5 to 10 minutes before serving.

Serve these pork chops with buttermilk mashed potatoes and a seasonal vegetable.

Spicy Whey Marinade

If cheesemaking is a hobby of yours, you probably have more whey around than you know what to do with. One way to use it up is to put it in a marinade.

TOOLS: mortar and pestle • 1-gallon zip-top bag

YIELD: about 2/3 cup (enough for about 4 servings)

1/2 CUP WHEY

1/4 TEASPOON TABASCO SAUCE

1/4 TEASPOON WORCESTERSHIRE SAUCE

1 GARLIC CLOVE, MINCED

1 JALAPEÑO, THINLY SLICED

1/4 TEASPOON ONION POWDER

1/8 TEASPOON CELERY SEEDS, GROUND WITH A MORTAR AND PESTLE
(SEE PAGE 118)

GENEROUS PINCH OF CAYENNE PEPPER

KOSHER SALT

FRESHLY GROUND BLACK PEPPER

MEASURE the whey, Tabasco, Worcestershire, garlic, jalapeño, onion powder, ground celery seeds, and cayenne into a 1-gallon zip-top bag and shake or squeeze until blended. Season to taste with salt and black pepper.

SUGGESTED USES: chicken pieces or pork chops (marinated 2 hours to overnight) or beef cube steaks (marinated 2 to 4 hours), deep-fried or pan-fried

CHICKEN-FRIED STEAK WITH GRAVY

FOR 4 SERVINGS, add 4 beef cube steaks (about 6 ounces each) to the Spicy Whey Marinade in the zip-top bag and turn to coat. Seal the bag, letting out all the air. Marinate for at least 2 hours and up to 4 hours in the refrigerator.

Set the bag aside at room temperature for about half an hour. Shaking off any excess marinade and picking off any jalapeño slices, dip each cube steak into all-purpose flour to coat and shake off any excess. Then dip each steak into an egg wash (1 egg beaten with $1/4$ cup milk) and finally back into the all-purpose flour to coat. Heat about $1/4$ inch of canola oil in a large, heavy sauté pan over medium heat until a pinch of flour sizzles immediately when added. Add the steaks and pan-fry until golden brown and crisp and just cooked through, 6 to 8 minutes, turning once. The cube steaks will be firm to the touch when they are just cooked through. Transfer the cube steaks to a paper towel–lined baking sheet and season to taste with salt. Tent the cube steaks with foil to keep warm.

For country-style white gravy, pour all but about 2 tablespoons oil out of the pan. Return the pan to medium heat and stir in 3 tablespoons all-purpose flour. Whisk in $1^1/2$ cups milk. Bring to a boil, stirring constantly and scraping up the brown bits from the bottom of the pan with a heatproof spatula. Simmer until thickened and saucy, 2 to 3 minutes. Season to taste with salt and lots of black pepper. Serve the cube steaks with the gravy immediately.

Mashed potatoes and a seasonal vegetable would be a nice accompaniment to these cube steaks.

Feta-Herb Marinade

Feta imparts its tangy, salty sheep's milk flavor to this marinade. Of course, it's a natural choice for lamb but is also delicious with chicken. Use a bold feta for the best results.

TOOL: 1-gallon zip-top bag

YIELD: about 1/2 cup (enough for 2 to 4 servings)

1/4 CUP EXTRA-VIRGIN OLIVE OIL

1 TABLESPOON RED WINE VINEGAR

1 1/2 OUNCES (GENEROUS 1/4 CUP) FETA CRUMBLES

2 GARLIC CLOVES, MINCED

1 TEASPOON MINCED FRESH ROSEMARY

1 TEASPOON MINCED FRESH OREGANO

1 TEASPOON MINCED FRESH MINT LEAVES

1/4 TEASPOON CRUSHED RED PEPPER

KOSHER SALT

FRESHLY GROUND BLACK PEPPER

MEASURE the oil, vinegar, feta, garlic, rosemary, oregano, mint, and crushed red pepper into a 1-gallon zip-top bag and shake or squeeze, breaking up the feta crumbles as you do, until blended. Season to taste with salt and black pepper.

SUGGESTED USES: chicken breasts or lamb chops (marinated 2 hours to overnight), grilled; shrimp (marinated 20 to 45 minutes), grilled or broiled

GRILLED LAMB RIB CHOPS

FOR 2 SERVINGS, add 6 frenched lamb rib chops (about 1 inch thick) to the Feta-Herb Marinade in the zip-top bag and turn to coat. Seal the bag, letting out all the air. Marinate for at least 2 hours and up to overnight in the refrigerator.

Set the bag aside at room temperature for about half an hour. Remove the chops from the marinade, pat dry with paper towels, then grill over direct high heat until medium-rare, 10 to 12 minutes (or until the desired doneness), turning once. Moisture will just begin to accumulate on the surface of the chops when they are medium-rare. Tent the chops with foil and let rest for 5 to 10 minutes before serving.

Serve these lamb chops with warm pita bread and a salad of tomato, cucumber, red onion, and kalamata olives dressed with a red wine vinegar vinaigrette. Alternatively, serve with orzo tossed with sliced kalamata olives, lemon zest, garlic, and olive oil.

Blue Cheese Marinade

Blue cheese might seem like an odd ingredient to use in a marinade, but its umami quality really brings out the beefy flavor in steak.

TOOL: 1-gallon zip-top bag

YIELD: about 1/2 cup (enough for about 4 servings)

1/3 CUP EXTRA-VIRGIN OLIVE OIL

1 TABLESPOON RED WINE VINEGAR

1 OUNCE (SCANT 1/4 CUP) BLUE CHEESE CRUMBLES

1 TABLESPOON MINCED FRESH CHIVES

KOSHER SALT

FRESHLY GROUND BLACK PEPPER

MEASURE the oil, vinegar, blue cheese, and chives into a 1-gallon zip-top bag and shake or squeeze, breaking up the blue cheese crumbles as you do, until blended. Season to taste with salt and pepper.

SUGGESTED USES: chicken breasts, pork chops, or beef steaks (marinated 2 hours to overnight), grilled

GRILLED RIB-EYE OR STRIP STEAKS

FOR 4 SERVINGS, add 4 boneless rib-eye or strip steaks (1 to 1 1/4 inches thick) to the Blue Cheese Marinade in the zip-top bag and turn to coat. Seal the bag, letting out all the air. Marinate for at least 2 hours and up to overnight in the refrigerator.

Set the bag aside at room temperature for about half an hour. Remove the steaks from the marinade, pat dry with paper towels, then grill over direct high heat until medium-rare, 12 to 14 minutes (or until the desired doneness), turning once. Moisture will just begin to accumulate on the surface of the steaks when they are medium-rare. Tent the steaks with foil and let rest for 5 to 10 minutes before carving and serving.

These steaks will go with just about anything—serve with any starch and seasonal vegetable you'd like. Alternatively, serve the steak, thinly sliced, over a salad of butter lettuce, strips of roasted red bell pepper, and sliced scallions dressed with blue cheese dressing and topped with crisp onion straws.

COFFEE, SODA, BEER, WINE, AND SPIRIT
MARINADES

MARINADES WITH BEER, WINE, AND LIQUOR MAY COME AS NO SURPRISE, BUT HAVE YOU EVER CONSIDERED USING COFFEE OR COLA? THE RECIPES IN THIS CHAPTER PROVE THAT ALMOST ANY TASTY BEVERAGE, ALCOHOLIC OR NOT, CAN FORM THE BASE OF A MARINADE. ESPRESSO, SODA POP, AND DIFFERENT TYPES OF BEER AND WINE INSPIRE MARINADES SUCH AS STOUT-MOLASSES MARINADE AND SHERRY-GARLIC MARINADE. FUN FLAVORS SUCH AS BLOODY MARY-NADE AND MARGARITA MARINADE ARE BASED ON POPULAR MIXED DRINKS.

Espresso Marinade

Coffee has long been used in such savory applications as redeye gravy, so I figured why not use espresso in a marinade? The result is delicious, with notes of caramel and anise coming through in the meat.

TOOL: 1-gallon zip-top bag

YIELD: about 1 cup (enough for 4 to 8 servings)

1 DOUBLE SHOT ESPRESSO (ABOUT $1/3$ CUP), AT ROOM TEMPERATURE

$1/4$ CUP SOY SAUCE

2 TABLESPOONS CANOLA OIL

$1/2$ TEASPOON WORCESTERSHIRE SAUCE

$1/4$ CUP PACKED LIGHT BROWN SUGAR

1 TEASPOON GRANULATED GARLIC

$1/2$ TEASPOON CHIPOTLE CHILE POWDER

GENEROUS PINCH OF GROUND CINNAMON

FRESHLY GROUND BLACK PEPPER

MEASURE the espresso, soy sauce, oil, Worcestershire, brown sugar, granulated garlic, chile powder, and cinnamon into a 1-gallon zip-top bag and shake or squeeze until blended. Season to taste with pepper.

SUGGESTED USES: pork chops or beef steaks (marinated 2 hours to overnight) or beef ribs (marinated overnight), grilled

GRILLED RIB-EYE OR STRIP STEAKS

FOR 8 SERVINGS, add 8 boneless rib-eye or strip steaks (1 to $1^1/4$ inches thick) to the Espresso Marinade in the zip-top bag and turn to coat. Seal the bag, letting out all the air. Marinate for at least 2 hours and up to overnight in the refrigerator.

Set the bag aside at room temperature for about half an hour. Remove the steaks from the marinade, pat dry with paper towels, then grill over direct high heat until medium-rare, 12 to 14 minutes (or until the desired doneness), turning once. Moisture will just begin to accumulate on the surface of the steaks when they are medium-rare. Tent the steaks with foil and let rest for 5 to 10 minutes before serving.

Serve these steaks with cornbread, grits, or a sweet potato casserole.

Cola Marinade

Soda marinades are common in the South, and it's no wonder—cola is sweet, acidic, and flavorful, and it has all of the characteristics necessary to make a good marinade.

TOOL: 1-gallon zip-top bag

YIELD: about 1 1/4 cups (enough for 4 to 10 servings)

1/2 CUP COLA (NOT DIET)

1/4 CUP SOY SAUCE

1/4 CUP KETCHUP

2 TABLESPOONS CANOLA OIL

1 TEASPOON WORCESTERSHIRE SAUCE

3/4 TEASPOON TABASCO SAUCE

1 TABLESPOON NEW MEXICO CHILE POWDER

1 TEASPOON GRANULATED GARLIC

3/4 TEASPOON ONION POWDER

FRESHLY GROUND BLACK PEPPER

MEASURE the cola, soy sauce, ketchup, oil, Worcestershire, Tabasco, chile powder, granulated garlic, and onion powder into a 1-gallon zip-top bag and shake or squeeze until blended. Season to taste with pepper.

SUGGESTED USES: whole chicken or pieces or beef brisket or ribs (marinated overnight), grilled or smoked; pork ribs (marinated overnight), grilled; ham steak (marinated 2 hours to overnight), sautéed or grilled

GRILLED BABY BACK RIBS

POUR ABOUT HALF of the Cola Marinade into a second 1-gallon zip-top bag. For 4 servings, cut 2 racks pork baby back ribs (2 to 2 1/2 pounds each) in half and add 1 rack (2 halves) to the marinade in each of the zip-top bags; turn to coat. Seal the bags, letting out all the air. Marinate overnight in the refrigerator.

Set the bags aside at room temperature for about half an hour. Remove the ribs from the marinade and place them on the grill, meaty side up. Grill the ribs, covered, over indirect medium-low heat until fork-tender, 2 to 2 1/2 hours. The meat will have noticeably shrunk away from the ends of the bones when it is done. Tent the ribs with foil and let rest for 5 to 10 minutes before carving and serving.

Serve the ribs with any side dishes that you might serve at a barbecue, such as cornbread, baked beans, or coleslaw.

Root Beer Marinade

Root beer and a variety of sweet spices impart a unique flavor to this marinade.

TOOL: 1-gallon zip-top bag

YIELD: about 1 1/4 cups (enough for 4 to 10 servings)

1/3 CUP ROOT BEER

1/4 CUP KETCHUP

2 TABLESPOONS CANOLA OIL

2 TABLESPOONS CIDER VINEGAR

2 TABLESPOONS SOY SAUCE

2 TABLESPOONS MOLASSES

1 TABLESPOON YELLOW MUSTARD

1/2 TEASPOON WORCESTERSHIRE SAUCE

2 GARLIC CLOVES, MINCED

1/2 TEASPOON ONION POWDER

1/8 TEASPOON GROUND GINGER

1/8 TEASPOON GROUND ALLSPICE

PINCH OF GROUND CLOVES

PINCH OF CAYENNE PEPPER

KOSHER SALT

FRESHLY GROUND BLACK PEPPER

MEASURE the root beer, ketchup, oil, cider vinegar, soy sauce, molasses, mustard, Worcestershire, garlic, onion powder, ginger, allspice, cloves, and cayenne into a 1-gallon zip-top bag and shake or squeeze until blended. Season to taste with salt and black pepper.

SUGGESTED USES: whole chicken (marinated overnight), smoked; pork butt, belly, or ribs or beef brisket or ribs (marinated overnight), grilled or smoked; ham steak (marinated 2 hours to overnight), sautéed or grilled

SMOKED CHICKEN

FOR 4 TO 6 SERVINGS, add 1 whole chicken (3 1/2 to 4 pounds) to the Root Beer Marinade in the zip-top bag and turn to coat, trying to get some of the marinade into the cavity. Seal the bag, letting out all the air. Marinate overnight in the refrigerator.

Set the bag aside at room temperature for about half an hour. Remove the chicken from the marinade, pat dry with paper towels, and truss. Smoke the chicken in a 200° to 225°F smoker until just cooked through, 3 to 4 hours. The drumsticks will wiggle freely in their joints, the meat of the drumsticks will have noticeably shrunk away from the knuckles, the juices will run clear, and a meat thermometer inserted in the thickest part of the breast will register 160°F when it is just cooked through. Tent the chicken with foil and let rest for 15 to 20 minutes before carving and serving (the internal temperature should rise to 165°F).

Serve the chicken with baked beans and coleslaw.

Brown Ale Marinade

Brown ale is lightly hopped and made from brown malt. This simple marinade lets the sweet, malty character of the beer shine through.

TOOL: 1-gallon zip-top bag

YIELD: about 2/3 cup (enough for 4 to 6 servings)

1/3 CUP BROWN ALE

1 TABLESPOON CANOLA OIL

1 TABLESPOON SOY SAUCE

1/2 TEASPOON WORCESTERSHIRE SAUCE

1 GARLIC CLOVE, MINCED

2 TABLESPOONS PACKED LIGHT BROWN SUGAR

1 TEASPOON NEW MEXICO CHILE POWDER

1/4 TEASPOON MUSTARD POWDER

KOSHER SALT

FRESHLY GROUND BLACK PEPPER

MEASURE the ale, oil, soy sauce, Worcestershire, garlic, brown sugar, chile powder, and mustard into a 1-gallon zip-top bag and shake or squeeze until blended. Season to taste with salt and pepper.

SUGGESTED USES: chicken pieces, pork chops, or beef steaks (marinated 2 hours to overnight), grilled

GRILLED PORK LOIN OR RIB CHOPS

FOR 4 SERVINGS, add 4 boneless pork loin or rib chops (about 1 inch thick) to the Brown Ale Marinade in the zip-top bag and turn to coat. Seal the bag, letting out all the air. Marinate for at least 2 hours and up to overnight in the refrigerator.

Set the bag aside at room temperature for about half an hour. Remove the chops from the marinade, pat dry with paper towels, then grill over direct high heat until medium, 13 to 15 minutes (or until the desired doneness), turning once. Moisture will just begin to pool on the surface of the chops when they are medium. Tent the chops with foil and let rest for 5 to 10 minutes before serving.

These pork chops will go with just about anything—serve with any starch and seasonal vegetable you'd like.

IPA-Jalapeño Marinade

My husband's love for India Pale Ale is what prompted me to create this marinade. IPAs are extremely floral but often aggressively bitter, so I used a good helping of brown sugar for balance.

TOOL: 1-gallon zip-top bag

YIELD: about 1¼ cups (enough for about 10 servings)

3/4 CUP INDIA PALE ALE

1 TABLESPOON CANOLA OIL

1 TABLESPOON FRESHLY SQUEEZED LIME JUICE

1/2 TEASPOON WORCESTERSHIRE SAUCE

1 GARLIC CLOVE, MINCED

2 JALAPEÑOS, SEEDED AND MINCED

1/4 CUP PACKED LIGHT BROWN SUGAR

KOSHER SALT

FRESHLY GROUND BLACK PEPPER

MEASURE the ale, oil, lime juice, Worcestershire, garlic, jalapeños, and brown sugar into a 1-gallon zip-top bag and shake or squeeze until blended. Season to taste with salt and pepper.

SUGGESTED USES: chicken breasts, pork chops, or beef steaks (marinated 2 hours to overnight), grilled

GRILLED SIRLOIN STEAKS

FOR 10 SERVINGS, add **5 sirloin steaks (1 to 1¼ inches thick)** to the IPA-Jalapeño Marinade in the zip-top bag and turn to coat. Seal the bag, letting out all the air. Marinate for **at least 2 hours and up to overnight** in the refrigerator.

Set the bag aside at room temperature for about half an hour. Remove the steaks from the marinade, pat dry with paper towels, then grill over direct high heat until medium-rare, 10 to 14 minutes (or until the desired doneness), turning once. Moisture will just begin to accumulate on the surface of the steaks when they are medium-rare. Tent the steaks with foil and let rest for 5 to 10 minutes before carving and serving.

These steaks will go with just about anything—serve with any starch and seasonal vegetable you'd like.

Stout-Mustard Marinade

Guinness stout is often used in this kind of marinade, but it's fun to experiment with Imperial stout, porter, or other types of stout, and with different mustards.

TOOL: 1-gallon zip-top bag

YIELD: about 3/4 cup (enough for about 6 servings)

1/2 CUP STOUT

3 TABLESPOONS COARSE-GRAIN MUSTARD

1 TABLESPOON CANOLA OIL

1 SHALLOT, MINCED

1/2 TEASPOON MINCED FRESH ROSEMARY

KOSHER SALT

FRESHLY GROUND BLACK PEPPER

MEASURE the stout, mustard, oil, shallot, and rosemary into a 1-gallon zip-top bag and shake or squeeze until blended. Season to taste with salt and pepper.

SUGGESTED USES: chicken breasts, pork chops, or beef steaks (marinated 2 hours to overnight), grilled

GRILLED PORK LOIN OR RIB CHOPS

FOR 6 SERVINGS, add 6 boneless pork loin or rib chops (about 1 inch thick) to the Stout-Mustard Marinade in the zip-top bag and turn to coat. Seal the bag, letting out all the air. Marinate for at least 2 hours and up to overnight in the refrigerator.

Set the bag aside at room temperature for about half an hour. Remove the chops from the marinade, pat dry with paper towels, then grill over direct high heat until medium, 13 to 15 minutes (or until the desired doneness), turning once. Moisture will just begin to pool on the surface of the chops when they are medium. Tent the chops with foil and let rest for 5 to 10 minutes before serving.

Serve these pork chops with roasted new potatoes with rosemary and a seasonal vegetable.

Stout-Molasses Marinade

The bitterness and malt flavor of stout is perfectly balanced by molasses.

TOOL: 1-gallon zip-top bag

YIELD: about 1/2 cup (enough for 2 to 4 servings)

1/4 CUP STOUT

2 TABLESPOONS MOLASSES

1 TABLESPOON CANOLA OIL

1 TEASPOON WORCESTERSHIRE SAUCE

1 GARLIC CLOVE, MINCED

KOSHER SALT

FRESHLY GROUND BLACK PEPPER

MEASURE the stout, molasses, oil, Worcestershire, and garlic into a 1-gallon zip-top bag and shake or squeeze until blended. Season to taste with salt and pepper.

SUGGESTED USES: chicken breasts, pork tenderloin medallions or chops, or beef steaks (marinated 2 hours to overnight), grilled or broiled

GRILLED PORK TENDERLOIN MEDALLIONS

FOR 2 SERVINGS, add 1 pork tenderloin (12 to 14 ounces), cut on a bias into 1-inch-thick medallions, to the Stout-Molasses Marinade in the zip-top bag and turn to coat. Seal the bag, letting out all the air. Marinate for at least 2 hours and up to overnight in the refrigerator.

Set the bag aside at room temperature for about half an hour. Remove the pork from the marinade, pat dry with paper towels, then grill over direct high heat until medium, 13 to 15 minutes (or until the desired doneness), turning once. Moisture will just begin to pool on the surface of the medallions when they are medium. Tent the medallions with foil and let rest for 5 to 10 minutes before serving.

Serve the pork medallions with roasted winter squash or sweet potatoes.

Stout-Chocolate Marinade

Stout and chocolate are often paired in sweets and desserts, but the combination lends itself to savory pairings just as well.

TOOL: 1-gallon zip-top bag

YIELD: about 1/2 cup (enough for about 4 servings)

1/4 CUP STOUT

1 TABLESPOON CANOLA OIL

1 GARLIC CLOVE, MINCED

2 TABLESPOONS PACKED LIGHT BROWN SUGAR

2 TABLESPOONS UNSWEETENED COCOA POWDER

1/2 TEASPOON ANCHO CHILE POWDER

KOSHER SALT

FRESHLY GROUND BLACK PEPPER

MEASURE the stout, oil, garlic, brown sugar, cocoa powder, and chile powder into a 1-gallon zip-top bag and shake or squeeze until blended. Season to taste with salt and pepper.

SUGGESTED USES: chicken breasts, pork chops, or beef steaks (marinated 2 hours to overnight), grilled

GRILLED SIRLOIN STEAKS

FOR 4 SERVINGS, add 2 sirloin steaks (1 to 1 1/4 inches thick) to the Stout-Chocolate Marinade in the zip-top bag and turn to coat. Seal the bag, letting out all the air. Marinate for at least 2 hours and up to overnight in the refrigerator.

Set the bag aside at room temperature for about half an hour. Remove the steaks from the marinade, pat dry with paper towels, then grill over direct high heat until medium-rare, 10 to 14 minutes (or until the desired doneness), turning once. Moisture will just begin to accumulate on the surface of the steaks when they are medium-rare. Tent the steaks with foil and let rest for 5 to 10 minutes before carving and serving.

Serve the steaks with roasted winter squash or sweet potatoes.

Hard Cider–Maple Marinade

Another great choice for fall, this recipe is sweeter than the Apple-Sage Marinade (page 75).

TOOL: 1-gallon zip-top bag

YIELD: about 1/2 cup (enough for about 4 servings)

1/3 CUP HARD CIDER

2 TABLESPOONS PURE MAPLE SYRUP

1 TABLESPOON CANOLA OIL

1 FRESH THYME SPRIG

1 SHALLOT, MINCED

1/8 TEASPOON GROUND CINNAMON

KOSHER SALT

FRESHLY GROUND BLACK PEPPER

MEASURE the cider, maple syrup, oil, thyme, shallot, and cinnamon into a 1-gallon zip-top bag and shake or squeeze until blended. Season to taste with salt and pepper.

SUGGESTED USES: chicken breasts, turkey breast cutlets, or pork chops (marinated 2 hours to overnight), grilled or broiled

GRILLED TURKEY BREAST CUTLETS

FOR 4 SERVINGS, add 4 turkey breast cutlets (about 4 ounces each and 1/2 inch thick) to the Hard Cider–Maple Marinade in the zip-top bag and turn to coat. Seal the bag, letting out all the air. Marinate for at least 2 hours and up to overnight in the refrigerator.

Set the bag aside at room temperature for about half an hour. Remove the turkey from the marinade, pat dry with paper towels, then grill on an oiled grill grate over direct high heat until just cooked through, 8 to 10 minutes, turning once. The turkey will be firm to the touch and the juices will run clear when it is just cooked through. Tent the turkey with foil and let rest for 5 to 10 minutes before serving.

Serve these turkey cutlets with baked apples or applesauce or a sweet potato casserole.

Rosé-Herb Marinade

Travels to Provence, where I experienced the rosé wines of Tavel and the ubiquitous use of herbes de Provence, led me to blend the two in this marinade.

TOOL: 1-gallon zip-top bag

YIELD: about 1/2 cup (enough for 2 to 4 servings)

1/3 CUP ROSÉ

1 TABLESPOON EXTRA-VIRGIN OLIVE OIL

2 TEASPOONS DIJON MUSTARD

1/2 TEASPOON GRATED LEMON ZEST

2 GARLIC CLOVES, MINCED

2 TEASPOONS HERBES DE PROVENCE (SEE PAGE 188)

1/4 TEASPOON DRIED LAVENDER FLOWERS, CRUSHED (SEE PAGE 287)

KOSHER SALT

FRESHLY GROUND BLACK PEPPER

MEASURE the rosé, oil, mustard, zest, garlic, herbes de Provence, and lavender into a 1-gallon zip-top bag and shake or squeeze until blended. Season to taste with salt and pepper.

SUGGESTED USES: chicken breasts, pork chops, or lamb leg steaks or chops (marinated 2 hours to overnight), grilled

GRILLED LAMB LEG STEAKS

FOR 4 SERVINGS, add 2 lamb leg steaks (1 to 1 1/4 inches thick) to the Rosé-Herb Marinade in the zip-top bag and turn to coat. Seal the bag, letting out all the air. Marinate for at least 2 hours and up to overnight in the refrigerator.

Set the bag aside at room temperature for about half an hour. Remove the steaks from the marinade, pat dry with paper towels, then grill over direct high heat until medium-rare, 10 to 14 minutes (or until the desired doneness), turning once. Moisture will just begin to accumulate on the surface of the steaks when they are medium-rare. Tent the steaks with foil and let rest for 5 to 10 minutes before carving and serving.

Serve the steaks with a sautéed medley of zucchini, yellow squash, red bell peppers, and eggplant.

Sherry-Garlic Marinade

I've been making this marinade for as long as I can remember. It's one of my favorites for steak, though it's also a good choice for chicken or shrimp. When I make it with beef, I like to marinate and cook at least two flank steaks, one to eat immediately and one to have cold in a sandwich or on a salad the next day.

TOOL: 1-gallon zip-top bag

YIELD: about 1/2 cup (enough for 2 to 6 servings)

2 TABLESPOONS CANOLA OIL

2 TABLESPOONS DRY SHERRY

2 TABLESPOONS SOY SAUCE

2 TABLESPOONS HONEY

2 GARLIC CLOVES, MINCED

PINCH OF CRUSHED RED PEPPER

FRESHLY GROUND BLACK PEPPER

MEASURE the oil, sherry, soy sauce, honey, garlic, and crushed red pepper into a 1-gallon zip-top bag and shake or squeeze until blended. Season to taste with black pepper.

SUGGESTED USES: chicken breasts or beef steaks (marinated 2 hours to overnight) or shrimp (marinated 20 to 45 minutes), grilled

GRILLED FLANK STEAKS

FOR 4 TO 6 SERVINGS, add 2 flank steaks (1 to 1 1/2 pounds each) to the Sherry-Garlic Marinade in the zip-top bag and turn to coat. Seal the bag, letting out all the air. Marinate for at least 2 hours and up to overnight in the refrigerator.

Set the bag aside at room temperature for about half an hour. Remove the steaks from the marinade, pat dry with paper towels, then grill over direct high heat until medium-rare, 10 to 12 minutes (or until the desired doneness), turning once. Moisture will just begin to accumulate on the surface of the steaks when they are medium-rare. Tent the steaks with foil and let rest for 5 to 10 minutes before carving and serving.

For a main-course salad, serve the steaks, thinly sliced, over mesclun greens with a sherry vinegar vinaigrette. The flank steak is also fantastic, either hot or cold, in a steak sandwich.

Marsala-Rosemary Marinade

Marsala is a fortified wine made in Sicily. You may know it from the popular Italian restaurant dish veal (or chicken) Marsala. Rich, oaky Marsala needs few additions to make a tasty marinade.

TOOL: 1-gallon zip-top bag

YIELD: about $1/3$ cup (enough for about 2 servings)

2 TABLESPOONS EXTRA-VIRGIN OLIVE OIL

2 TABLESPOONS DRY MARSALA

1 SHALLOT, MINCED

$1/2$ TEASPOON MINCED FRESH ROSEMARY

KOSHER SALT

FRESHLY GROUND BLACK PEPPER

MEASURE the oil, Marsala, shallot, and rosemary into a 1-gallon zip-top bag and shake or squeeze until blended. Season to taste with salt and pepper.

SUGGESTED USES: chicken breasts, pork tenderloin medallions, or veal chops (marinated 2 hours to overnight), grilled; ham steak (marinated 2 hours to overnight), sautéed or grilled

GRILLED CHICKEN BREASTS

FOR 2 SERVINGS, add 2 boneless, skinless chicken breasts (about 8 ounces each), pounded to an even thickness of $1/2$ to $3/4$ inch, to the Marsala-Rosemary Marinade in the zip-top bag and turn to coat. Seal the bag, letting out all the air. Marinate for at least 2 hours and up to overnight in the refrigerator.

Set the bag aside at room temperature for about half an hour. Remove the chicken from the marinade, pat dry with paper towels, then grill on an oiled grill grate over direct high heat until just cooked through, 10 to 12 minutes, turning once. The chicken will be firm to the touch and the juices will run clear when it is just cooked through. Tent the chicken with foil and let rest for 5 to 10 minutes before serving.

Serve the chicken breasts with mushroom risotto.

Madeira-Thyme Marinade

Madeira, a fortified wine from Portugal, can be used in a marinade in much the same way as Marsala. The flavors are similar, but Madeira differs in that it has toasty caramel notes from being heated during the aging process.

TOOL: 1-gallon zip-top bag

YIELD: about 1/2 cup (enough for 2 to 4 servings)

1/4 CUP DRY MADEIRA

2 TABLESPOONS EXTRA-VIRGIN OLIVE OIL

1 TABLESPOON HONEY

2 GARLIC CLOVES, MINCED

1/2 TEASPOON MINCED FRESH THYME

KOSHER SALT

FRESHLY GROUND BLACK PEPPER

MEASURE the Madeira, oil, honey, garlic, and thyme into a 1-gallon zip-top bag and shake or squeeze until blended. Season to taste with salt and pepper.

SUGGESTED USES: chicken breasts, pork tenderloin medallions, or veal chops (marinated 2 hours to overnight), grilled

GRILLED VEAL RIB CHOPS

FOR 4 SERVINGS, add 4 boneless veal rib chops (1 to 1 1/4 inches thick) to the Madeira-Thyme Marinade in the zip-top bag and turn to coat. Seal the bag, letting out all the air. Marinate for at least 2 hours and up to overnight in the refrigerator.

Set the bag aside at room temperature for about half an hour. Remove the chops from the marinade, pat dry with paper towels, then grill over direct high heat until medium-rare, 10 to 14 minutes (or until the desired doneness), turning once. Moisture will just begin to accumulate on the surface of the chops when they are medium-rare. Tent the chops with foil and let rest for 5 to 10 minutes before serving.

Serve these veal chops with wild mushroom pasta.

Bourbon-Maple Marinade

A Southern favorite, this marinade highlights the flavors of oaky bourbon and sweet maple syrup.

TOOL: 1-gallon zip-top bag

YIELD: about 3/4 cup (enough for about 6 servings)

3 TABLESPOONS PURE MAPLE SYRUP

2 TABLESPOONS CANOLA OIL

2 TABLESPOONS BOURBON

2 TABLESPOONS SOY SAUCE

1 TABLESPOON CIDER VINEGAR

1 TABLESPOON KETCHUP

1 TEASPOON DIJON MUSTARD

1/2 TEASPOON TABASCO SAUCE

1/4 TEASPOON WORCESTERSHIRE SAUCE

1 GARLIC CLOVE, MINCED

1/4 TEASPOON CRUSHED RED PEPPER

KOSHER SALT

FRESHLY GROUND BLACK PEPPER

MEASURE the maple syrup, oil, bourbon, soy sauce, cider vinegar, ketchup, mustard, Tabasco, Worcestershire, garlic, and crushed red pepper into a 1-gallon zip-top bag and shake or squeeze until blended. Season to taste with salt and black pepper.

SUGGESTED USES: chicken breasts, pork chops, or beef steaks (marinated 2 hours to overnight), grilled

GRILLED CHICKEN BREASTS

FOR 6 SERVINGS, add 6 boneless, skinless chicken breasts (about 8 ounces each), pounded to an even thickness of $1/2$ to $3/4$ inch, to the Bourbon-Maple Marinade in the zip-top bag and turn to coat. Seal the bag, letting out all the air. Marinate for at least 2 hours and up to overnight in the refrigerator.

Set the bag aside at room temperature for about half an hour. Remove the chicken from the marinade, pat dry with paper towels, then grill on an oiled grill grate over direct high heat until just cooked through, 10 to 12 minutes, turning once. The chicken will be firm to the touch and the juices will run clear when it is just cooked through. Tent the chicken with foil and let rest for 5 to 10 minutes before serving.

Serve the chicken breasts with buttered corn on the cob or your favorite Southern-style comfort food sides.

Whiskey-Peppercorn Marinade

Variations of this marinade, often made with Jack Daniel's, are extremely popular in the South.

TOOL: 1-gallon zip-top bag

YIELD: about 1/3 cup (enough for about 2 servings)

2 TABLESPOONS WHISKEY

2 TABLESPOONS SOY SAUCE

1 TABLESPOON CANOLA OIL

1 TEASPOON TABASCO SAUCE

1 TEASPOON WORCESTERSHIRE SAUCE

2 GARLIC CLOVES, MINCED

2 TABLESPOONS PACKED LIGHT BROWN SUGAR

1/2 TEASPOON FRESHLY CRACKED BLACK PEPPERCORNS

MEASURE the whiskey, soy sauce, oil, Tabasco, Worcestershire, garlic, brown sugar, and black pepper into a 1-gallon zip-top bag and shake or squeeze until blended.

SUGGESTED USES: chicken breasts, pork chops, or beef steaks (marinated 2 hours to overnight), grilled

GRILLED SIRLOIN STEAK

FOR 2 SERVINGS, add 1 sirloin steak (1 to 1 1/4 inches thick) to the Whiskey-Peppercorn Marinade in the zip-top bag and turn to coat. Seal the bag, letting out all the air. Marinate for at least 2 hours and up to overnight in the refrigerator.

Set the bag aside at room temperature for about half an hour. Remove the steak from the marinade, pat dry with paper towels, then grill over direct high heat until medium-rare, 10 to 14 minutes (or until the desired doneness), turning once. Moisture will just begin to accumulate on the surface of the steak when it is medium-rare. Tent the steak with foil and let rest for 5 to 10 minutes before carving and serving.

This steak will go with just about anything—serve with baked potatoes and a green salad or any side dishes you desire.

Marinade for Pâté

Chicken livers are often seasoned with nothing but salt and pepper before being sautéed for pâté. Soaking them first for a short time in a cognac marinade adds a new dimension to the finished pâté.

TOOL: 1-gallon zip-top bag

YIELD: about 1/4 cup (enough for 1 pound chicken livers)

3 TABLESPOONS COGNAC

1 SHALLOT, SLICED

PINCH OF FRESHLY GROUND MACE

PINCH OF FRESHLY GROUND WHITE PEPPER

KOSHER SALT

MEASURE the cognac, shallot, mace, and white pepper into a 1-gallon zip-top bag and shake until blended. Season to taste with salt.

CHICKEN LIVER PÂTÉ

FOR 6 TO 10 SERVINGS, add 1 pound chicken livers to the Marinade for Pâté in the zip-top bag and turn to coat. Seal the bag, letting out all the air. Marinate for at least 45 minutes and up to 1 hour at room temperature.

Remove the livers from the marinade and pat dry with paper towels, picking off any shallots. Heat a large, heavy sauté pan over medium-low heat. Add 3 tablespoons unsalted butter and 1 julienned yellow onion (see page 297) and cook, stirring frequently, until caramelized. Increase the heat to medium-high, add the livers, and sauté until crusty and brown on the outside but still quite pink inside. If desired, add 1 tablespoon cognac and bring to a boil, scraping up the brown bits from the bottom of the pan with a heatproof spatula. Remove from the heat and let cool to room temperature. Transfer the livers and onions to a food processor, add 1/4 cup softened unsalted butter, and process until smooth. Force through a fine-mesh sieve to remove any veins or gristly bits. Season to taste with salt and pepper and pack into a large ramekin or small terrine mold.

Serve the pâté with baguette slices and cornichons or caper berries. Leftovers can be stored, tightly covered in the refrigerator, for a day or two.

Gin Marinade

With its double hit of juniper in the form of gin and crushed berries, this marinade has a woodsy flavor that's particularly well suited to pork and wild game. Juniper berries can be found at most gourmet shops.

TOOL: 1-gallon zip-top bag

YIELD: about 1/3 cup (enough for about 2 servings)

2 TABLESPOONS EXTRA-VIRGIN OLIVE OIL

2 TABLESPOONS GIN

1 TABLESPOON WHITE WINE VINEGAR

1 GARLIC CLOVE, MINCED

1 BAY LEAF, CRUMBLED

1/4 TEASPOON JUNIPER BERRIES, CRUSHED

1/4 TEASPOON MUSTARD SEEDS

1/4 TEASPOON CRUSHED RED PEPPER

4 ALLSPICE BERRIES

2 WHOLE CLOVES

KOSHER SALT

FRESHLY GROUND BLACK PEPPER

MEASURE the oil, gin, vinegar, garlic, bay leaf, juniper berries, mustard seeds, crushed red pepper, allspice, and cloves into a 1-gallon zip-top bag and shake or squeeze until blended. Season to taste with salt and black pepper.

SUGGESTED USES: pork chops, boneless, skin-on duck breasts, butterflied Cornish hens, venison or boar medallions, or other game (marinated 2 hours to overnight), grilled or seared

GRILLED PORK LOIN OR RIB CHOPS

FOR 2 SERVINGS, add 2 boneless pork loin or rib chops (about 1 inch thick) to the Gin Marinade in the zip-top bag and turn to coat. Seal the bag, letting out all the air. Marinate for at least 2 hours and up to overnight in the refrigerator.

Set the bag aside at room temperature for about half an hour. Remove the chops from the marinade and pat dry with paper towels, picking off any spices. Grill over direct high heat until medium, 13 to 15 minutes (or until the desired doneness), turning once. Moisture will just begin to pool on the surface of the chops when they are medium. Tent the chops with foil and let rest for 5 to 10 minutes before serving.

Serve the pork chops with roasted rosemary potatoes and a seasonal vegetable.

Brandy–Vanilla Bean Marinade

Ice cream and crème brûlée may be the first things that come to mind when you think of vanilla, but its use outside of sweets and desserts is becoming more and more common among creative chefs. Try this marinade if you'd like to begin to explore the potential of vanilla in savory applications yourself.

TOOL: 1-gallon zip-top bag

YIELD: about 2/3 cup (enough for about 4 servings)

1/2 VANILLA BEAN

1/4 CUP FRESHLY SQUEEZED ORANGE JUICE

2 TABLESPOONS CANOLA OIL

2 TABLESPOONS BRANDY

1 SHALLOT, MINCED

1 TABLESPOON PACKED LIGHT BROWN SUGAR

KOSHER SALT

FRESHLY GROUND BLACK PEPPER

WITH A paring knife, cut the vanilla bean in half lengthwise. With the tip of the knife, scrape out the seeds, reserving the pod for another use (see page 295). Measure the vanilla seeds, orange juice, oil, brandy, shallot, and brown sugar into a 1-gallon zip-top bag and shake or squeeze until blended. Season to taste with salt and pepper.

SUGGESTED USES: split lobster tails (marinated 20 to 45 minutes), grilled or broiled; boneless, skin-on duck breasts (marinated 2 hours to overnight), seared; butterflied Cornish hens, whole quail, squab, or other game birds (marinated 2 hours to overnight), pan-roasted

SEARED DUCK BREASTS

FOR 4 SERVINGS, add **4 boneless, skin-on duck breasts** (about 8 ounces each), skin scored with a diamond pattern, to the Brandy–Vanilla Bean Marinade in the zip-top bag and turn to coat. Seal the bag, letting out all the air. Marinate for **at least 2 hours and up to overnight** in the refrigerator.

Set the bag aside at room temperature for about half an hour. Remove the duck from the marinade and pat dry with paper towels. Heat a large, heavy sauté pan over medium heat until a few water droplets dance and look like ball bearings rolling around when flicked into the pan. Sear the duck, starting with the skin side down, until medium-rare, 10 to 12 minutes (or until the desired doneness), turning once. The duck will just begin to feel firm to the touch when it is medium-rare, and the temperature will register 130°F when an instant-read thermometer is inserted sideways into the center of the breast. Tent the duck with foil and let rest for 5 to 10 minutes before carving and serving.

Serve the duck breasts with a medley of maple-glazed roasted carrots, parsnips, and sweet potatoes.

Dirty Martini Marinade

Olive brine and vodka are the main ingredients in this marinade, just as they are in the mixed drink. If you like, you can substitute gin for the vodka.

TOOL: 1-gallon zip-top bag

YIELD: about 2/3 cup (enough for 4 to 6 servings)

1/4 CUP OLIVE BRINE (FROM A JAR OF GREEN OLIVES)

2 TABLESPOONS EXTRA-VIRGIN OLIVE OIL

2 TABLESPOONS VODKA

1 TABLESPOON FRESHLY SQUEEZED LEMON JUICE

1 TEASPOON DRY VERMOUTH

1/4 TEASPOON WORCESTERSHIRE SAUCE

1 GARLIC CLOVE, MINCED

1/2 TEASPOON ONION POWDER

KOSHER SALT

FRESHLY GROUND BLACK PEPPER

MEASURE the olive brine, oil, vodka, lemon juice, vermouth, Worcestershire, garlic, and onion powder into a 1-gallon zip-top bag and shake or squeeze until blended. Season to taste with salt and pepper.

SUGGESTED USES: cubes of boneless, skinless chicken thighs or beef sirloin (marinated 2 hours to overnight), skewered and grilled; salmon fillets (marinated 20 to 45 minutes), baked *en papillote*

GRILLED CHICKEN KABOBS

FOR 8 APPETIZER SERVINGS, add 8 boneless, skinless chicken thighs (about 4 ounces each), cut into $1^1/2$-inch pieces, to the Dirty Martini Marinade in the zip-top bag and turn to coat. Seal the bag, letting out all the air. Marinate for at least 2 hours and up to overnight in the refrigerator.

Set the bag aside at room temperature for about half an hour. Remove the chicken from the marinade, pat dry with paper towels, and skewer, alternating with green olives (either pitted or pimiento-stuffed) and pearl onions, onto bamboo skewers that have been soaked in water. Grill the skewers, covered, on an oiled grill grate over direct medium heat until just cooked through, 10 to 12 minutes, turning once. The chicken will be firm to the touch and the juices will run clear when it is just cooked through. Tent the skewers with foil and let rest for 5 to 10 minutes before serving.

Serve with martinis, of course!

Bloody Mary-nade

The **savory flavors** of the ever-popular cocktail translate nicely into marinade form.

TOOLS: mortar and pestle • 1-gallon zip-top bag

YIELD: about $1/2$ cup (enough for 2 to 4 servings)

1/3 CUP TOMATO JUICE

2 TABLESPOONS VODKA

1 TABLESPOON CANOLA OIL

1 TABLESPOON FRESHLY SQUEEZED LEMON JUICE

1 TEASPOON PREPARED HORSERADISH

1/2 TEASPOON TABASCO SAUCE

1/4 TEASPOON WORCESTERSHIRE SAUCE

1/4 TEASPOON CELERY SEEDS, GROUND WITH A MORTAR AND PESTLE
  (SEE PAGE 118)

KOSHER SALT

FRESHLY GROUND BLACK PEPPER

MEASURE the tomato juice, vodka, oil, lemon juice, horseradish, Tabasco, Worcestershire, and celery seeds into a 1-gallon zip-top bag and shake or squeeze until blended. Season to taste with salt and pepper.

SUGGESTED USES: chicken breasts or beef steaks (marinated 2 hours to overnight) or shrimp (marinated 20 to 45 minutes), grilled

GRILLED SHRIMP

FOR 2 SERVINGS, add $^1/_2$ to $^3/_4$ pound peeled, deveined large shrimp (21/25 count) to the Bloody Mary-nade in the zip-top bag and turn to coat. Seal the bag, letting out all the air. Marinate for **at least 20 minutes and up to 45 minutes** at room temperature.

Remove the shrimp from the marinade, pat dry with paper towels, then grill on an oiled grill grate over direct high heat until just cooked through, 4 to 5 minutes, turning once. The shrimp will be firm to the touch, opaque and pink, and beginning to curl when they are just cooked through.

Serve these as shrimp cocktail, with shredded iceberg lettuce and thinly sliced celery (because every good Bloody Mary requires a crisp stalk of celery) and plenty of cocktail sauce for dipping. Or toss with diced onion and celery and dress with mayonnaise, lemon juice, and Tabasco sauce for a zesty salad.

Margarita Marinade

When you use tequila in a marinade, you get all of the lovely agave flavor without any of the harshness.

TOOL: 1-gallon zip-top bag

YIELD: about 1/3 cup (enough for about 2 servings)

2 TABLESPOONS CANOLA OIL

1 TEASPOON GRATED LIME ZEST

2 TABLESPOONS FRESHLY SQUEEZED LIME JUICE

1 TABLESPOON TEQUILA

1 GARLIC CLOVE, MINCED

2 TEASPOONS SUGAR

1/8 TEASPOON GROUND CUMIN

KOSHER SALT

FRESHLY GROUND BLACK PEPPER

MEASURE the oil, lime zest, lime juice, tequila, garlic, sugar, and cumin into a 1-gallon zip-top bag and shake or squeeze until blended. Season to taste with salt and pepper.

SUGGESTED USES: chicken breasts or beef (especially skirt) steaks (marinated 2 hours to overnight) or shrimp or sea scallops (marinated 20 to 45 minutes), grilled

GRILLED SCALLOPS

FOR 2 SERVINGS, add 6 jumbo sea scallops (about 2 ounces each), side muscles removed, to the Margarita Marinade in the zip-top bag and turn to coat. Seal the bag, letting out all the air. Marinate for at least 20 minutes and up to 45 minutes at room temperature.

Remove the scallops from the marinade, pat dry with paper towels, then grill on an oiled grill grate over direct high heat until medium-rare, 6 to 7 minutes (or until the desired doneness), turning once. Moisture will just begin to accumulate on the surface of the scallops when they are medium-rare.

Serve these scallops with any south-of-the-border-style side dishes, such as refried beans and Mexican rice.

Mojito Marinade

Just like the Cuban cocktail, this recipe features rum, mint, and lime juice.

TOOL: 1-gallon zip-top bag

YIELD: about 1/2 cup (enough for 2 to 4 servings)

1/4 CUP FRESHLY SQUEEZED LIME JUICE

2 TABLESPOONS CANOLA OIL

2 TABLESPOONS LIGHT RUM

2 GARLIC CLOVES, MINCED

1/4 CUP LIGHTLY PACKED FRESH MINT LEAVES, TORN

1 TABLESPOON PLUS 1 TEASPOON LIGHT BROWN SUGAR

KOSHER SALT

FRESHLY GROUND BLACK PEPPER

MEASURE the lime juice, oil, rum, garlic, mint leaves, and brown sugar into a 1-gallon zip-top bag and shake or squeeze until blended and the mint leaves are bruised. Season to taste with salt and pepper.

SUGGESTED USES: chicken breasts, pork chops, or beef steaks (marinated 2 hours to overnight) or shrimp (marinated 20 to 45 minutes), grilled

GRILLED CHICKEN BREASTS

FOR 4 SERVINGS, add 4 boneless, skinless chicken breasts (about 8 ounces each), pounded to an even thickness of 1/2 to 3/4 inch, to the Mojito Marinade in the zip-top bag and turn to coat. Seal the bag, letting out all the air. Marinate for at least 2 hours and up to overnight in the refrigerator.

Set the bag aside at room temperature for about half an hour. Remove the chicken from the marinade, pat dry with paper towels, then grill on an oiled grill grate over direct high heat until just cooked through, 10 to 12 minutes, turning once. The chicken will be firm to the touch and the juices will run clear when it is just cooked through. Tent the chicken with foil and let rest for 5 to 10 minutes before serving.

Serve these chicken breasts with Cuban beans and rice.

Arnold Palmer Marinade

The flavors of the classic beverage—iced tea and lemonade—are front and center in this marinade, along with a hint of bourbon for good measure.

TOOL: 1-gallon zip-top bag

YIELD: about 2/3 cup (enough for 4 to 6 servings)

2 TABLESPOONS BERGAMOT TEA LEAVES, SUCH AS EARL GREY

1/4 CUP PLUS 2 TABLESPOONS BOILING WATER

1 TEASPOON GRATED LEMON ZEST

2 TABLESPOONS FRESHLY SQUEEZED LEMON JUICE

2 TABLESPOONS BOURBON

1 TABLESPOON CANOLA OIL

1 GARLIC CLOVE, MINCED

2 TABLESPOONS SUGAR

1/4 TEASPOON CRUSHED RED PEPPER

KOSHER SALT

FRESHLY GROUND BLACK PEPPER

COMBINE the tea leaves and boiling water in a small bowl and let stand until the tea is steeped to the desired degree, 2 to 3 minutes. Strain through a fine-mesh sieve and let cool. Measure the tea, lemon zest, lemon juice, bourbon, oil, garlic, sugar, and crushed red pepper into a 1-gallon zip-top bag and shake or squeeze until blended. Season to taste with salt and black pepper.

SUGGESTED USES: chicken breasts or turkey breast cutlets (marinated 2 hours to overnight) or shrimp or sea scallops (marinated 20 to 45 minutes), grilled

GRILLED CHICKEN BREASTS

FOR 4 SERVINGS, add 4 boneless, skinless chicken breasts (about 8 ounces each), pounded to an even thickness of $1/2$ to $3/4$ inch, to the Arnold Palmer Marinade in the zip-top bag and turn to coat. Seal the bag, letting out all the air. Marinate for at least 2 hours and up to overnight in the refrigerator.

Set the bag aside at room temperature for about half an hour. Remove the chicken from the marinade, pat dry with paper towels, then grill on an oiled grill grate over direct high heat until just cooked through, 10 to 12 minutes, turning once. The chicken will be firm to the touch and the juices will run clear when it is just cooked through. Tent the chicken with foil and let rest for 5 to 10 minutes before carving and serving.

For a light main-course salad, serve the chicken breasts, thinly sliced, over baby spinach or mesclun greens dressed with a lemon vinaigrette.

Piña Colada Marinade

Pineapple juice, coconut milk, and rum work as well in a marinade as they do in a tropical beverage. Be sure to use pasteurized pineapple juice, as fresh pineapple juice contains an enzyme that can cause marinated foods to become mushy.

TOOL: 1-gallon zip-top bag

YIELD: about $1/2$ cup (enough for about 2 servings)

$1/4$ CUP PASTEURIZED PINEAPPLE JUICE

3 TABLESPOONS COCONUT MILK

1 TABLESPOON LIGHT RUM

1 TABLESPOON SOY SAUCE

1 $1/2$ TEASPOONS FRESHLY SQUEEZED LIME JUICE

1 GARLIC CLOVE, MINCED

1 TABLESPOON PACKED LIGHT BROWN SUGAR

GENEROUS PINCH OF CRUSHED RED PEPPER

FRESHLY GROUND BLACK PEPPER

MEASURE the pineapple juice, coconut milk, rum, soy sauce, lime juice, garlic, brown sugar, and crushed red pepper into a 1-gallon zip-top bag and shake or squeeze until blended. Season to taste with black pepper.

SUGGESTED USES: cubes of chicken breast (marinated 2 hours to overnight) or cubes of mahi-mahi or swordfish, shrimp, or sea scallops (marinated 20 to 45 minutes), skewered and grilled

GRILLED MAHI-MAHI OR SWORDFISH KABOBS

FOR 2 SERVINGS, add 2 skinned, boneless mahi-mahi fillets or swordfish steaks (6 to 8 ounces each; the swordfish should be about 1 inch thick), cut into $1 1/4$-inch pieces, to the Piña Colada Marinade in the zip-top bag and turn to coat. Seal the bag, letting out all the air. Marinate for at least 20 minutes and up to 45 minutes at room temperature.

Remove the fish from the marinade, pat dry with paper towels and skewer, alternating with chunks of red and green bell peppers, red onion, and pineapple, onto bamboo skewers that have been soaked in water. Grill the skewers on an oiled grill grate over direct high heat until the fish is just cooked through, 10 to 12 minutes, turning once. The fish will begin to flake when it is just cooked through.

Serve these fish kabobs over coconut rice.

Amaretto Sour Marinade

This marinade is a riff on the flavors of the almond liqueur–based cocktail.

TOOL: 1-gallon zip-top bag

YIELD: about 1/2 cup (enough for about 4 servings)

1/4 CUP AMARETTO

2 TABLESPOONS CANOLA OIL

1/2 TEASPOON GRATED LEMON ZEST

2 TABLESPOONS FRESHLY SQUEEZED LEMON JUICE

1 GARLIC CLOVE, MINCED

GENEROUS PINCH OF CRUSHED RED PEPPER

KOSHER SALT

FRESHLY GROUND BLACK PEPPER

MEASURE the amaretto, oil, lemon zest, lemon juice, garlic, and red pepper into a 1-gallon zip-top bag and shake or squeeze until blended. Season to taste with salt and black pepper.

SUGGESTED USES: chicken breasts or pork chops (marinated 2 hours to overnight) or salmon fillets (marinated 20 to 45 minutes), grilled

GRILLED SALMON FILLETS

FOR 4 SERVINGS, add 4 skinned, boneless salmon fillets (6 to 8 ounces each) to the Amaretto Sour Marinade in the zip-top bag and turn to coat. Seal the bag, letting out all the air. Marinate for at least 20 minutes and up to 45 minutes at room temperature.

Remove the fillets from the marinade, pat dry with paper towels, then grill on an oiled grill grate over direct high heat until medium-rare, 8 to 10 minutes (or until the desired doneness), turning once. The fillets will barely begin to flake when they are medium-rare.

Serve the salmon fillets with almond rice pilaf and a seasonal vegetable—green beans are a particularly good choice.

SOUTHWESTERN
MARINADES

Growing up in Texas and traveling throughout New Mexico and Arizona have given me a special appreciation for the flavors of the Southwest and especially for chiles, both fresh and dried. Some of my most loved marinade recipes inspired by those years appear in this chapter, including my all-time favorites Chile-Lime Marinade and All-Purpose Tex-Mex Marinade, both of which I picked up when I was first learning to cook. I still make them on a regular basis, and once you taste them I'm sure you will, too. Though the recipes in this chapter are packed with chile flavor, most are not particularly hot.

Salsa Marinade

Whether it's homemade or store-bought, salsa has all the right stuff to make a great marinade—it's aromatic, spicy, and acidic. Chile-based and tomato-based salsas are best for marinades, but most any variety will work. You can find a variety of recipes in the salsa series I did for my blog, Hungry Cravings (see page 297).

TOOL: 1-gallon zip-top bag

YIELD: about 1/2 cup (enough for 2 to 4 servings)

1/2 CUP SALSA

2 TABLESPOONS CANOLA OIL

MEASURE the salsa and oil into a 1-gallon zip-top bag and shake or squeeze until blended.

SUGGESTED USES: chicken breasts, pork chops, or beef steaks (marinated 2 hours to overnight), grilled

GRILLED SKIRT STEAKS

FOR 4 TO 6 SERVINGS, add 2 skirt steaks (1 to 1 1/2 pounds each) to the Salsa Marinade in the zip-top bag and turn to coat. Seal the bag, letting out all the air. Marinate for at least 2 hours and up to overnight in the refrigerator.

Set the bag aside at room temperature for about half an hour. Remove the steaks from the marinade, pat dry with paper towels, picking off any large chunks of salsa, then grill over direct high heat until medium-rare, 10 to 12 minutes (or until the desired doneness), turning once. Moisture will just begin to accumulate on the surface of the steaks when they are medium-rare. Tent the steaks with foil and let rest for 5 to 10 minutes before carving and serving.

Dice the skirt steaks and use in any Tex-Mex favorites—from fajitas and burritos to nachos and quesadillas to tortilla soup.

Chile-Lime Marinade

This recipe appears in my first cookbook, *Seared to Perfection*, but since it's my all-time favorite marinade, I had to include it here, too. Steaks soaked in this marinade are equally delicious whether grilled or seared in a pan. Well, maybe grilling is better.

TOOL: 1-gallon zip-top bag

YIELD: about ³/4 cup (enough for about 6 servings)

2 TABLESPOONS FRESHLY SQUEEZED LIME JUICE

2 TABLESPOONS SOY SAUCE

2 TABLESPOONS HONEY

2 TABLESPOONS WORCESTERSHIRE SAUCE

2 GARLIC CLOVES, MINCED

3 TABLESPOONS NEW MEXICO CHILE POWDER

MEASURE the lime juice, soy sauce, honey, Worcestershire, garlic, and chile powder into a 1-gallon zip-top bag and shake or squeeze until blended.

SUGGESTED USES: chicken breasts, pork chops, or beef steaks (marinated 2 hours to overnight), grilled

GRILLED OR SEARED RIB-EYE OR STRIP STEAKS

FOR 6 SERVINGS, add 6 boneless rib-eye or strip steaks (1 to 1¹/4 inches thick) to the Chile-Lime Marinade in the zip-top bag and turn to coat. Seal the bag, letting out all the air. Marinate for at least 2 hours and up to overnight in the refrigerator.

Set the bag aside at room temperature for about half an hour. Remove the steaks from the marinade, pat dry with paper towels, then grill over direct high heat until medium-rare, 12 to 14 minutes (or until the desired doneness), turning once. Moisture will just begin to accumulate on the surface of the steaks when they are medium-rare. Tent the steaks with foil and let rest for 5 to 10 minutes before serving.

Alternatively, heat a large, heavy sauté pan over medium-high heat until a few water droplets dance and look like ball bearings rolling around when flicked into the pan. Add 2 tablespoons canola oil and sear the steaks until medium-rare, 6 to 8 minutes (or until the desired doneness), turning once.

Serve the steaks topped with a tropical fruit salsa of diced mango and/or pineapple, plum tomatoes, red onion, jalapeños, minced cilantro, and freshly squeezed lime juice.

Chile de Arbol Marinade

This marinade is really nothing but an infused oil. You can add a splash of lemon or lime juice if you like, but I really enjoy the richness and pure, unadulterated flavor of toasted chiles and garlic as is. Chiles de árbol, which are available at Mexican markets and many grocery stores, pack a lot of heat, but toasting does seem to mellow them slightly. When tearing the chiles, it's a good idea to wear gloves.

TOOLS: saucepan • blender • 1-gallon zip-top bag
YIELD: about 1/2 cup (enough for 2 to 4 servings)

1/2 CUP CANOLA OIL
24 CHILES DE ÁRBOL, STEMMED, SEEDED, AND TORN
1 GARLIC CLOVE, SLICED
KOSHER SALT

COMBINE the oil, chiles, and garlic in a small, heavy saucepan. Bring to a boil, then reduce the heat and simmer, stirring frequently, until the chiles and garlic are golden brown, 2 to 3 minutes. Remove from the heat and let cool to room temperature. Transfer to a blender, blend until smooth, and season to taste with salt.

SUGGESTED USES: chicken breasts, pork chops, or beef steaks (marinated 2 hours to overnight) or white fish fillets, shrimp, or sea scallops (marinated 20 to 45 minutes), grilled or broiled

GRILLED SHRIMP

FOR 2 SERVINGS, combine the Chile de Arbol Marinade and 1/2 to 3/4 pound peeled, deveined large shrimp (21/25 count) in a 1-gallon zip-top bag and turn to coat. Seal the bag, letting out all the air. Marinate for at least 20 minutes and up to 45 minutes at room temperature.

Remove the shrimp from the marinade, pat dry with paper towels, then grill on an oiled grill grate over direct high heat until just cooked through, 4 to 5 minutes, turning once. The shrimp will be firm to the touch, opaque and pink, and beginning to curl when they are just cooked through.

Serve the shrimp with any south-of-the-border-style side dishes, such as refried beans and Mexican rice.

Chipotle Marinade

If you like your food to have a little heat, this spicy and smoky marinade is sure to become a go-to. Use more or less chipotles as you wish to adjust the heat level. Leftover chipotles keep well in the freezer.

TOOL: 1-gallon zip-top bag

YIELD: about 1/2 cup (enough for 2 to 4 servings)

6 TO 8 CANNED CHIPOTLE CHILES IN ADOBO SAUCE

2 TABLESPOONS CANOLA OIL

2 TABLESPOONS FRESHLY SQUEEZED LIME JUICE

1 GARLIC CLOVE, MINCED

1 TABLESPOON PACKED LIGHT BROWN SUGAR

1/4 TEASPOON GROUND CUMIN

1/8 TEASPOON MEXICAN OREGANO (SEE PAGE 170)

KOSHER SALT

FORCE the chipotles through a fine-mesh sieve to remove the skins and seeds. Measure the chipotle puree, oil, lime juice, garlic, brown sugar, cumin, and Mexican oregano into a 1-gallon zip-top bag and shake or squeeze until blended. Season to taste with salt.

SUGGESTED USES: chicken breasts, pork ribs or chops, or beef steaks (marinated 2 hours to overnight) or salmon fillets or shrimp (marinated 20 to 45 minutes), grilled

GRILLED RIB-EYE OR STRIP STEAKS

FOR 4 SERVINGS, add 4 boneless rib-eye or strip steaks (1 to 1 1/4 inches thick) to the Chipotle Marinade in the zip-top bag and turn to coat. Seal the bag, letting out all the air. Marinate for at least 2 hours and up to overnight in the refrigerator.

Set the bag aside at room temperature for about half an hour. Remove the steaks from the marinade, pat dry with paper towels, then grill over direct high heat until medium-rare, 12 to 14 minutes (or until the desired doneness), turning once. Moisture will just begin to accumulate on the surface of the steaks when they are medium-rare. Tent the steaks with foil and let rest for 5 to 10 minutes before serving.

Serve the steaks with guacamole and any other side dishes that you might serve with Mexican food or barbecue.

Chipotle-Ale Marinade

When you're craving meat smothered in smoky, spicy chipotles but don't feel inclined to fuss with seeding them, try this marinade. It cleverly shortcuts all the work by using Tabasco chipotle sauce.

TOOL: 1-gallon zip-top bag

YIELD: about 3/4 cup (enough for about 6 servings)

1/3 CUP PALE ALE

2 TABLESPOONS CANOLA OIL

2 TABLESPOONS TABASCO CHIPOTLE SAUCE

1 TABLESPOON MALT VINEGAR

1/2 TEASPOON WORCESTERSHIRE SAUCE

1 GARLIC CLOVE, MINCED

2 TABLESPOONS PACKED LIGHT BROWN SUGAR

KOSHER SALT

FRESHLY GROUND BLACK PEPPER

MEASURE the ale, oil, Tabasco, malt vinegar, Worcestershire, garlic, and brown sugar into a 1-gallon zip-top bag and shake or squeeze until blended. Season to taste with salt and pepper.

SUGGESTED USES: chicken breasts, pork chops, or beef steaks (marinated 2 hours to overnight), grilled

GRILLED PORK LOIN OR RIB CHOPS

FOR 6 SERVINGS, add **6 boneless pork loin or rib chops (about 1 inch thick)** to the Chipotle-Ale Marinade in the zip-top bag and turn to coat. Seal the bag, letting out all the air. Marinate for **at least 2 hours and up to overnight** in the refrigerator.

Set the bag aside at room temperature for about half an hour. Remove the chops from the marinade, pat dry with paper towels, then grill over direct high heat until medium, 13 to 15 minutes (or until the desired doneness), turning once. Moisture will just begin to pool on the surface of the chops when they are medium. Tent the chops with foil and let rest for 5 to 10 minutes before serving.

Serve the pork chops with potato salad or baked beans.

All-Purpose Tex-Mex Marinade

I grew up in Texas, so there's a soft spot in my heart for Tex-Mex food. Now that I live in the Pacific Northwest, I rely on this zesty marinade whenever I need a fix. The versatile recipe is as easy as throwing a few ingredients into a blender, and I developed it to make a very large batch so that there's always some on hand in case of emergency Tex-Mex cravings. It can be portioned into zip-top bags and frozen for a few weeks.

TOOLS: blender • three 1-gallon zip-top bags

YIELD: about 2 3/4 cups (enough for 14 to 24 servings)

1/2 CUP CANOLA OIL

2 TABLESPOONS DISTILLED WHITE VINEGAR

2 TABLESPOONS FRESHLY SQUEEZED LIME JUICE

1 BUNCH FRESH CILANTRO, STEM ENDS TRIMMED

1 YELLOW ONION, CUT INTO EIGHTHS

3 JALAPEÑOS, STEMMED

1/4 CUP PICKLED JALAPEÑO SLICES

1 TEASPOON GROUND CUMIN

KOSHER SALT

FRESHLY GROUND BLACK PEPPER

COMBINE the oil, vinegar, lime juice, cilantro, onion, jalapeños, pickled jalapeños, and cumin in a blender and blend until smooth. Season to taste with salt and pepper.

SUGGESTED USES: chicken breasts or beef (especially skirt) steaks (marinated 2 hours to overnight) or white fish fillets, shrimp, or sea scallops (marinated 20 to 45 minutes), grilled

GRILLED CHICKEN BREASTS

FOR 8 SERVINGS, combine about one-third of the All-Purpose Tex-Mex Marinade and 8 boneless, skinless chicken breasts (about 8 ounces each), pounded to an even thickness of $1/2$ to $3/4$ inch, in a zip-top bag and turn to coat. Seal the bag, letting out all the air. Marinate for at least 2 hours and up to overnight in the refrigerator. (Divide the remaining marinade between two 1-gallon zip-top bags and freeze for future use.)

Set the bag aside at room temperature for about half an hour. Remove the chicken from the marinade, pat dry with paper towels, then grill on an oiled grill grate over direct high heat until just cooked through, 10 to 12 minutes, turning once. The chicken will be firm to the touch and the juices will run clear when it is just cooked through. Tent the chicken with foil and let rest for 5 to 10 minutes before carving and serving.

Dice the chicken breasts and use in any Tex-Mex favorites—from fajitas and burritos to nachos and quesadillas to tortilla soup. Slice and serve on a Caesar salad. For a particularly satisfying sandwich, stack marinated and grilled chicken breasts, bacon, Swiss or cheddar cheese, garlicky guacamole, lettuce, and tomato on artisan-style hamburger buns. Or simply serve the chicken breasts with refried beans and Mexican rice.

Hatch Green Chile Marinade

Hatch green chiles have an almost cult following. During the brief New Mexico green chile season (late August to September), devotees will go to tremendous lengths to hoard the chiles, which are charred and blistered in roadside open-fire chile roasters, stashing them in their freezers for use throughout the year. As a chile lover who has made the pilgrimage to Hatch, I can attest that the chiles do indeed live up to their reputation of deliciousness. They imbue dishes with warm heat and campfire smokiness. In season, Hatch green chiles are available at many better markets and online. If Hatch or New Mexico green chiles are unavailable, Anaheims will yield similarly tasty results.

TOOLS: blender • 1-gallon zip-top bag

YIELD: about 1/2 cup (enough for 2 to 4 servings)

2 TABLESPOONS CANOLA OIL

2 TABLESPOONS FRESHLY SQUEEZED LIME JUICE

2 HATCH GREEN CHILES, ROASTED, PEELED, AND SEEDED (SEE PAGE 297)

2 GARLIC CLOVES, SLICED

1/4 TEASPOON GROUND CUMIN

1/8 TEASPOON MEXICAN OREGANO (SEE BELOW)

KOSHER SALT

FRESHLY GROUND BLACK PEPPER

COMBINE the oil, lime juice, green chiles, garlic, cumin, and Mexican oregano in a blender and blend until smooth. Season to taste with salt and pepper.

MEXICAN OREGANO	Dried Mexican oregano lends its unique floral and slightly musky flavor to many Mexican and Southwestern dishes. It can be found at some gourmet shops and (usually for less than a dollar) at any Mexican market. If you can't find it, just omit it from the recipe; don't substitute common oregano.

SUGGESTED USES: boneless, skinless chicken thighs, pork chops, or beef steaks (marinated 2 hours to overnight) or fish fillets, shrimp, or sea scallops (marinated 20 to 45 minutes), grilled

GRILLED CHICKEN THIGHS

FOR 4 SERVINGS, combine the Hatch Green Chile Marinade and 8 boneless, skinless chicken thighs (about 4 ounces each) in a 1-gallon zip-top bag and turn to coat. Seal the bag, letting out all the air. Marinate for **at least 2 hours and up to overnight** in the refrigerator.

Set the bag aside at room temperature for about half an hour. Remove the chicken from the marinade, pat dry with paper towels, then grill, covered, on an oiled grill grate over direct medium heat until just cooked through, 12 to 14 minutes, turning once. The chicken will be firm to the touch and the juices will run clear when it is just cooked through. Tent the chicken with foil and let rest for 5 to 10 minutes before carving and serving.

Serve these chicken thighs with refried beans and Mexican rice. They also make a fantastic burrito filling.

MEXICAN AND SOUTH AMERICAN
MARINADES

THE MARINADES IN THIS CHAPTER WILL TAKE YOU ON A TOUR OF MEXICO WITH A SIDE TRIP TO ARGENTINA AND PERU. TYPICAL INGREDIENTS INCLUDE CHILES, CUMIN, MEXICAN OREGANO, AND LIME. MANY RECIPES—SUCH AS CARNE ASADA MARINADE, MARINADE FOR TACOS AL PASTOR, ACHIOTE MARINADE, AND CHIMICHURRI MARINADE—STAY MORE OR LESS TRUE TO THEIR TRADITIONAL ROOTS, WHILE MY INTERPRETATION OF *MOLE* BREAKS ALL THE RULES AND REIMAGINES THE TRADITIONAL LONG-COOKING, LABOR-INTENSIVE DISH IN MARINADE FORM.

Carne Asada Marinade

Next time you're craving authentic carne asada, use this mixture to flavor the skirt steak before grilling it.

TOOLS: blender • 1-gallon zip-top bag

YIELD: about 3/4 cup (enough for 4 to 9 servings)

1/4 CUP FRESHLY SQUEEZED ORANGE JUICE

2 TABLESPOONS FRESHLY SQUEEZED LIME JUICE

2 TABLESPOONS CANOLA OIL

1 GARLIC CLOVE, SLICED

2 JALAPEÑOS, ROASTED AND SEEDED (SEE PAGE 297)

1/2 TEASPOON GROUND CUMIN

1/4 TEASPOON MEXICAN OREGANO (SEE PAGE 170)

KOSHER SALT

FRESHLY GROUND BLACK PEPPER

COMBINE the orange juice, lime juice, oil, garlic, jalapeños, cumin, and Mexican oregano in a blender and blend until smooth. Season to taste with salt and pepper.

SUGGESTED USES: chicken breasts or skirt steaks (marinated 2 hours to overnight) or fish fillets, shrimp, or sea scallops (marinated 20 to 45 minutes), grilled

CARNE ASADA

FOR 6 TO 9 SERVINGS, combine the Carne Asada Marinade and 3 skirt steaks (1 to 1 1/2 pounds each) in a 1-gallon zip-top bag and turn to coat. Seal the bag, letting out all the air. Marinate for at least 2 hours and up to overnight in the refrigerator.

Set the bag aside at room temperature for about half an hour. Remove the steaks from the marinade, pat dry with paper towels, then grill over direct high heat until medium-rare, 10 to 12 minutes (or until the desired doneness), turning once. Moisture will just begin to accumulate on the surface of the steak when it is medium-rare. Tent the steak with foil and let rest for 5 to 10 minutes before carving and serving.

For authentic Mexican taqueria-style tacos, dice the steak and serve along with diced white onion, minced fresh cilantro, and salsa folded inside of warm corn tortillas. Offer sliced radishes and pickled jalapeños on the side.

Marinade for Tacos al Pastor

I learned this delicious red-hued marinade for pork tacos al pastor, a popular Mexican street food, over a dozen years ago from the guy behind the counter at a small taqueria in Austin. It packs a ton of chile flavor without being hot, and the fresh pineapple lends a fruity sweetness and makes the pork very tender (don't be tempted to increase the proportion of fresh pineapple in the recipe, as it will make the pork mushy). In all these years, I haven't found another taco that can compare. Mexican markets are the best source for dried guajillo chiles.

TOOLS: sauté pan • blender • 1-gallon zip-top bag

YIELD: about 2/3 cup (enough for 2 to 3 servings)

6 GUAJILLO CHILES, STEMMED

1 GARLIC CLOVE, SLICED

PINCH OF GROUND CLOVES, OPTIONAL

1/3 CUP DICED PINEAPPLE

KOSHER SALT

HEAT a medium-size, heavy sauté pan over medium heat until very hot but not smoking. Add 2 of the chiles and toast, pressing down on them firmly with a spatula, for 10 to 15 seconds, or until golden brown in spots. Turn the chiles and continue to toast, pressing down on them firmly with the spatula, another 10 to 15 seconds, or until fragrant, golden brown, and pliable. Transfer the toasted chiles to a bowl and toast the remaining chiles in the same manner. Add enough boiling water to the chiles to cover, and let soak until rehydrated, 10 to 12 minutes. Transfer the chiles and 1/4 cup of the soaking liquid to a blender, add the garlic and cloves, and blend until smooth. Force the mixture through a fine-mesh sieve to remove the skins and seeds. Stir in the pineapple and season to taste with salt.

TACOS AL PASTOR

FOR 2 TO 3 SERVINGS, combine the Marinade for Tacos al Pastor and 1 to 1¼ pounds boneless pork butt, cut into ½-inch cubes, in a 1-gallon zip-top bag and turn to coat. Seal the bag, letting out all the air. Marinate overnight in the refrigerator.

Set the bag aside at room temperature for about half an hour. Remove the pork from the marinade and pat it dry with paper towels. Heat a large, heavy sauté pan over medium-high heat until a few water droplets dance and look like ball bearings rolling around when flicked into the pan. Add 2 tablespoons canola oil and pan-fry the pork until tender and golden brown, 10 to 12 minutes, tossing a few times (don't worry if some of the marinade seems to stick to the bottom of the pan—it'll be okay as long as it doesn't burn). Season the pork to taste with salt.

Serve the pork tucked inside warm corn tortillas along with some diced white onion, minced fresh cilantro, and Guajillo Salsa (visit hungrycravings.com for the recipe).

Mole Marinade

Mole, pride of the Mexican kitchen, is a rich sauce with a long list of ingredients including a variety of dried chiles, garlic, onion, tomatoes, tomatillos, sesame seeds, pumpkin seeds, almonds, raisins, bread, tortillas, spices, sugar, and chocolate. Making *mole* is a laborious process of toasting and grinding each component separately and then cooking them all together. This recipe, though far simpler than the complex sauce that inspired it, captures the essential flavors, and it can be used as both a marinade and a sauce. Mexican markets are the best source for dried mulato and pasilla chiles. Ancho chiles may be substituted if mulatos are unavailable.

TOOLS: sauté pan • blender • 1-gallon zip-top bag

YIELD: about 1 3/4 cups (enough for 4 to 12 servings)

- **3 MULATO CHILES, STEMMED**
- **2 PASILLA CHILES, STEMMED**
- **2 TABLESPOONS FRESHLY SQUEEZED LIME JUICE**
- **1/2 TEASPOON TOASTED SESAME OIL**
- **2 GARLIC CLOVES, SLICED**
- **1/4 CUP PACKED LIGHT BROWN SUGAR**
- **1 TABLESPOON UNSWEETENED COCOA POWDER**
- **1/4 TEASPOON GROUND CINNAMON**
- **GENEROUS PINCH OF GROUND CLOVES**
- **KOSHER SALT**
- **FRESHLY GROUND BLACK PEPPER**

HEAT a medium-size, heavy sauté pan over medium heat until very hot but not smoking. Add 2 of the chiles and toast, pressing down on them firmly with a spatula, for 10 to 15 seconds, or until golden brown. Turn the chiles and continue to toast, pressing down on them firmly with the spatula, another 10 to 15 seconds, or until fragrant, golden brown, and pliable. Transfer the toasted chiles to a bowl and toast the remaining chiles in the same manner. Add enough boiling water to the chiles to cover, and let soak until rehydrated, 10 to 12 minutes. Transfer the chiles and 1 1/4 cups of the soaking liquid to a blender; add the lime juice, sesame oil, garlic, brown sugar, cocoa powder, cinnamon, and cloves, and blend until smooth. Force the mixture through a fine-mesh sieve to remove the skins and seeds. Season to taste with salt and pepper.

SUGGESTED USES: chicken pieces, turkey breast cutlets, pork chops, or beef steaks (marinated 2 hours to overnight), or pork ribs (marinated overnight), or salmon fillets or shrimp (marinated 20 to 45 minutes), grilled

GRILLED BABY BACK RIBS

POUR about $3/4$ cup of the *Mole* Marinade into a small bowl; cover and refrigerate. Pour about half of the remaining marinade into a second 1-gallon zip-top bag. For 4 servings, cut 2 racks pork baby back ribs (2 to $2^{1}/2$ pounds each) in half and add 1 rack (2 halves) to the marinade in each of the zip-top bags; turn to coat. Seal the bags, letting out all the air. Marinate overnight in the refrigerator.

Set the bags aside at room temperature for about half an hour. Remove the ribs from the marinade and place them on the grill, meaty side up. Grill the ribs, covered, over indirect medium-low heat until fork-tender, 2 to $2^{1}/2$ hours, brushing occasionally with the reserved $3/4$ cup marinade. The meat will have noticeably shrunk away from the ends of the bones when it is done. Tent the ribs with foil and let rest for 5 to 10 minutes before carving and serving.

Serve the ribs with black beans, Mexican rice, and corn tortillas.

Achiote Marinade

Mexico's Yucatan is the origin of this bright red annatto-based marinade. Annatto, also known as achiote, has a subtle earthy flavor. While many recipes start with store-bought achiote paste, which contains food coloring and preservatives, I prefer to start from scratch and use ground annatto seeds. Whole and ground annatto seeds are most readily found at Mexican markets.

TOOL: 1-gallon zip-top bag

YIELD: about 1/3 cup (enough for about 2 servings)

1/4 CUP FRESHLY SQUEEZED ORANGE JUICE

2 TABLESPOONS FRESHLY SQUEEZED LIME JUICE

1 TABLESPOON CANOLA OIL

3 GARLIC CLOVES, MINCED

3/4 TEASPOON GROUND ANNATTO SEEDS

1/2 TEASPOON GROUND CUMIN

1/4 TEASPOON MEXICAN OREGANO (SEE PAGE 170)

GENEROUS PINCH OF GROUND CLOVES

KOSHER SALT

FRESHLY GROUND BLACK PEPPER

MEASURE the orange juice, lime juice, oil, garlic, annatto seeds, cumin, Mexican oregano, and cloves into a 1-gallon zip-top bag and shake or squeeze until blended. Season to taste with salt and pepper.

SUGGESTED USES: chicken breasts or pork chops (marinated 2 hours to overnight) or white fish fillets, shrimp, or sea scallops (marinated 20 to 45 minutes), grilled

GRILLED SNAPPER OR ROCKFISH FILLETS

FOR 2 SERVINGS, add 2 skinned, boneless snapper or rockfish fillets (6 to 8 ounces each) to the Achiote Marinade in the zip-top bag and turn to coat. Seal the bag, letting out all the air. Marinate for at least 20 minutes and up to 45 minutes at room temperature.

Remove the fillets from the marinade, pat dry with paper towels, then grill on an oiled grill grate over direct high heat until just cooked through, 5 to 6 minutes, turning once. The fillets will begin to flake when they are just cooked through.

Serve the fish fillets with black beans and Mexican rice.

Mexican Tamarind Marinade

Tamarind is a favorite ingredient in Mexico, where it's used in everything from candy and *aguas frescas* to marinades such as this.

TOOL: 1-gallon zip-top bag

YIELD: about 1/2 cup (enough for 2 to 4 servings)

1/4 CUP WATER

3 TABLESPOONS TAMARIND CONCENTRATE (SEE PAGE 240)

2 TABLESPOONS CANOLA OIL

2 GARLIC CLOVES, MINCED

1 TABLESPOON PACKED LIGHT BROWN SUGAR

2 TEASPOONS ANCHO CHILE POWDER

1/4 TEASPOON MEXICAN OREGANO (SEE PAGE 170)

1/8 TEASPOON GROUND CUMIN

GENEROUS PINCH OF CAYENNE PEPPER

KOSHER SALT

FRESHLY GROUND BLACK PEPPER

MEASURE the water, tamarind concentrate, oil, garlic, brown sugar, chile powder, Mexican oregano, cumin, and cayenne into a 1-gallon zip-top bag and shake or squeeze until blended. Season to taste with salt and black pepper.

SUGGESTED USES: chicken breasts or pork chops (marinated 2 hours to overnight) or fish fillets or shrimp (marinated 20 to 45 minutes), grilled

GRILLED SHRIMP

FOR 2 SERVINGS, add 1/2 to 3/4 pound peeled, deveined large shrimp (21/25 count) to the Mexican Tamarind Marinade in the zip-top bag and turn to coat. Seal the bag, letting out all the air. Marinate for at least 20 minutes and up to 45 minutes at room temperature.

Remove the shrimp from the marinade, pat dry with paper towels, then grill on an oiled grill grate over direct high heat until just cooked through, 4 to 5 minutes, turning once. The shrimp will be firm to the touch, opaque and pink, and beginning to curl when they are just cooked through.

Serve the shrimp with black beans and Mexican rice.

Marinade for Ceviche

Ceviche is a dish of lime-marinated raw seafood popular in coastal regions in Mexico and other parts of Central and South America. The lime juice "cooks" the seafood (this is possibly the only dish where that's actually considered desirable; usually, you want a marinade to flavor the seafood and then use heat to cook it), and you can tell it's ready when it's gone from translucent to white throughout. While some recipes call for relatively short marination times, I find a longer soak allows the flavors to marry and results in tastier ceviche. Key limes pack a lot of flavor compared to Persian limes, the kind commonly found in grocery stores, but the juice of either variety will work. Use only pristine seafood from a reputable fishmonger to make ceviche.

TOOL: 1-gallon zip-top bag

YIELD: about 2 1/2 cups (enough for 6 to 8 servings)

3/4 CUP FRESHLY SQUEEZED KEY LIME JUICE

1 TABLESPOON EXTRA-VIRGIN OLIVE OIL

1 1/4 CUPS DICED TOMATOES

1 CUP DICED RED ONION

1 JALAPEÑO, SEEDED AND MINCED

1/3 CUP MINCED FRESH CILANTRO

KOSHER SALT

FRESHLY GROUND BLACK PEPPER

MEASURE the lime juice, oil, tomatoes, onion, jalapeño, and cilantro into a 1-gallon zip-top bag and shake or squeeze until blended. Season to taste with salt and pepper.

CEVICHE

FOR 6 TO 8 SERVINGS, add 1 1/2 pounds (total weight) white ocean fish fillets (such as sea bass, snapper, or rockfish) cut into 1/2-inch cubes, peeled, and deveined small shrimp (51/60 count), and/or bay scallops to the Marinade for Ceviche in the zip-top bag and turn to coat. Seal the bag, letting out all the air. Marinate for at least 8 hours and up to overnight in the refrigerator.

Serve the chilled ceviche, marinade and all, with diced avocados, Key lime wedges, and tostadas. Pass a bottle of hot sauce at the table.

Chimichurri Marinade

Chimichurri is a concoction of Argentinean origin, and it's used as both a marinade and a sauce for grilled meat.

TOOLS: food processor • 1-gallon zip-top bag

YIELD: about 1/2 cup (enough for 2 to 4 servings)

1/3 CUP EXTRA-VIRGIN OLIVE OIL

1 TABLESPOON WHITE WINE VINEGAR

1 CUP PACKED FRESH FLAT-LEAF PARSLEY LEAVES

2 TABLESPOONS FRESH OREGANO LEAVES

2 GARLIC CLOVES, SLICED

1/2 TEASPOON CRUSHED RED PEPPER

KOSHER SALT

FRESHLY GROUND BLACK PEPPER

COMBINE the oil, vinegar, parsley, oregano, garlic, and crushed red pepper in a food processor and process until smooth. Season to taste with salt and black pepper.

SUGGESTED USES: chicken breasts, pork chops, beef steaks, or lamb chops (marinated 2 hours to overnight) or white fish fillets, shrimp, or sea scallops (marinated 20 to 45 minutes), grilled

GRILLED FLATIRON STEAKS

FOR 2 SERVINGS, combine about half of the Chimichurri Marinade and 2 flatiron steaks (about 8 ounces each) in a 1-gallon zip-top bag and turn to coat. Seal the bag, letting out all the air. Marinate for at least 2 hours and up to overnight in the refrigerator.

Set the bag aside at room temperature for about half an hour. Remove the steaks from the marinade, pat dry with paper towels, then grill over direct high heat until medium-rare, 10 to 12 minutes (or until the desired doneness), turning once. Moisture will just begin to accumulate on the surface of the steaks when they are medium-rare. Tent the steaks with foil and let rest for 5 to 10 minutes before serving.

Serve the steaks with the remaining marinade as a sauce. These steaks will go with just about anything—serve any starch and seasonal vegetable you desire on the side. Personally, I'd go with simple grilled vegetables and crusty bread.

Marinade for Pollo a la Brasa

Pollo a la Brasa, or Peruvian-style chicken, is marinated in a blend of lime juice, soy sauce, and spices before being cooked on the grill or rotisserie.

TOOL: 1-gallon zip-top bag

YIELD: about 3/4 cup (enough for 4 to 6 servings)

1/4 CUP FRESHLY SQUEEZED LIME JUICE

1/4 CUP SOY SAUCE

3 TABLESPOONS EXTRA-VIRGIN OLIVE OIL

4 GARLIC CLOVES, MINCED

1/2 TEASPOON DRIED OREGANO

1/4 TEASPOON DRIED MINT

1/2 TEASPOON PAPRIKA

1/2 TEASPOON GROUND CUMIN

1/4 TEASPOON GROUND ANNATTO SEEDS

1/4 TEASPOON CAYENNE PEPPER

FRESHLY GROUND BLACK PEPPER

MEASURE the lime juice, soy sauce, oil, garlic, oregano, mint, paprika, cumin, annatto, and cayenne into a 1-gallon zip-top bag and shake or squeeze until blended. Season to taste with black pepper.

POLLO A LA BRASA

FOR 4 TO 6 SERVINGS, add 1 butterflied whole chicken (3$\frac{1}{2}$ to 4 pounds) to the Marinade for *Pollo a la Brasa* in the zip-top bag and turn to coat. Seal the bag, letting out all the air. Marinate **overnight** in the refrigerator.

Set the bag aside at room temperature for about half an hour. Remove the chicken from the marinade, pat dry with paper towels, then grill over indirect medium heat until just cooked through, 55 to 65 minutes, turning occasionally. The chicken will be firm to the touch, the meat of the drumsticks will have noticeably shrunk away from the knuckles, and the juices will run clear when it is just cooked through. Tent the chicken with foil and let rest for 15 to 20 minutes before carving and serving.

Alternatively, use a whole (unbutterflied) chicken and marinate it overnight. Set the chicken aside at room temperature for about half an hour. Pat the chicken dry with paper towels and truss. Roast the chicken on a rack in a roasting pan in a preheated 400°F oven until just cooked through, 55 to 65 minutes. The drumsticks will wiggle freely in their joints, the meat of the drumsticks will have noticeably shrunk away from the knuckles, the juices will run clear, and a meat thermometer inserted in the thickest part of the breast will register 160°F when it is just cooked through. Tent the chicken with foil and let rest for 15 to 20 minutes before carving and serving (the internal temperature should rise to 165°F).

If you prefer, bone-in chicken pieces may also be used; marinate them overnight as well and roast them in a preheated 450°F oven until just cooked through, 22 to 26 minutes for legs, thighs, and wings and 30 to 35 minutes for breasts.

Serve the chicken with black beans and rice.

EUROPEAN
MARINADES

The marinades in this chapter explore the varied cuisines of France, Italy, Spain, Greece, and Germany. Just to name a few, the French Red Wine Marinade will unlock the secret to both Boeuf Bourguignon and Coq au Vin, the Porchetta Marinade will enable you to roast the most succulent pork, redolent of herbs and spices in the Italian tradition, and the Sauerbraten Marinade will show you the way to a hearty sweet and sour German pot roast.

Tapenade Marinade

Tapenade is generally eaten spread on bread or crackers, but the olive and caper puree also makes an intensely flavorful marinade.

TOOLS: food processor • 1-gallon zip-top bag

YIELD: about 3/4 cup (enough for 4 to 6 servings)

1/2 CUP EXTRA-VIRGIN OLIVE OIL

1/3 CUP PITTED KALAMATA OLIVES

2 TEASPOONS CAPERS

1 ANCHOVY FILLET

1 GARLIC CLOVE, SLICED

1/4 TEASPOON HERBES DE PROVENCE (SEE PAGE 188)

FRESHLY GROUND BLACK PEPPER

COMBINE the oil, olives, capers, anchovy, garlic, and herbes de Provence in a food processor and process until smooth. Season to taste with pepper.

SUGGESTED USES: chicken breasts, pork chops, or lamb chops (marinated 2 hours to overnight), butterflied lamb leg (marinated overnight), or white fish fillets (marinated 20 to 45 minutes), grilled

GRILLED LAMB RIB CHOPS

FOR 4 SERVINGS, combine the Tapenade Marinade and 12 frenched lamb rib chops (about 1 inch thick) in a 1-gallon zip-top bag and turn to coat. Seal the bag, letting out all the air. Marinate for at least 2 hours and up to overnight in the refrigerator.

Set the bag aside at room temperature for about half an hour. Remove the chops from the marinade, pat dry with paper towels, then grill over direct high heat until medium-rare, 10 to 12 minutes (or until the desired doneness), turning once. Moisture will just begin to accumulate on the surface of the chops when they are medium-rare. Tent the chops with foil and let rest for 5 to 10 minutes before serving.

Serve the lamb chops with orzo tossed with crumbled feta, diced red onion, halved cherry tomatoes, torn fresh basil, minced garlic, and olive oil.

French Red Wine Marinade

This simple red wine marinade is used for both boeuf bourguignon and coq au vin. Some cooks add the mirepoix to the marinade, but I prefer to sauté the onion, celery, and carrot mixture to bring out its sweetness and let the sauce simmer with it.

TOOL: 1-gallon zip-top bag

YIELD: about 3 cups (enough for 4 to 6 servings)

3 CUPS PINOT NOIR OR OTHER DRY RED WINE

2 OR 3 FRESH THYME SPRIGS

4 GARLIC CLOVES, MINCED

1 BAY LEAF

KOSHER SALT

FRESHLY GROUND BLACK PEPPER

MEASURE the wine, thyme, garlic, and bay leaf into a 1-gallon zip-top bag and shake until blended. Season to taste with salt and pepper.

FRENCH WHITE WINE MARINADE: Substitute a dry, unoaked Chardonnay or other dry white wine for the Pinot Noir and use the marinade for white coq au vin.

BOEUF BOURGUIGNON OR COQ AU VIN

FOR 4 TO 6 SERVINGS, add 2 to 2¹/₂ pounds beef chuck, cut into 2-inch cubes, or 8 chicken drumsticks and/or thighs to the French Red Wine Marinade in the zip-top bag and turn to coat. Seal the bag, letting out all the air. Marinate overnight in the refrigerator.

Set the bag aside at room temperature for about half an hour. Remove the meat from the marinade, reserving the marinade to use for the sauce, and pat the meat dry with paper towels. Heat a large, heavy pot over medium-high heat until a few water droplets dance and look like ball bearings rolling around when flicked into the pot. Add 2 tablespoons olive oil and sear the meat in batches until crusty and brown all over, 8 to 10 minutes, turning occasionally. Transfer the meat to a plate. Reduce the heat to medium-low, add 1 diced large yellow onion, 2 diced celery ribs, and 1 diced carrot to the pot, and cook until the vegetables are soft. Add 3 or 4 minced garlic cloves and 1 tablespoon tomato paste and cook until fragrant, 1 to 2 minutes more. Add 2 tablespoons brandy and simmer for a minute or so, scraping up the brown bits from the bottom of the pan with a heatproof spatula. Return the meat to the pot and add the reserved marinade, several fresh flat-leaf parsley sprigs, 1 fresh thyme sprig, 1 bay leaf, and 3 cups beef broth for boeuf bourguignon or chicken broth for coq au vin. Bring to a boil, then reduce the heat and simmer slowly until the meat is fork-tender—about 1 hour for chicken and 3 hours for beef.

Meanwhile, in a separate pan, brown about 8 ounces whole small button mushrooms in a knob of butter, then brown about 1 cup pearl onions (thawed if frozen), and finally render 2 slices of diced bacon.

When the meat is tender, remove it to a plate and tent with foil to keep warm. Remove the pot from the heat, skim off any fat from the surface of the cooking liquid, and strain the liquid through a fine-mesh sieve. Return it to the pot and bring it to a boil. Make a paste of 3 tablespoons softened unsalted butter blended with 3 tablespoons all-purpose flour. Whisk the paste into the boiling liquid a little at a time until the sauce is thickened to the desired consistency. Return the meat to the pot, add the mushrooms, pearl onions, and bacon, and reheat gently. Season to taste with salt and pepper.

Serve the stew with the classic side dishes of parsleyed potatoes and buttered peas.

Provençal Marinade

This recipe is inspired by the flavors of southern France, where lavender honey, green peppercorns, and herbes de Provence are all common ingredients. Lavender honey and dried green peppercorns (you don't want the ones preserved in brine in this recipe) can be found at most gourmet shops as well as many supermarkets.

Since this marinade is mostly honey, a little bit goes a long way. The honey can cause the duck breasts (or whatever you marinate) to brown more quickly than usual, so watch them carefully and turn the heat down if they darken too soon.

TOOL: 1-gallon zip-top bag

YIELD: about 1/4 cup (enough for 2 to 4 servings)

3 TABLESPOONS LAVENDER HONEY

1 GARLIC CLOVE, MINCED

1 TEASPOON HERBES DE PROVENCE (SEE BELOW)

1 TEASPOON FRESHLY CRACKED DRIED GREEN PEPPERCORNS

KOSHER SALT

MEASURE the honey, garlic, herbes de Provence, and green peppercorns into a 1-gallon zip-top bag and shake or squeeze until blended. Season to taste with salt.

HERBES DE PROVENCE	The aromatic herb mixture herbes de Provence hails from the sunny South of France, where it's used liberally on everything from pizza to rotisserie chicken. Authentic blends consist of just rosemary, thyme, basil, marjoram, and summer savory, but some interpretations include other ingredients such as lavender, fennel, and orange peel. Having traveled to Provence and tasted the real deal, I think it's worth seeking out imported herbes de Provence, and I'll scour every corner of the Internet to find it. But most gourmet shops and specialty spice merchants offer a passable, if not 100 percent authentic, version.

SUGGESTED USES: boneless, skin-on duck breasts (marinated 2 hours to overnight), seared; butterflied Cornish hens or whole quail (marinated 2 hours to overnight), grilled or pan-roasted

SEARED DUCK BREASTS

FOR 4 SERVINGS, add 4 boneless, skin-on duck breasts (about 8 ounces each), skin scored with a diamond pattern, to the Provençal Marinade in the zip-top bag and turn to coat. Seal the bag, letting out all the air. Marinate for at least 2 hours and up to overnight in the refrigerator.

Set the bag aside at room temperature for about half an hour. Remove the duck breasts from the marinade and pat dry with paper towels. Heat a large, heavy sauté pan over medium heat until a few water droplets dance and look like ball bearings rolling around when flicked into the pan. Sear the duck, starting with the skin side down, until medium-rare, 10 to 12 minutes (or until the desired doneness), turning once. The duck will just begin to feel firm to the touch when it is medium-rare. Tent the duck with foil and let rest for 5 to 10 minutes before carving and serving.

For a main-course salad, serve the duck, thinly sliced, over butter lettuce with a red wine vinegar and shallot vinaigrette. For a heartier meal, try it with potatoes fried or roasted in duck fat.

Pimentón Marinade

The smoky, earthy flavor of pimentón, also known as Spanish paprika, makes it one of my favorite spices and this one of my favorite marinades. I also love it for chicken thighs used as a jumping off point for arroz con pollo or along with shrimp in a pan of paella. Or, for a tapas-style appetizer, sauté marinated shrimp with slices of Spanish chorizo and serve with a baguette for soaking up the aromatic red-hued oil.

Pimentón is available in sweet and hot varieties, with sweet pimentón being preferable for this recipe since it can be used in ample quantities without adding too much heat. You can find both pimentón and sherry vinegar at most gourmet shops.

TOOL: 1-gallon zip-top bag

YIELD: about 2/3 cup (enough for 4 to 6 servings)

1/2 CUP EXTRA-VIRGIN OLIVE OIL

2 TABLESPOONS SHERRY VINEGAR

2 GARLIC CLOVES, MINCED

2 TABLESPOONS SWEET SPANISH PAPRIKA

KOSHER SALT

FRESHLY GROUND BLACK PEPPER

MEASURE the oil, vinegar, garlic, and Spanish paprika into a 1-gallon zip-top bag and shake or squeeze until blended. Season to taste with salt and pepper.

SUGGESTED USES: whole chicken (marinated overnight), roasted; boneless, skinless chicken thighs (marinated 2 hours to overnight) or shrimp (marinated 20 to 45 minutes), sautéed

ROASTED CHICKEN WITH POTATOES

FOR 4 TO 6 SERVINGS, add 1 whole chicken (3$\frac{1}{2}$ to 4 pounds) to the Pimentón Marinade in the zip-top bag and turn to coat, trying to get some of the marinade into the cavity. Seal the bag, letting out all the air. Marinate **overnight** in the refrigerator.

Set the bag aside at room temperature for about half an hour. Remove the chicken from the marinade, pat dry with paper towels, and truss. Set the chicken on a rack in a roasting pan. Peel and quarter 2 large russet potatoes; toss them in olive oil and scatter them in the bottom of the pan around the chicken. Roast in a preheated 400°F oven until the potatoes are tender and the chicken is just cooked through, 55 to 65 minutes. The drumsticks will wiggle freely in their joints, the meat of the drumsticks will have noticeably shrunk away from the knuckles, the juices will run clear, and a meat thermometer inserted in the thickest part of the breast will register 160°F when it is just cooked through. Tent the chicken with foil and let rest for 15 to 20 minutes before carving and serving (the internal temperature should rise to 165°F).

Serve the chicken with the roasted potatoes.

Basil Pesto Marinade

Pesto works just as well as a marinade as it does as a pasta sauce. If time is short, use a high-quality purchased pesto.

TOOLS: food processor • 1-gallon zip-top bag

YIELD: about 3/4 cup (enough for 4 to 6 servings)

1/3 CUP EXTRA-VIRGIN OLIVE OIL

1/2 OUNCE PARMIGIANO-REGGIANO, GRATED (ABOUT 1/3 CUP LIGHTLY PACKED)

1 1/2 CUPS LIGHTLY PACKED FRESH BASIL LEAVES

2 TABLESPOONS PINE NUTS

2 GARLIC CLOVES, SLICED

KOSHER SALT

COMBINE the oil, Parmigiano, basil, pine nuts, and garlic in a food processor and process until smooth. Season to taste with salt.

SUGGESTED USES: chicken breasts, pork chops, or lamb chops (marinated 2 hours to overnight), fish fillets, shrimp, or sea scallops (marinated 20 to 45 minutes), or vegetables (marinated 30 minutes to 1 hour), grilled

GRILLED CHICKEN BREASTS

FOR 6 SERVINGS, combine the Basil Pesto Marinade and 6 boneless, skinless chicken breasts (about 8 ounces each), pounded to an even thickness of 1/2 to 3/4 inch, in a 1-gallon zip-top bag and turn to coat. Seal the bag, letting out all the air. Marinate for at least 2 hours and up to overnight in the refrigerator.

Set the bag aside at room temperature for about half an hour. Remove the chicken from the marinade, pat dry with paper towels, then grill on an oiled grill grate over direct high heat until just cooked through, 10 to 12 minutes, turning once. The chicken will be firm to the touch and the juices will run clear when it is just cooked through. Tent the chicken with foil and let rest for 5 to 10 minutes before carving and serving.

Serve the chicken breasts, thinly sliced, over a bed of pasta. Or serve with Caprese salad, or use to make panini.

Italian Salsa Verde Marinade

Salsa verde is an Italian condiment for grilled meat and seafood. It's typically served as a dipping sauce, but it works nicely as a marinade as well. For double the flavor, I like to use it as both a marinade before cooking and a sauce for serving.

TOOLS: food processor • 1-gallon zip-top bag

YIELD: about 1/2 cup (enough for 2 to 4 servings)

1/4 CUP PLUS 2 TABLESPOONS EXTRA-VIRGIN OLIVE OIL

2 TEASPOONS RED WINE VINEGAR

1 TABLESPOON CAPERS

2 ANCHOVY FILLETS

1/2 CUP LIGHTLY PACKED FRESH FLAT-LEAF PARSLEY LEAVES

1 SHALLOT, SLICED

KOSHER SALT

FRESHLY GROUND BLACK PEPPER

COMBINE the oil, vinegar, capers, anchovies, parsley, and shallot in a food processor and process until smooth. Season to taste with salt and pepper.

SUGGESTED USES: chicken breasts, pork chops, beef steaks, or lamb chops (marinated 2 hours to overnight), fish fillets, shrimp, or sea scallops (marinated 20 to 45 minutes), or vegetables (marinated 30 minutes to 1 hour), grilled

GRILLED RIB-EYE OR STRIP STEAKS

FOR 2 SERVINGS, combine about half of the Italian Salsa Verde Marinade and 2 boneless rib-eye or strip steaks (1 to 1 1/4 inches thick) in a 1-gallon zip-top bag and turn to coat. Seal the bag, letting out all the air. Marinate for at least 2 hours and up to overnight in the refrigerator.

Set the bag aside at room temperature for about half an hour. Remove the steaks from the marinade, pat dry with paper towels, then grill over direct high heat until medium-rare, 12 to 14 minutes (or until the desired doneness), turning once. Moisture will just begin to accumulate on the surface of the steaks when they are medium-rare. Tent the steaks with foil and let rest for 5 to 10 minutes before serving.

Serve the steaks with the remaining marinade as a sauce, alongside simple grilled vegetables and crusty bread.

Porchetta Marinade

This paste-like marinade of garlic, rosemary, fennel, and a variety of other herbs and spices is what flavors the famous Italian pork roast.

TOOL: 1-gallon zip-top bag

YIELD: about 1/2 cup (enough for 4 to 6 servings)

1/4 CUP PLUS 2 TABLESPOONS EXTRA-VIRGIN OLIVE OIL

1 TEASPOON GRATED LEMON ZEST

6 GARLIC CLOVES, MINCED

2 TABLESPOONS MINCED FRESH ROSEMARY

2 TEASPOONS MINCED FRESH THYME

1 TEASPOON FENNEL SEEDS, TOASTED AND CRACKED

1/4 TEASPOON FRESHLY GROUND BLACK PEPPER

GENEROUS PINCH OF CRUSHED RED PEPPER

KOSHER SALT

MEASURE the oil, lemon zest, garlic, rosemary, thyme, fennel seeds, black pepper, and crushed red pepper into a 1-gallon zip-top bag and shake or squeeze until blended. Season to taste with salt.

SUGGESTED USES: pork loin or belly, or whole suckling pig (quadruple the recipe for a 12-pound pig) (marinated overnight), roasted

PORCHETTA

FOR 4 TO 6 SERVINGS, add 1 boneless pork loin roast (about 2 pounds) to the Porchetta Marinade in the zip-top bag and turn to coat. Seal the bag, letting out all the air. Marinate overnight in the refrigerator.

Set the bag aside at room temperature for about half an hour. Remove the pork from the marinade and place on a rack in a roasting pan. Roast the pork in a preheated 350°F oven until medium (or until the desired doneness), 65 to 80 minutes. A meat thermometer inserted in the center will register 140°F when the roast is medium. Tent the roast with foil and let rest for 15 to 20 minutes before carving and serving.

Serve this pork roast with your favorite Italian-style side dishes.

Basic Greek Marinade

The ease of this marinade belies its deliciousness.

TOOL: 1-gallon zip-top bag

YIELD: about 1/2 cup (enough for 2 to 4 servings)

1/4 CUP EXTRA-VIRGIN OLIVE OIL

1 TABLESPOON PLUS 1 TEASPOON RED WINE VINEGAR

1 TABLESPOON PLUS 1 TEASPOON FRESHLY SQUEEZED LEMON JUICE

4 GARLIC CLOVES, MINCED

2 TEASPOONS DRIED OREGANO

KOSHER SALT

FRESHLY GROUND BLACK PEPPER

MEASURE the oil, vinegar, lemon juice, garlic, and oregano into a 1-gallon zip-top bag and shake or squeeze until blended. Season to taste with salt and pepper.

SUGGESTED USES: chicken breasts, pork chops, beef steaks, or lamb chops (marinated 2 hours to overnight), fish fillets, shrimp, or sea scallops (marinated 20 to 45 minutes), or vegetables (marinated 30 minutes to 1 hour), grilled

GRILLED CHICKEN BREASTS

FOR 4 SERVINGS, add 4 boneless, skinless chicken breasts (about 8 ounces each), pounded to an even thickness of 1/2 to 3/4 inch, to the Basic Greek Marinade in the zip-top bag and turn to coat. Seal the bag, letting out all the air. Marinate for at least 2 hours and up to overnight in the refrigerator.

Set the bag aside at room temperature for about half an hour. Remove the chicken from the marinade, pat dry with paper towels, then grill on an oiled grill grate over direct high heat until just cooked through, 10 to 12 minutes, turning once. The chicken will be firm to the touch and the juices will run clear when it is just cooked through. Tent the chicken with foil and let rest for 5 to 10 minutes before carving and serving.

Serve the chicken breasts, thinly sliced, over a Greek salad or wrap in a pita, gyro style. Or chop it and serve tossed into orzo with grilled vegetables and crumbled feta.

Herbed Gyro Marinade

Most restaurants with gyros on the menu are just reheating a commercially prepared, mass-produced finely ground meat product that's a lot like a meatloaf. Homemade gyros using this marinade are far tastier—and healthier.

TOOL: 1-gallon zip-top bag

YIELD: about 1/2 cup (enough for about 4 servings)

1/4 CUP EXTRA-VIRGIN OLIVE OIL

1/4 CUP FRESHLY SQUEEZED LEMON JUICE

2 GARLIC CLOVES, MINCED

2 TABLESPOONS MINCED FRESH OREGANO

2 TEASPOONS MINCED FRESH THYME

2 TEASPOONS MINCED FRESH ROSEMARY

2 TEASPOONS GROUND CORIANDER

1 TEASPOON GROUND CUMIN

1/4 TEASPOON CAYENNE PEPPER

KOSHER SALT

FRESHLY GROUND BLACK PEPPER

MEASURE the oil, lemon juice, garlic, oregano, thyme, rosemary, coriander, cumin, and cayenne into a 1-gallon zip-top bag and shake or squeeze until blended. Season to taste with salt and black pepper.

SUGGESTED USES: boneless, skinless chicken thighs, beef steaks, or lamb leg steaks (marinated 2 hours to overnight), grilled

GYROS

FOR 4 SERVINGS, add 2 lamb leg steaks (1 to 1¼ inches thick) to the Herbed Gyro Marinade in the zip-top bag and turn to coat. Seal the bag, letting out all the air. Marinate for at least 2 hours and up to overnight in the refrigerator.

Set the bag aside at room temperature for about half an hour. Remove the steaks from the marinade, pat dry with paper towels, then grill over direct high heat until medium-rare, 10 to 14 minutes (or until the desired doneness), turning once. Moisture will just begin to accumulate on the surface of the steaks when they are medium-rare. Tent the steaks with foil and let rest for 5 to 10 minutes before carving and serving.

Serve the lamb, thinly sliced, wrapped in Greek pita bread with shredded lettuce, sliced tomatoes and onions, crumbled feta, and a sauce of Greek yogurt, lemon juice, diced cucumber, garlic, and minced fresh mint or dill.

Souvlaki Marinade

The popular Greek fast food of grilled meat skewers is made using this marinade.

TOOL: 1-gallon zip-top bag

YIELD: about 1/2 cup (enough for about 2 servings)

1/4 CUP EXTRA-VIRGIN OLIVE OIL

1 TABLESPOON RED WINE VINEGAR

1 TABLESPOON FRESHLY SQUEEZED LEMON JUICE

1/4 CUP MINCED YELLOW ONION

3 GARLIC CLOVES, MINCED

2 TEASPOONS MINCED FRESH FLAT-LEAF PARSLEY

2 TEASPOONS MINCED FRESH MINT LEAVES

1 TEASPOON DRIED OREGANO

KOSHER SALT

FRESHLY GROUND BLACK PEPPER

MEASURE the oil, vinegar, lemon juice, onion, garlic, parsley, mint, and oregano into a 1-gallon zip-top bag and shake or squeeze until blended. Season to taste with salt and pepper.

SUGGESTED USES: cubes of chicken breast, pork sirloin, or lamb leg (marinated 2 hours to overnight) or cubes of swordfish, shrimp, or sea scallops (marinated 20 to 45 minutes), skewered and grilled

SWORDFISH SOUVLAKI

FOR 2 SERVINGS, add 2 skinned swordfish steaks (6 to 8 ounces each and about 1 inch thick), cut into 1 1/4-inch cubes, to the Souvlaki Marinade in the zip-top bag and turn to coat. Seal the bag, letting out all the air. Marinate for at least 20 minutes and up to 45 minutes at room temperature.

Remove the fish from the marinade, pat dry with paper towels, and skewer onto bamboo skewers that have been soaked in water. Grill the skewers on an oiled grill grate over direct high heat until just cooked through, 10 to 12 minutes, turning once. The fish will begin to flake when it is just cooked through.

Serve these kabobs over rice or wrap in Greek pita bread with shredded lettuce, sliced tomatoes and onions, and a sauce of Greek yogurt, lemon juice, diced cucumber, garlic, and minced fresh mint or dill.

Marinade for Sauerbraten

Sauerbraten is a traditional German pot roast in a sweet-and-sour sauce. The meat has a lengthy soak in a mixture of red wine, red wine vinegar, vegetables, herbs, and spices and is then braised, with the strained marinade becoming the base for the sauce. When making sauerbraten, plan well enough ahead to allow the meat to marinate for at least 3 days.

TOOLS: saucepan • 1-gallon zip-top bag

YIELD: about 6 cups (enough for 8 to 10 servings)

2 CUPS PINOT NOIR OR OTHER DRY RED WINE

2 CUPS RED WINE VINEGAR

1 LARGE YELLOW ONION, DICED

2 CELERY RIBS, DICED

1 CARROT, DICED

6 GARLIC CLOVES, SLICED

1/2 CUP PACKED LIGHT BROWN SUGAR

3 BAY LEAVES

1 TABLESPOON CORIANDER SEEDS

1 TABLESPOON BLACK PEPPERCORNS

1 TABLESPOON MUSTARD POWDER

1 TABLESPOON JUNIPER BERRIES, CRUSHED

6 ALLSPICE BERRIES

5 WHOLE CLOVES

1 CINNAMON STICK

KOSHER SALT

COMBINE the wine, vinegar, onion, celery, carrot, garlic, brown sugar, bay leaves, coriander, peppercorns, mustard, juniper, allspice, cloves, and cinnamon in a saucepan and bring to a boil. Remove from the heat, season to taste with salt, and let cool to room temperature.

RECIPE CONTINUES →

SAUERBRATEN

FOR 8 TO 10 SERVINGS, combine the Marinade for Sauerbraten and 1 beef chuck roast (about 4 pounds) in a 1-gallon zip-top bag and turn to coat. Seal the bag, letting out all the air. Marinate for at least 3 days and up to 5 days in the refrigerator, turning over the bag once a day.

Set the bag aside at room temperature for about half an hour. Remove the beef from the marinade, reserving the marinade to use for the sauce. Pat the beef dry with paper towels, picking off any spices, and season it generously with salt and pepper. Strain the marinade through a fine-mesh sieve into a glass measuring cup until you have 2 cups (discard the rest). Heat a large, heavy pot over medium-high heat until a few water droplets dance and look like ball bearings rolling around when flicked into the pot. Add 2 tablespoons canola oil and sear the beef until crusty and brown all over, 15 to 17 minutes, turning occasionally. Transfer the beef to a plate. Reduce the heat to medium-low, add 2 julienned medium yellow onions (see page 297) and 2 slices diced bacon to the pot, and cook, stirring frequently, until the onions are caramelized. Stir in $1/4$ cup plus 2 tablespoons all-purpose flour, and then 4 cups beef broth and the 2 cups strained marinade. Bring to a boil, scraping up the brown bits from the bottom of the pan with a heatproof spatula. Return the beef to the pot, cover, and bake in a preheated 350°F oven until the beef is fork-tender, about 3 hours. About halfway through the cooking time, turn the beef and make sure that the sauce is simmering slowly for the duration of the cooking time. If the sauce is simmering quickly, reduce the heat to 325°F.

To finish, transfer the beef to a plate and tent with foil to keep warm. Skim off any fat from the surface of the sauce and season it to taste with salt and pepper. Some cooks add gingersnap crumbs to sweeten and thicken the sauce, but I like it just as it is (besides, at my house any cookies would be eaten long before they could ever make it into the pot). Slice the beef against the grain and serve immediately with the sauce.

Buttered spaetzle or egg noodles are the perfect accompaniment for this pot roast.

CHINESE, JAPANESE, AND KOREAN
MARINADES

THE VARIED CUISINES OF CHINA, JAPAN, AND KOREA INSPIRE THIS GROUP OF MARINADES. THEY FEATURE SUCH INTERESTING UMAMI-RICH INGREDIENTS AS HOISIN SAUCE, XO SAUCE, FERMENTED BLACK BEANS, MISO, AND KIMCHEE, AS WELL AS THE REQUISITE SOY SAUCE, GARLIC, AND GINGER. SOME, SUCH AS THE BASIC WOK MARINADE, ARE MEANT FOR STIR-FRYING; OTHERS, SUCH AS THE SIMPLE SOY MARINADE, ARE INTENDED FOR THINLY SLICED MEATS SIMMERED IN BROTH AND THEN SERVED IN NOODLE SOUP. SOME RECIPES ARE PERFECT FOR GRILLING, SUCH AS THE LAPSANG SOUCHONG MARINADE, WHICH FEATURES A TEA WITH A DISTINCTLY SMOKY FLAVOR.

Basic Wok Marinade

This marinade is versatile enough to be used for any type of stir-fry, from meat to seafood to tofu.

TOOL: 1-gallon zip-top bag

YIELD: about 1/2 cup (enough for about 4 servings)

2 TABLESPOONS CANOLA OIL

2 TABLESPOONS SOY SAUCE

1 TABLESPOON SHAOXING RICE WINE (SEE BELOW)

2 TABLESPOONS SLICED SCALLIONS

1 TABLESPOON MINCED FRESH GINGER

3 GARLIC CLOVES, MINCED

2 TEASPOONS SUGAR

MEASURE the oil, soy sauce, wine, scallions, ginger, garlic, and sugar into a 1-gallon zip-top bag and shake or squeeze until blended.

SHAOXING RICE WINE	Shaoxing rice wine, which is made from fermented rice, is used extensively in Chinese cooking. It is vaguely similar to sherry, and in fact, sherry can be substituted if it's not available. Another good stand-in would be sake. Look for Shaoxing rice wine at Asian markets.

SUGGESTED USES: bite-size pieces of chicken, pork, or beef, or shrimp, bay scallops, squid rings, or bite-size pieces of tofu (marinated 20 to 45 minutes), stir-fried

STIR-FRIED SHRIMP WITH VEGETABLES

FOR 4 SERVINGS, add 1 pound peeled, deveined large shrimp (21/25 count) to the Basic Wok Marinade in the zip-top bag and turn to coat. Seal the bag, letting out all the air. Marinate for at least 20 minutes and up to 45 minutes at room temperature.

Remove the shrimp from the marinade and pat dry with paper towels. Heat a large wok over high heat until very hot and smoking. Add 1 tablespoon canola oil and swirl to coat the bottom of the wok. Stir-fry 3 cups vegetables of your choice (such as broccoli, bell peppers, mushrooms, cabbage, carrots, celery, or onions) cut into bite-size pieces until almost tender-crisp, 2 to 3 minutes. Transfer the vegetables to a plate. Add another 1 tablespoon canola oil to the wok and stir-fry the shrimp until almost cooked through, 2 to 3 minutes. Toss the vegetables back into the wok and stir-fry until the vegetables are tender-crisp and the shrimp is just cooked through, about 1 minute longer. The shrimp will be firm to the touch, opaque and pink, and beginning to curl when they are just cooked through. Season to taste with soy sauce.

Serve the stir-fry over sticky rice. Alternatively, toss some noodles into the stir-fry.

Simple Soy Marinade

With just three ingredients, this is perhaps the simplest of all Asian-style marinades. I have relied on it—along with a package of thinly sliced pork butt or beef short ribs from the Asian market—on many a weeknight to whip up a healthy and delicious noodle soup. The marinade needs only a couple of minutes to do its magic if you use meat that's cut paper-thin on a slicer.

TOOL: 1-gallon zip-top bag

YIELD: about 1/4 cup (enough for about 2 servings)

3 TABLESPOONS SOY SAUCE

2 GARLIC CLOVES, MINCED

1 TABLESPOON SUGAR

MEASURE the soy sauce, garlic, and sugar into a 1-gallon zip-top bag and shake until blended.

SUGGESTED USES: bite-size pieces of chicken, thinly sliced pork butt, or boneless beef short ribs, or shrimp, bay scallops, squid rings, or bite-size pieces of tofu (marinated 20 to 45 minutes), simmered or stir-fried

PORK OR BEEF, BOK CHOY, AND SHIITAKE UDON NOODLE SOUP

FOR 2 SERVINGS, add 2/3 to 3/4 pound very thinly sliced pork butt or boneless beef short ribs to the Simple Soy Marinade in the zip-top bag and turn to coat. Seal the bag, letting out all the air. Marinate for at least 5 minutes and up to 15 minutes at room temperature.

Combine 4 to 6 dried shiitake mushrooms and enough boiling water to cover in a small bowl and let soak until the mushrooms are rehydrated and pliable, 10 to 12 minutes. Strain the soaking liquid through a fine-mesh sieve and slice the mushrooms. Bring 4 cups chicken broth to a boil in a medium-size pot. Add the sliced mushrooms and the separated leaves of 3 heads baby bok choy to the pot and simmer until the bok choy begins to soften, 2 to 3 minutes. Add the meat, marinade and all, and 2 individual-serving packages (about 7 ounces each) of refrigerated udon noodles to the pot and simmer, stirring gently, until the meat is just cooked through and the noodles soften, 3 to 5 minutes. Remove from the heat, add the shiitake soaking liquid, if desired, and stir in 3 tablespoons miso thinned with 3 tablespoons water and a handful of sliced scallions.

Shiitake-Soy Marinade

This unusual marinade features the soaking liquid from rehydrating dried shiitake mushrooms, which is loaded with flavor. Your guests may have trouble putting their finger on exactly what's in it, but they are certain to love it, as it's loaded with umami. Dried shiitake mushrooms and mushroom-flavored soy sauce are available at Asian markets.

TOOL: 1-gallon zip-top bag

YIELD: about 3/4 cup (enough for about 6 servings)

---

8 DRIED SHIITAKE MUSHROOMS

3/4 CUP BOILING WATER

2 TABLESPOONS MUSHROOM-FLAVORED SOY SAUCE

1 TABLESPOON CANOLA OIL

2 GARLIC CLOVES, MINCED

COMBINE the shiitakes and boiling water in a small bowl and let soak until the mushrooms are rehydrated and pliable, 10 to 12 minutes. Strain the soaking liquid through a fine-mesh sieve and let cool to room temperature. Reserve the shiitakes to stir-fry for a side dish.

Measure the soaking liquid, mushroom-flavored soy sauce, oil, and garlic into a 1-gallon zip-top bag and shake or squeeze until blended.

SUGGESTED USES: beef steaks, salmon fillets, boneless, skin-on duck breasts, or tofu (marinated overnight), grilled or seared

GRILLED RIB-EYE OR STRIP STEAKS

FOR 6 SERVINGS, add 6 boneless rib-eye or strip steaks (1 to 1^1/4 inches thick) to the Shiitake-Soy Marinade in the zip-top bag and turn to coat. Seal the bag, letting out all the air. Marinate overnight in the refrigerator.

Set the bag aside at room temperature for about half an hour. Remove the steaks from the marinade, pat dry with paper towels, then grill over direct high heat until medium-rare, 12 to 14 minutes (or until the desired doneness), turning once. Moisture will just begin to accumulate on the surface of the steaks when they are medium-rare. Tent the steaks with foil and let rest for 5 to 10 minutes before carving and serving.

Serve the steaks, thinly sliced, with stir-fried vegetables (including the reserved shiitake mushrooms) over sticky rice.

Ginger-Orange Marinade

Orange gives a little twist to the usual Asian flavors.

TOOL: 1-gallon zip-top bag

YIELD: about 3/4 cup (enough for 4 to 6 servings)

1 TABLESPOON GRATED ORANGE ZEST

1/4 CUP FRESHLY SQUEEZED ORANGE JUICE

1/4 CUP SOY SAUCE

3 TABLESPOONS HONEY

2 TABLESPOONS CANOLA OIL

1/4 TEASPOON TOASTED SESAME OIL

1 TABLESPOON MINCED FRESH GINGER

1 GARLIC CLOVE, MINCED

GENEROUS PINCH OF CRUSHED RED PEPPER

MEASURE the orange zest, orange juice, soy sauce, honey, canola oil, sesame oil, ginger, garlic, and crushed red pepper into a 1-gallon zip-top bag and shake or squeeze until blended.

SUGGESTED USES: chicken breasts, pork chops, or tofu (marinated 2 hours to overnight) or salmon fillets, shrimp, or sea scallops (marinated 20 to 45 minutes), grilled

GRILLED SALMON FILLETS

FOR 6 SERVINGS, add 6 skinned, boneless salmon fillets (6 to 8 ounces each) to the Ginger-Orange Marinade in the zip-top bag and turn to coat. Seal the bag, letting out all the air. Marinate for at least 20 minutes and up to 45 minutes at room temperature.

Remove the fillets from the marinade, pat dry with paper towels, then grill on an oiled grill grate over direct high heat until medium-rare, 8 to 10 minutes (or until the desired doneness), turning once. The fillets will barely begin to flake when they are medium-rare.

Serve the salmon fillets on a bed of steaming sticky rice along with a steamed vegetable such as bok choy, snow peas, or broccoli.

Sesame Marinade

Toasted sesame oil is usually used a drop at a time, but not so here. This marinade calls for sesame oil by the spoonful, along with a generous quantity of toasted sesame seeds, for over-the-top sesame flavor.

TOOL: 1-gallon zip-top bag

YIELD: about 1/2 cup (enough for 2 to 4 servings)

3 TABLESPOONS SOY SAUCE

2 TABLESPOONS TOASTED SESAME OIL

1/2 CUP SLICED SCALLIONS

1 TABLESPOON SUGAR

1 TEASPOON TOASTED SESAME SEEDS

FRESHLY GROUND BLACK PEPPER

MEASURE the soy sauce, sesame oil, scallions, sugar, and sesame seeds into a 1-gallon zip-top bag and shake or squeeze until blended. Season to taste with pepper.

SUGGESTED USES: boneless, skinless chicken breasts, pork chops, or beef steaks (marinated 2 hours to overnight) or white fish fillets, shrimp, or scallops (marinated 20 to 45 minutes) or tofu (marinated 30 to 60 minutes), grilled or seared

SEARED TOFU

FOR 4 SERVINGS, add one 14-ounce package extra-firm tofu, drained and cut into four 1-inch-thick slices, to the Sesame Marinade in the zip-top bag and turn to coat. Seal the bag, letting out all the air. Marinate for at least 30 minutes and up to 1 hour at room temperature.

Remove the tofu from the marinade and pat dry with paper towels. Heat a large, heavy sauté pan over medium-high heat until a few water droplets dance and look like ball bearings rolling around when flicked into the pan. Add 3 tablespoons canola oil and sear the tofu until heated through, 5 to 7 minutes, turning once.

Serve the tofu with sticky rice or noodles and stir-fried vegetables such as yard-long green beans or bok choy.

Marinade for Char Siu

Chinese food lovers will be delighted to learn how easy it is to make outstanding succulent Chinese barbecued pork at home. Chinese five-spice powder and maltose, the sweet syrup that gives the pork its shiny appearance, are available at Asian markets. Additional honey may be used in place of the maltose (in which case you can forgo heating the mixture on the stovetop and simply blend in the bag instead). Though many char siu recipes include food coloring for that recognizable red hue, I prefer to go without.

TOOLS: saucepan • 1-gallon zip-top bag

YIELD: about 1 cup (enough for 6 to 8 servings)

1/4 CUP SOY SAUCE

1/4 CUP HOISIN SAUCE

2 TABLESPOONS SHAOXING RICE WINE (SEE PAGE 202)

2 TABLESPOONS MALTOSE

2 TABLESPOONS HONEY

1/2 TEASPOON TOASTED SESAME OIL

1/2 TEASPOON CHINESE FIVE-SPICE POWDER

GENEROUS PINCH OF FRESHLY GROUND WHITE PEPPER

2 GARLIC CLOVES, MINCED

COMBINE the soy sauce, hoisin sauce, rice wine, maltose, honey, sesame oil, five-spice, and white pepper in a small saucepan and heat, stirring constantly, until the maltose dissolves. Let cool to room temperature and stir in the garlic.

CHAR SIU PORK

FOR 6 TO 8 SERVINGS, combine the Marinade for Char Siu and 2 to 3 pounds country-style pork ribs in a 1-gallon zip-top bag and turn to coat. Seal the bag, letting out all the air. Marinate at least overnight and up to 3 days in the refrigerator, turning over the bag once a day.

Set the bag aside at room temperature for about half an hour. Remove the pork from the marinade, reserving the marinade to use for basting, and place the pork on a rack on a rimmed baking sheet. Roast in a preheated 350°F oven until just cooked through, 75 to 90 minutes, basting occasionally with the marinade during the first 45 minutes of roasting. The pork will look burnished and juicy and be firm to the touch, and a meat thermometer inserted in the center of a rib will register 160°F when it is just cooked through. Tent the pork with foil and let rest for 5 to 10 minutes before carving and serving.

Serve the pork with sticky rice and steamed vegetables, atop a bowl of ramen, or tucked inside steamed buns with hoisin sauce and scallions. Make extra for leftovers to use in fried rice or lo mein.

Chinese Five-Spice Marinade

Chinese five-spice powder, which is a common ingredient in Chinese cuisine, is a fragrant, warm, and slightly sweet mixture of ground cinnamon, cloves, star anise, fennel seed, and Sichuan peppercorns. The flavor is bold and pungent, and a little bit goes a long way. Chinese five-spice powder is available at most gourmet shops and many supermarkets.

TOOL: 1-gallon zip-top bag

YIELD: about 1/2 cup (enough for 2 to 4 servings)

1/4 CUP SOY SAUCE

2 TABLESPOONS CANOLA OIL

1/2 TEASPOON TOASTED SESAME OIL

2 TEASPOONS MINCED FRESH GINGER

4 GARLIC CLOVES, MINCED

1/4 CUP PACKED LIGHT BROWN SUGAR

2 TEASPOONS CHINESE FIVE-SPICE POWDER

MEASURE the soy sauce, canola oil, sesame oil, ginger, garlic, brown sugar, and five-spice into a 1-gallon zip-top bag and shake or squeeze until blended.

SUGGESTED USES: pork tenderloin medallions or boneless, skin-on duck breasts (marinated 2 hours to overnight), grilled or seared; whole duck (marinated overnight), roasted

GRILLED PORK TENDERLOIN MEDALLIONS

FOR 2 SERVINGS, add 1 pork tenderloin (12 to 14 ounces), cut on a bias into 1-inch-thick medallions, to the Chinese Five-Spice Marinade in the zip-top bag and turn to coat. Seal the bag, letting out all the air. Marinate for at least 2 hours and up to overnight in the refrigerator.

Set the bag aside at room temperature for about half an hour. Remove the pork medallions from the marinade, pat dry with paper towels, then grill over direct high heat until medium, 13 to 15 minutes (or until the desired doneness), turning once. Moisture will just begin to pool on the surface of the medallions when they are medium. Tent the medallions with foil and let rest for 5 to 10 minutes before serving.

Serve the pork medallions with sticky rice and steamed vegetables. Leftovers make fantastic fried rice and lo mein.

Asian Plum Marinade

This fruity, sweet, and savory marinade is delicious with bone-in chicken or pork.

TOOL: 1-gallon zip-top bag

YIELD: about 1 cup (enough for 4 to 8 servings)

1/4 CUP PLUM JAM

3 TABLESPOONS HOISIN SAUCE

2 TABLESPOONS CANOLA OIL

2 TABLESPOONS RICE VINEGAR

2 TABLESPOONS SOY SAUCE

1 TABLESPOON OYSTER SAUCE

1 TABLESPOON SRIRACHA SAUCE

2 TABLESPOONS SLICED SCALLIONS

1 TEASPOON MINCED FRESH GINGER

2 GARLIC CLOVES, MINCED

1/8 TEASPOON CHINESE FIVE-SPICE POWDER

MEASURE the jam, hoisin sauce, oil, rice vinegar, soy sauce, oyster sauce, sriracha sauce, scallions, ginger, garlic, and five-spice into a 1-gallon zip-top bag and shake or squeeze until blended.

SUGGESTED USES: bone-in chicken pieces (especially wings) or boneless, skin-on duck breasts (marinated 2 hours to overnight), or pork ribs (marinated overnight), grilled

GRILLED BABY BACK RIBS

POUR ABOUT HALF of the Asian Plum Marinade into a second 1-gallon zip-top bag. For 4 servings, cut 2 racks pork baby back ribs (2 to 2 1/2 pounds each) in half and add 1 rack (2 halves) to the marinade in each of the zip-top bags; turn to coat. Seal the bags, letting out all the air. Marinate overnight in the refrigerator.

Set the bags aside at room temperature for about half an hour. Remove the ribs from the marinade and place them on the grill, meaty side up. Grill the ribs, covered, over indirect medium-low heat until fork-tender, 2 to 2 1/2 hours. The meat will have noticeably shrunk away from the ends of the bones when it is done. Tent the ribs with foil and let rest for 5 to 10 minutes before carving and serving.

Serve the ribs sprinkled with sliced scallions and toasted sesame seeds and with sides of sticky rice and steamed Chinese greens.

Douchi Marinade

Douchi, roughly translated into English as fermented or salted black beans, is a widely used flavoring ingredient in Chinese cuisine. It's salty and pungent and often used in seafood dishes, making this marinade a good choice for scallops, shrimp, or squid. Douchi is available at Asian markets.

TOOLS: blender • 1-gallon zip-top bag

YIELD: about 1/2 cup (enough for about 4 servings)

3 TABLESPOONS DOUCHI (FERMENTED BLACK BEANS)

2 TABLESPOONS CANOLA OIL

1 TABLESPOON SHAOXING RICE WINE (SEE PAGE 202)

1 TABLESPOON SOY SAUCE

1/4 CUP SLICED SCALLIONS

1 TEASPOON MINCED FRESH GINGER

1 GARLIC CLOVE, SLICED

1 TABLESPOON SUGAR

COMBINE the douchi, oil, rice wine, soy sauce, scallions, ginger, garlic, and sugar in a blender and blend until smooth.

SUGGESTED USES: bite-size pieces of chicken, pork, or beef, or shrimp, bay scallops, squid rings, or bite-size pieces of tofu (marinated 20 to 45 minutes), stir-fried

STIR-FRIED SCALLOPS WITH VEGETABLES

FOR 4 SERVINGS, combine the Douchi Marinade and 1 pound bay scallops in a 1-gallon zip-top bag and turn to coat. Seal the bag, letting out all the air. Marinate for at least 20 minutes and up to 45 minutes at room temperature.

Remove the scallops from the marinade and drain on paper towels. Heat a large wok over high heat until very hot and smoking. Add 1 tablespoon canola oil and swirl to coat the bottom of the wok. Stir-fry 3 cups vegetables of your choice (such as broccoli, bell peppers, mushrooms, cabbage, carrots, celery, or onions) cut into bite-size pieces until almost tender-crisp, 2 to 3 minutes. Remove the vegetables to a plate. Add another 1 tablespoon canola oil to the wok and stir-fry the scallops until almost cooked through, 2 to 3 minutes. Toss the vegetables back into the wok and stir-fry until the vegetables are tender-crisp and the scallops are just cooked through, about 1 minute longer. The scallops will be opaque and white and firm to the touch. Season to taste with soy sauce. Serve the stir-fry immediately.

Serve the stir-fry over sticky rice. Alternatively, toss some noodles into the stir-fry.

XO Marinade

XO sauce—which is made with dried shrimp and scallops, ham, shallots, garlic, and chile—is considered a luxury ingredient in Chinese cooking. It's relatively expensive, but just a little bit will add quite an umami kick to any dish—and it will keep indefinitely in the refrigerator. Look for it at any Chinese market.

TOOL: 1-gallon zip-top bag

YIELD: about 1/2 cup (enough for about 4 servings)

1/4 CUP SOY SAUCE

2 TABLESPOONS CANOLA OIL

2 TABLESPOONS XO SAUCE

2 GARLIC CLOVES, MINCED

1 TEASPOON SUGAR

MEASURE the soy sauce, oil, XO sauce, garlic, and sugar into a 1-gallon zip-top bag and shake or squeeze until blended.

SUGGESTED USES: shrimp, bay scallops, or squid rings (marinated 20 to 45 minutes), stir-fried

SCALLOP FRIED RICE

FOR 4 SERVINGS, add 1 pound bay scallops to the XO Marinade in the zip-top bag and turn to coat. Seal the bag, letting out all the air. Marinate for at least 20 minutes and up to 45 minutes at room temperature.

Remove the scallops from the marinade and drain on paper towels. Beat 2 large eggs. Heat a large wok over high heat until very hot and smoking. Add 1 tablespoon canola oil and swirl to coat the bottom of the wok. Stir-fry the eggs until scrambled, 30 seconds to 1 minute. Transfer the eggs to a plate. Add another 1 tablespoon canola oil to the wok and stir-fry 1/2 cup diced carrots and 1/2 cup thawed frozen peas until golden brown, 1 to 2 minutes. Toss in 2 minced garlic cloves. Transfer the vegetables to the plate. Add another 2 tablespoons canola oil to the wok and stir-fry the scallops until almost cooked through, 2 to 3 minutes. Return the eggs and vegetables to the wok and add 6 cups cold cooked long-grain white rice and 3/4 cup sliced scallions. Stir-fry until the rice is heated through and the scallops are just cooked through, 2 to 3 minutes. The scallops will be opaque and white and firm to the touch. Season to taste with soy sauce.

Lapsang Souchong Marinade

Lapsang Souchong is a smoked black tea from China. Its intense smoky flavor comes through loud and clear in this marinade. Loose-leaf Lapsang Souchong tea is available wherever fine teas are sold.

TOOL: 1-gallon zip-top bag

YIELD: about $1/3$ cup (enough for 2 to 3 servings)

2 TABLESPOONS LAPSANG SOUCHONG TEA LEAVES

$1/3$ CUP BOILING WATER

1 TABLESPOON CANOLA OIL

1 TABLESPOON SOY SAUCE

1 GARLIC CLOVE, MINCED

1 TEASPOON SUGAR

$1/4$ TEASPOON CRUSHED RED PEPPER

COMBINE the tea and boiling water in a small bowl and let stand until the tea is steeped to the desired strength, 2 to 3 minutes. Strain through a fine-mesh sieve and let cool. Measure the tea, oil, soy sauce, garlic, sugar, and crushed red pepper into a 1-gallon zip-top bag and shake or squeeze until blended.

SUGGESTED USES: boneless, skinless chicken thighs, pork belly, beef steaks, fish fillets, or boneless, skin-on duck breasts (marinated overnight), grilled

GRILLED FLANK STEAK

FOR 2 TO 3 SERVINGS, add 1 flank steak (1 to 1 $1/2$ pounds) to the Lapsang Souchong Marinade in the zip-top bag and turn to coat. Seal the bag, letting out all the air. Marinate overnight in the refrigerator.

Set the bag aside at room temperature for about half an hour. Remove the steak from the marinade, pat dry with paper towels, then grill over direct high heat until medium-rare, 10 to 12 minutes (or until the desired doneness), turning once. Moisture will just begin to accumulate on the surface of the steak when it is medium-rare. Tent the steak with foil and let rest for 5 to 10 minutes before carving and serving.

Serve the steak with sticky rice and a vegetable stir-fry.

Teriyaki Marinade

Though grocery store shelves are loaded with bottled teriyaki marinades and sauces, homemade is far superior and couldn't be easier to make.

TOOL: 1-gallon zip-top bag

YIELD: about 3/4 cup (enough for 4 to 6 servings)

1/4 CUP SAKE

1/4 CUP MIRIN (SEE BELOW)

1/4 CUP SOY SAUCE

1 TEASPOON MINCED FRESH GINGER

1 GARLIC CLOVE, MINCED

2 TABLESPOONS SUGAR

MEASURE the sake, mirin, soy sauce, ginger, garlic, and sugar into a 1-gallon zip-top bag and shake or squeeze until blended.

MIRIN	Mirin, an essential ingredient in Japanese cooking, is a sweetened rice wine. It's commonly used in sauces and glazes, and marinades made with mirin tend to become lacquer-like glazes. Mirin is available at Asian markets and many large supermarkets.

SUGGESTED USES: boneless, skinless chicken thighs, pork chops, or beef steaks (marinated 2 hours to overnight), salmon fillets or shrimp (marinated 20 to 45 minutes), or vegetables (especially zucchini and yellow squash) (marinated 30 minutes to 1 hour), grilled

CHICKEN TERIYAKI

FOR 6 SERVINGS, add 12 boneless, skinless chicken thighs (about 4 ounces each) to the Teriyaki Marinade in the zip-top bag and turn to coat. Seal the bag, letting out all the air. Marinate for at least 2 hours and up to overnight in the refrigerator.

Set the bag aside at room temperature for about half an hour. Remove the chicken from the marinade, pat dry with paper towels, then grill, covered, on an oiled grill grate over direct medium heat until just cooked through, 12 to 14 minutes, turning once. The chicken will be firm to the touch and the juices will run clear when it is just cooked through. Tent the chicken with foil and let rest for 5 to 10 minutes before carving and serving.

Serve the chicken thighs over sticky rice and topped with sliced scallions and toasted sesame seeds. If desired, make an extra batch of marinade, simmer it until thickened and slightly syrupy, and use it as a drizzling sauce.

Miso Marinade

A traditional Japanese ingredient, miso is fermented soybean paste. It has a flavor that's both salty and umami. Asian markets and most well-stocked grocery stores carry miso.

TOOL: 1-gallon zip-top bag

YIELD: about 1/2 cup (enough for 2 to 4 servings)

2 TABLESPOONS CANOLA OIL

2 TABLESPOONS SAKE

2 TABLESPOONS MISO

1 SCALLION, SLICED

1 GARLIC CLOVE, MINCED

MEASURE the oil, sake, miso, scallion, and garlic into a 1-gallon zip-top bag and shake or squeeze until blended.

SUGGESTED USES: boneless, skinless chicken thighs, pork chops, or beef steaks (marinated 2 hours to overnight), salmon fillets, shrimp, or sea scallops (marinated 20 to 45 minutes), or vegetables (marinated 30 minutes to 1 hour), grilled or broiled

GRILLED SALMON FILLETS

FOR 4 SERVINGS, add 4 skinned, boneless salmon fillets (6 to 8 ounces each) to the Miso Marinade in the zip-top bag and turn to coat. Seal the bag, letting out all the air. Marinate for at least 20 minutes and up to 45 minutes at room temperature.

Remove the fillets from the marinade, pat dry with paper towels, then grill on an oiled grill grate over direct high heat until medium-rare, 8 to 10 minutes (or until the desired doneness), turning once. The fillets will barely begin to flake when they are medium-rare.

Serve the salmon fillets on a bed of steaming sticky rice along with steamed vegetables such as bok choy, snow peas, or broccoli and shiitake mushrooms.

Wasabi Marinade

This recipe calls for wasabi powder, but check the ingredient label on the can to make sure it's the real thing—often powdered "wasabi" is just horseradish and food coloring. If you can get your hands on fresh wasabi, by all means use that instead.

TOOL: 1-gallon zip-top bag

YIELD: about 1/2 cup (enough for 2 to 4 servings)

2 TABLESPOONS CANOLA OIL

2 TABLESPOONS SAKE

2 TABLESPOONS SOY SAUCE

1 TEASPOON RICE VINEGAR

2 TEASPOONS SUGAR

1 TABLESPOON WASABI POWDER

MEASURE the oil, sake, soy sauce, vinegar, sugar, and wasabi into a 1-gallon zip-top bag and shake or squeeze until blended.

SUGGESTED USES: chicken breasts or beef steaks (marinated 2 hours to overnight) or salmon fillets or shrimp (marinated 20 to 45 minutes), grilled or broiled

GRILLED SALMON FILLETS

FOR 4 SERVINGS, add 4 skinned, boneless salmon fillets (6 to 8 ounces each) to the Wasabi Marinade in the zip-top bag and turn to coat. Seal the bag, letting out all the air. Marinate for at least 20 minutes and up to 45 minutes at room temperature.

Remove the fillets from the marinade, pat dry with paper towels, then grill on an oiled grill grate over direct high heat until medium-rare, 8 to 10 minutes (or until the desired doneness), turning once. The fillets will barely begin to flake when they are medium-rare.

Serve the salmon fillets over sushi rice or soba noodles with soy sauce, scallions, and sesame seeds.

Yuzu Marinade

Yuzu, a citrus fruit common to Japanese cuisine, lends its tart, piney flavor to this marinade. Fresh yuzu is hard to find, though it does appear at gourmet markets from time to time. Bottled yuzu juice can be found at Japanese markets.

TOOL: 1-gallon zip-top bag

YIELD: about 3/4 cup (enough for 4 to 6 servings)

1/4 CUP SAKE

3 TABLESPOONS YUZU JUICE

2 TABLESPOONS SOY SAUCE

1 TABLESPOON CANOLA OIL

1 TABLESPOON MIRIN (SEE PAGE 216)

1 GARLIC CLOVE, MINCED

1 TABLESPOON SUGAR

GENEROUS PINCH OF FRESHLY GROUND WHITE PEPPER

MEASURE the sake, yuzu juice, soy sauce, oil, mirin, garlic, sugar, and pepper into a 1-gallon zip-top bag and shake or squeeze until blended.

SUGGESTED USES: chicken breasts or pork tenderloin medallions (marinated 2 hours to overnight), fish fillets (especially salmon), shrimp, or scallops (marinated 20 to 45 minutes), grilled or broiled

GRILLED SHRIMP

FOR 4 SERVINGS, add 1 to 1 1/2 pounds peeled, deveined large shrimp (21/25 count) to the Yuzu Marinade in the zip-top bag and turn to coat. Seal the bag, letting out all the air. Marinate for at least 20 minutes and up to 45 minutes at room temperature.

Remove the shrimp from the marinade, pat dry with paper towels, then grill on an oiled grill grate over direct high heat until just cooked through, 4 to 5 minutes, turning once. The shrimp will be firm to the touch, opaque and pink, and beginning to curl when they are just cooked through.

Serve the shrimp with sticky rice and grilled vegetables.

Shiso-Lime Marinade

Shiso (also known as perilla) is an herb used commonly in Japanese cooking. A member of the mint family, shiso comes in two varieties. Green shiso tastes like cumin seeds, while red shiso has an anise-like flavor. Personally, I'm partial to green shiso, but you can use whichever you prefer in this recipe. Japanese markets carry fresh shiso leaves.

TOOL: 1-gallon zip-top bag

YIELD: about 2/3 cup (enough for 4 to 6 servings)

1/4 CUP SAKE

2 TABLESPOONS CANOLA OIL

2 TABLESPOONS SOY SAUCE

1/2 TEASPOON GRATED LIME ZEST

1 TABLESPOON FRESHLY SQUEEZED LIME JUICE

1 GARLIC CLOVE, MINCED

8 FRESH SHISO LEAVES, MINCED

1 TABLESPOON SUGAR

MEASURE the sake, oil, soy sauce, lime zest, lime juice, garlic, shiso, and sugar into a 1-gallon zip-top bag and shake or squeeze until blended.

SUGGESTED USES: chicken breasts or pork chops (marinated 2 hours to overnight) or fish fillets (especially salmon) or shrimp (marinated 20 to 45 minutes), grilled

GRILLED PORK LOIN OR RIB CHOPS

FOR 4 SERVINGS, add 4 boneless pork loin or rib chops (about 1 inch thick) to the Shiso-Lime Marinade in the zip-top bag and turn to coat. Seal the bag, letting out all the air. Marinate for at least 2 hours and up to overnight in the refrigerator.

Set the bag aside at room temperature for about half an hour. Remove the chops from the marinade, pat dry with paper towels, then grill over direct high heat until medium, 13 to 15 minutes (or until the desired doneness), turning once. Moisture will just begin to pool on the surface of the chops when they are medium. Tent the chops with foil and let rest for 5 to 10 minutes before serving.

Serve the pork chops over sushi rice or soba noodles with soy sauce, scallions, and sesame seeds.

Tataki Marinade

Tataki, which is sometimes served in sushi restaurants, is unusual in that the meat or fish is marinated only after it is cooked. The food is always cooked rare and served chilled, so I marinate it overnight. Kelp and bonito flakes are available at any Asian market.

TOOLS: saucepan • fine-mesh sieve • 1-gallon zip-top bag

YIELD: about 1/2 cup (enough for about 4 servings)

1/4 CUP SAKE

1/4 CUP SOY SAUCE

2 TABLESPOONS RICE VINEGAR

1 TABLESPOON MINCED FRESH GINGER

1 GARLIC CLOVE, MINCED

2 TABLESPOONS SUGAR

1 (2-INCH SQUARE) PIECE KELP

1/2 CUP BONITO FLAKES

SEVERAL DROPS OF TOASTED SESAME OIL

COMBINE the sake, soy sauce, rice vinegar, ginger, garlic, sugar, and kelp in a small saucepan. Bring to a boil and simmer until the kelp is rehydrated, 2 to 3 minutes. Remove from the heat, add the bonito and sesame oil, and let stand until the bonito is rehydrated and sinks to the bottom, 2 to 3 minutes. Strain through a fine-mesh sieve and let cool to room temperature.

SUGGESTED USES: beef steaks (especially New York strips), ahi tuna steaks, or salmon fillets, grilled or seared, then marinated overnight

TUNA TATAKI

FOR 4 SERVINGS, set 4 ahi tuna steaks (6 ounces each and 1 1/4 to 1 1/2 inches thick) aside at room temperature for about half an hour. Pat the steaks dry with paper towels. Heat a large, heavy sauté pan over high heat until a few water droplets dance and look like ball bearings rolling around when flicked into the pan. Add 2 tablespoons canola oil and sear the steaks until rare, 3 to 4 minutes (or until the desired doneness), turning once. The steaks will be soft to the touch when they are rare. Let the steaks cool to room temperature.

Combine the Tataki Marinade and the steaks in a 1-gallon zip-top bag and turn to coat. Seal the bag, letting out all the air. Marinate overnight in the refrigerator.

Remove the steaks from the marinade, reserving the marinade to use as a dressing, and slice thinly.

Serve the chilled tuna over either sushi rice or plain sticky rice and topped with a salad of julienned daikon, carrot, and yellow onion tossed with enough of the marinade to coat. Alternatively, top with toasted sesame seeds, sliced scallions, and shredded nori.

Kalbi Marinade

Kalbi, or Korean grilled short ribs, is a mainstay of Korean barbecue restaurants. Before being grilled, the short ribs take a long soak in a salty-sweet marinade that's loaded with scallions, garlic, ginger, and sesame oil. Flanken-cut means that the short ribs are cut into thin slices across the bone.

Korean food aficionados should note that sliced steak or very thinly sliced boneless short ribs may also be soaked in this basic marinade and grilled or stir-fried as the base for other dishes such as bulgogi, bibimbap, and dang myun.

TOOL: 1-gallon zip-top bag

YIELD: about 1 1/4 cups (enough for 4 to 10 servings)

3/4 CUP SOY SAUCE

1/2 TEASPOON TOASTED SESAME OIL

1/2 CUP SLICED SCALLIONS

1 1/2 TABLESPOONS MINCED FRESH GINGER

6 GARLIC CLOVES, MINCED

1/2 CUP SUGAR

1/2 TEASPOON CRUSHED RED PEPPER

FRESHLY GROUND BLACK PEPPER

MEASURE the soy sauce, sesame oil, scallions, ginger, garlic, sugar, and crushed red pepper into a 1-gallon zip-top bag and shake or squeeze until blended. Season to taste with black pepper.

KALBI

FOR 4 TO 6 SERVINGS, add 2 pounds flanken-cut beef short ribs to the Kalbi Marinade in the zip-top bag and turn to coat. Seal the bag, letting out all the air. Marinate overnight in the refrigerator.

Set the bag aside at room temperature for about half an hour. Remove the ribs from the marinade, pat dry with paper towels, then grill over direct high heat until well-done, 7 to 9 minutes, turning once. The beef will look juicy and be firm to the touch and crisp around the edges when it is well-done. Tent the ribs with foil and let rest for 5 to 10 minutes before serving.

Sprinkle the kalbi with toasted sesame seeds and additional sliced scallions and serve over sticky rice. Offer kimchee on the side.

Kimchee Marinade

This marinade is made with the juice of napa cabbage kimchee, the national pickle of Korea. The flavor of kimchee grows in intensity as it ages, so use young kimchee for a milder marinade and aged kimchee for a more pungent marinade. Kimchee is available at Asian markets and many supermarkets.

TOOL: 1-gallon zip-top bag

YIELD: about $1/2$ cup (enough for 2 to 4 servings)

$1/4$ CUP PLUS 2 TABLESPOONS KIMCHEE JUICE

2 TABLESPOONS CANOLA OIL

2 TABLESPOONS SOY SAUCE

MEASURE the kimchee juice, oil, and soy sauce into a 1-gallon zip-top bag and shake until blended.

SUGGESTED USES: chicken breasts, pork chops, or beef steaks (marinated 2 hours to overnight) or fish fillets, shrimp, or sea scallops (marinated 20 to 45 minutes), grilled

GRILLED RIB-EYE OR STRIP STEAKS

FOR 4 SERVINGS, add 4 boneless rib-eye or strip steaks (1 to 1 $1/4$ inches thick) to the Kimchee Marinade in the zip-top bag and turn to coat. Seal the bag, letting out all the air. Marinate for at least 2 hours and up to overnight in the refrigerator.

Set the bag aside at room temperature for about half an hour. Remove the steaks from the marinade, pat dry with paper towels, then grill over direct high heat until medium-rare, 12 to 14 minutes (or until the desired doneness), turning once. Moisture will just begin to accumulate on the surface of the steaks when they are medium-rare. Tent the steaks with foil and let rest for 5 to 10 minutes before serving.

Serve these steaks with sticky rice and kimchee.

Gochujang Marinade

The Korean fermented sweet chile paste known as gochujang makes a spicy bright red marinade that takes no time or effort to whip together. Most Asian markets carry gochujang, which keeps for months in the refrigerator. Trader Joe's Seafood Blend (1-pound bag of frozen shrimp, bay scallops, and squid rings) is perfect for the stir-fry made with this marinade.

TOOL: 1-gallon zip-top bag

YIELD: about 1/2 cup (enough for about 4 servings)

1/4 CUP GOCHUJANG

2 TABLESPOONS CANOLA OIL

2 TABLESPOONS RICE VINEGAR

1/4 TEASPOON TOASTED SESAME OIL

MEASURE the gochujang, canola oil, rice vinegar, and sesame oil into a 1-gallon zip-top bag and shake or squeeze until blended.

SUGGESTED USES: chicken breasts, pork chops, or beef steaks (marinated 2 hours to overnight) or fish fillets (marinated 20 to 45 minutes), grilled; shrimp, bay scallops, or squid rings (marinated 20 to 45 minutes), stir-fried

STIR-FRIED SEAFOOD

FOR 4 SERVINGS, add 1 pound (total weight) peeled, deveined extra-small or tiny shrimp (more than 60 count), bay scallops, and/or 1/2-inch-wide squid rings to the Gochujang Marinade in the zip-top bag and turn to coat. Seal the bag, letting out all the air. Marinate for at least 20 minutes and up to 45 minutes at room temperature.

Remove the seafood from the marinade and drain on paper towels. Heat a large wok over high heat until very hot and smoking. Add 2 tablespoons canola oil and swirl to coat the bottom of the wok. Stir-fry the seafood until almost cooked through, 2 to 3 minutes. Toss 1 cup scallions cut into 1-inch pieces into the wok and stir-fry until the seafood is just cooked through, about 1 minute longer. The seafood will be firm to the touch, the shrimp will be opaque and pink and beginning to curl, and the scallops and squid will be opaque and white.

Serve the stir-fried seafood over sticky rice or use as an omelet filling.

Black Garlic Marinade

Black garlic, which seems to have originated in Korea, is a product of fermentation. The ink-colored cloves have a soft, gelatinous texture and a complex sweet and mellow garlic flavor with candy-like hints of molasses, caramel, smoke, and fruit. Fans of roasted garlic will most certainly fall in love with it. Black garlic is hard to find in stores, but it's available from many sources online.

TOOLS: blender • 1-gallon zip-top bag

YIELD: about 3/4 cup (enough for about 4 servings)

1/4 CUP CANOLA OIL

1/4 CUP SOY SAUCE

2 TABLESPOONS RICE VINEGAR

2 TABLESPOONS SHAOXING RICE WINE (SEE PAGE 202)

6 BLACK GARLIC CLOVES

COMBINE the oil, soy sauce, rice vinegar, rice wine, and black garlic in a blender and blend until smooth.

SUGGESTED USES: bite-size pieces of chicken, pork, or beef, or shrimp, bay scallops, or squid rings (marinated 20 to 45 minutes), stir-fried; sea scallops (marinated 20 to 45 minutes), grilled

GRILLED BACON-WRAPPED SEA SCALLOPS

FOR 4 SERVINGS, combine the Black Garlic Marinade and 12 jumbo sea scallops (about 2 ounces each), side muscles removed, in a 1-gallon zip-top bag and turn to coat. Seal the bag, letting out all the air. Marinate for at least 20 minutes and up to 45 minutes at room temperature.

Remove the scallops from the marinade and pat dry with paper towels. Wrap half a slice of par-cooked bacon around the circumference of each scallop and secure it with a toothpick. Grill the scallops on an oiled grill grate over direct high heat until the bacon is crisp and the scallops are medium-rare, 6 to 7 minutes (or until the desired doneness), turning once. Moisture will just begin to accumulate on the surface of the scallops when they are medium-rare.

Serve these scallops with sticky rice or noodles and stir-fried vegetables such as yard-long green beans or cabbage.

VIETNAMESE AND THAI
MARINADES

With ingredients like fish sauce, garlic, chiles, lemongrass, and lime leaves, the marinades in this chapter are inspired by the flavors of Southeast Asia. If you find yourself dining at Vietnamese and Thai restaurants with any regularity, you'll definitely want to try every one of the recipes. The authentic Lemongrass-Garlic-Chile Marinade is the secret to a great Vietnamese noodle bowl, and the colorful Satay Marinade makes an irresistible chicken skewer. Other recipes—such as the Thai Green Curry Marinade—reinterpret classic dishes in marinade form.

Sriracha Marinade

When you don't have time to start from scratch and mince garlic, chiles, and other ingredients, you can rely on sriracha, the popular chile and garlic sauce. It makes for an irresistible spicy marinade that takes just seconds to throw together.

TOOL: 1-gallon zip-top bag

YIELD: about 3/4 cup (enough for 4 to 6 servings)

1/4 CUP CANOLA OIL

1/4 CUP SRIRACHA SAUCE

3 TABLESPOONS SOY SAUCE

1/4 TEASPOON TOASTED SESAME OIL

2 TABLESPOONS SUGAR

MEASURE the canola oil, sriracha sauce, soy sauce, sesame oil, and sugar into a 1-gallon zip-top bag and shake or squeeze until blended.

SUGGESTED USES: boneless, skinless chicken thighs, pork chops, or beef steaks (marinated 2 hours to overnight) or white fish fillets, shrimp, sea scallops, or squid (marinated 20 to 45 minutes), grilled

GRILLED PORK LOIN OR RIB CHOPS

FOR 6 SERVINGS, add 6 boneless pork loin or rib chops (about 1 inch thick) to the Sriracha Marinade in the zip-top bag and turn to coat. Seal the bag, letting out all the air. Marinate for at least 2 hours and up to overnight in the refrigerator.

Set the bag aside at room temperature for about half an hour. Remove the chops from the marinade, pat dry with paper towels, then grill over direct high heat until medium, 13 to 15 minutes (or until the desired doneness), turning once. Moisture will just begin to pool on the surface of the chops when they are medium. Tent the chops with foil and let rest for 5 to 10 minutes before serving.

Serve the pork chops on a bed of sticky rice along with a steamed vegetable such as bok choy, snow peas, or broccoli.

Lemongrass-Garlic-Chile Marinade

If you've ever ordered a noodle bowl at a Vietnamese restaurant, the meat in it was likely soaked in a marinade like this one. Customize the heat level of the marinade by using more or less chile, and seed the chiles if you like it on the milder side. And here's a little secret: You can substitute a squirt of sriracha for the garlic and chile if you're pressed for time.

TOOL: 1-gallon zip-top bag

YIELD: about 1/2 cup (enough for 2 to 4 servings)

2 TABLESPOONS CANOLA OIL

2 TABLESPOONS FRESHLY SQUEEZED LIME JUICE

2 TABLESPOONS FISH SAUCE

2 TABLESPOONS HONEY

1 TABLESPOON MINCED LEMONGRASS (SEE BELOW)

2 GARLIC CLOVES, MINCED

2 OR 3 THAI RED CHILES, MINCED

MEASURE the oil, lime juice, fish sauce, honey, lemongrass, garlic, and chiles into a 1-gallon zip-top bag and shake or squeeze until blended.

LEMONGRASS	Lemongrass is an aromatic and fibrous herb. Use only the heart of the lemongrass stalk, and to get the most flavor out of it, bruise it by bashing it with the back of a heavy knife before you mince it.

SUGGESTED USES: boneless, skinless chicken thighs or thin-cut pork loin chops (marinated overnight) or shrimp (marinated 20 to 45 minutes), grilled

GRILLED CHICKEN THIGHS

FOR 4 SERVINGS, add 8 boneless, skinless chicken thighs (about 4 ounces each) to the Lemongrass-Garlic-Chile Marinade in the zip-top bag and turn to coat. Seal the bag, letting out all the air. Marinate overnight in the refrigerator.

Set the bag aside at room temperature for about half an hour. Remove the chicken from the marinade, pat dry with paper towels, then grill, covered, on an oiled grill grate over direct medium heat until just cooked through, 12 to 14 minutes, turning once. The chicken will be firm to the touch and the juices will run clear when it is just cooked through. Tent the chicken with foil and let rest for 5 to 10 minutes before carving and serving.

For light, crisp, and refreshing Vietnamese noodle bowls, arrange rice vermicelli that's been softened in warm water and drained and a salad of thinly sliced romaine lettuce, shredded red cabbage, julienned carrot and English cucumber, bean sprouts, minced fresh mint and cilantro leaves, and sliced scallions side by side in individual bowls. Arrange sliced chicken thighs over the top, and sprinkle with crushed roasted peanuts. Serve with a sauce made of equal parts freshly squeezed lime juice, fish sauce, sugar, and warm water, and some minced garlic and Thai chiles. If you prefer Vietnamese rice bowls, simply substitute hot cooked sticky rice for the rice noodles.

Vietnamese Caramel Marinade

The basis of this marinade is caramel syrup, an ingredient commonly used in Vietnamese cooking to add sweetness and flavor to a variety of dishes. It may seem surprising to have caramel in a savory application, but it offers a complexity that both sugar and honey lack.

TOOLS: saucepan • 1-gallon zip-top bag

YIELD: about $1/2$ cup (enough for 2 to 4 servings)

$1/4$ CUP SUGAR

$1/4$ CUP PLUS 3 TABLESPOONS WATER

2 TABLESPOONS CANOLA OIL

2 TABLESPOONS FISH SAUCE

1 TABLESPOON FRESHLY SQUEEZED LIME JUICE

2 GARLIC CLOVES, MINCED

$1/4$ TEASPOON CRUSHED RED PEPPER

$1/8$ TEASPOON FRESHLY GROUND BLACK PEPPER

COMBINE the sugar and 3 tablespoons of the water in a small, heavy saucepan. Bring to a boil, brush down the sides of the pan with water, and boil until the sugar is fragrant and a deep amber color. Remove the pan from the heat and carefully add the remaining $1/4$ cup water, stirring until the caramel is dissolved. Let cool to room temperature. Measure the caramel syrup, oil, fish sauce, lime juice, garlic, crushed red pepper, and black pepper into a 1-gallon zip-top bag and shake or squeeze until blended.

SUGGESTED USES: boneless, skinless chicken thighs or country-style pork ribs (marinated 2 hours to overnight) or shrimp or sea scallops (marinated 20 to 45 minutes), grilled

GRILLED SEA SCALLOPS

FOR 2 SERVINGS, add 6 jumbo sea scallops (about 2 ounces each), side muscles removed, to the Vietnamese Caramel Marinade in the zip-top bag and turn to coat. Seal the bag, letting out all the air. Marinate for at least 20 minutes and up to 45 minutes at room temperature.

Remove the scallops from the marinade, pat dry with paper towels, then grill on an oiled grill grate over direct high heat until medium-rare, 6 to 7 minutes (or until the desired doneness), turning once. Moisture will just begin to accumulate on the surface of the scallops when they are medium-rare.

Serve these scallops with sticky rice and a salad of romaine or butter lettuce, shredded carrots and daikon, fresh mint and cilantro leaves, and sliced scallions, and a dressing made of equal parts freshly squeezed lime juice, fish sauce, sugar, and warm water, and some minced garlic and Thai chiles.

Satay Marinade

If the small appetizer portions of satay served at Thai restaurants seem as unsatisfying to you as they do to me, then you must try making satay at home using this marinade and have an entire meal of it!

TOOL: 1-gallon zip-top bag

YIELD: about 1 1/4 cups (enough for about 6 servings)

3/4 CUP COCONUT MILK

3 TABLESPOONS SOY SAUCE

2 TABLESPOONS FRESHLY SQUEEZED LIME JUICE

1 TABLESPOON PLUS 1 TEASPOON MINCED FRESH GINGER

4 GARLIC CLOVES, MINCED

3 TABLESPOONS MINCED CILANTRO STEMS

2 TABLESPOONS PACKED LIGHT BROWN SUGAR

3/4 TEASPOON CURRY POWDER

1/2 TEASPOON GROUND TURMERIC

1/2 TEASPOON CAYENNE PEPPER

KOSHER SALT

MEASURE the coconut milk, soy sauce, lime juice, ginger, garlic, cilantro, brown sugar, curry powder, turmeric, and cayenne into a 1-gallon zip-top bag and shake or squeeze until blended. Season to taste with salt.

SUGGESTED USES: strips of chicken breast or pork sirloin (marinated 2 hours to overnight) or shrimp (marinated 20 to 45 minutes), skewered and grilled

CHICKEN SATAY

FOR 12 TO 18 APPETIZER or 6 main-course servings, add 6 boneless, skinless chicken breasts (about 8 ounces each), cut into $1/2$-inch-thick strips, to the Satay Marinade in the zip-top bag and turn to coat. Seal the bag, letting out all the air. Marinate for at least 2 hours and up to overnight in the refrigerator.

Set the bag aside at room temperature for about half an hour. Remove the chicken from the marinade, pat dry with paper towels, and thread onto bamboo skewers that have been soaked in water. Grill the skewers on an oiled grill grate over direct high heat until just cooked through, 7 to 8 minutes, turning once. The chicken will be firm to the touch and the juices will run clear when it is just cooked through. Tent the skewers with foil and let rest for 5 to 10 minutes before serving.

Serve the satay with jasmine rice and a dipping sauce of peanut butter thinned with coconut milk or water and flavored with soy sauce, lime juice, brown sugar, sesame oil, and minced fresh ginger, garlic, fresh cilantro, and Thai red chiles.

Thai Green Curry Marinade

If you're in the mood for the flavors of Thai green curry on a summer day when it's too hot for a steaming bowl of stew, try this marinade. You can use purchased Thai green curry paste blended with coconut milk and a bit of fish sauce as a shortcut. Galangal is similar to ginger in appearance but has a menthol-like flavor that's key to green curry. It is available at Southeast Asian markets, as is shrimp paste.

TOOLS: blender • 1-gallon zip-top bag

YIELD: about 1 1/4 cups (enough for 6 to 10 servings)

2/3 CUP COCONUT MILK

2 TABLESPOON FISH SAUCE

2 STRIPS LIME ZEST

1 TABLESPOON FRESHLY SQUEEZED LIME JUICE

1/4 TEASPOON SHRIMP PASTE

6 LARGE FRESH THAI BASIL LEAVES

1 SHALLOT, SLICED

2 TABLESPOONS SLICED LEMONGRASS (SEE PAGE 230)

2 TEASPOONS MINCED GALANGAL

2 GARLIC CLOVES, SLICED

2 TABLESPOONS MINCED CILANTRO STEMS

2 TO 3 THAI GREEN CHILES, SLICED

2 TABLESPOONS PACKED LIGHT BROWN SUGAR

1/2 TEASPOON CORIANDER SEEDS, TOASTED AND GROUND

1/4 TEASPOON CUMIN SEEDS, TOASTED AND GROUND

1/8 TEASPOON WHITE PEPPERCORNS, TOASTED AND GROUND

COMBINE the coconut milk, fish sauce, lime zest, lime juice, shrimp paste, basil, shallot, lemongrass, galangal, garlic, cilantro, chiles, brown sugar, coriander, cumin, and white pepper in a blender and blend until smooth.

SUGGESTED USES: boneless, skinless chicken thighs, pork chops, or tofu (marinated 2 hours to overnight) or shrimp or sea scallops (marinated 20 to 45 minutes), grilled

GRILLED CHICKEN THIGHS

FOR 10 SERVINGS, combine the Thai Green Curry Marinade and 20 boneless, skinless chicken thighs (about 4 ounces each) in a 1-gallon zip-top bag and turn to coat. Seal the bag, letting out all the air. Marinate for at least 2 hours and up to overnight in the refrigerator.

Set the bag aside at room temperature for about half an hour. Remove the chicken from the marinade, pat dry with paper towels, then grill, covered, on an oiled grill grate over direct medium heat until just cooked through, 12 to 14 minutes, turning once. The chicken will be firm to the touch and the juices will run clear when it is just cooked through. Tent the chicken with foil and let rest for 5 to 10 minutes before serving.

Serve these chicken thighs with grilled eggplant, green bell pepper, and red onion slices on a bed of jasmine rice.

Thai Peanut Marinade

Thai peanut sauce works just as well for marinating as it does for dipping salad rolls—in fact, some of this marinade is reserved to use as a sauce.

TOOLS: blender • 1-gallon zip-top bag

YIELD: about 1$\frac{1}{3}$ cups (enough for 4 to 10 servings)

$\frac{2}{3}$ CUP COCONUT MILK

3 TABLESPOONS SMOOTH PEANUT BUTTER

2 TABLESPOONS FISH SAUCE

1 TABLESPOON FRESHLY SQUEEZED LIME JUICE

$\frac{1}{4}$ TEASPOON TOASTED SESAME OIL

1 TEASPOON MINCED FRESH GINGER

2 GARLIC CLOVES, SLICED

2 THAI RED CHILES, SLICED

$\frac{1}{4}$ CUP LIGHTLY PACKED FRESH CILANTRO LEAVES

2 TABLESPOONS PACKED LIGHT BROWN SUGAR

COMBINE the coconut milk, peanut butter, fish sauce, lime juice, sesame oil, ginger, garlic, chiles, cilantro, and brown sugar in a blender and blend until smooth.

SUGGESTED USES: boneless, skinless chicken thighs, pork chops, or tofu (marinated 2 hours to overnight) or shrimp (marinated 20 to 45 minutes), grilled

GRILLED PORK LOIN OR RIB CHOPS

FOR 4 SERVINGS, combine about half of the Thai Peanut Marinade and 4 boneless pork loin or rib chops (about 1 inch thick) in a 1-gallon zip-top bag and turn to coat. Seal the bag, letting out all the air. Marinate for at least 2 hours and up to overnight in the refrigerator.

Set the bag aside at room temperature for about half an hour. Remove the chops from the marinade, pat dry with paper towels, then grill over direct high heat until medium, 13 to 15 minutes (or until the desired doneness), turning once. Moisture will just begin to pool on the surface of the chops when they are medium. Tent the chops with foil and let rest for 5 to 10 minutes before serving.

Serve the pork chops with jasmine rice and a salad of julienned cucumbers, carrots, red bell peppers, red onions, and cilantro leaves tossed with sweetened rice vinegar and a small squirt of sriracha. Use the remaining half of the marinade as the sauce for the pork and rice bowl.

Lemongrass–Lime Leaf Marinade

Lemongrass and lime leaves make an intensely aromatic marinade. Fresh kaffir lime leaves can be found at Southeast Asian markets. If fresh aren't available, thawed frozen will work fine.

TOOLS: blender • 1-gallon zip-top bag

YIELD: about 1 cup (enough for 4 to 8 servings)

2/3 CUP COCONUT MILK

1 1/2 TABLESPOONS FISH SAUCE

1 TABLESPOON SLICED LEMONGRASS (SEE PAGE 230)

2 GARLIC CLOVES, SLICED

4 KAFFIR LIME LEAVES, TORN

1 TO 2 THAI GREEN CHILES, SLICED

2 TABLESPOONS PACKED LIGHT BROWN SUGAR

COMBINE the coconut milk, fish sauce, lemongrass, garlic, lime leaves, chiles, and brown sugar in a blender and blend until smooth.

SUGGESTED USES: boneless, skinless chicken thighs, pork chops, or tofu (marinated 2 hours to overnight) or fish fillets (especially salmon) or shrimp (marinated 20 to 45 minutes), grilled

GRILLED SHRIMP

FOR 4 SERVINGS, combine the Lemongrass–Lime Leaf Marinade and 1 to 1 1/2 pounds peeled, deveined large shrimp (21/25 count) in a 1-gallon zip-top bag and turn to coat. Seal the bag, letting out all the air. Marinate for at least 20 minutes and up to 45 minutes at room temperature.

Remove the shrimp from the marinade, pat dry with paper towels, then grill on an oiled grill grate over direct high heat until just cooked through, 4 to 5 minutes, turning once. The shrimp will be firm to the touch, opaque and pink, and beginning to curl when they are just cooked through.

Serve these shrimp with jasmine rice and steamed vegetables such as baby bok choy and snow peas.

Tamarind–Fish Sauce Marinade

This recipe takes its cue from the Thai flavor pairing of tamarind and fish sauce, which is used in everything from marinades to pad thai.

TOOL: 1-gallon zip-top bag

YIELD: about 1/2 cup (enough for 2 to 4 servings)

2 TABLESPOONS CANOLA OIL

2 TABLESPOONS FISH SAUCE

2 TABLESPOONS TAMARIND CONCENTRATE (SEE BELOW)

2 TABLESPOONS WATER

2 GARLIC CLOVES, MINCED

3 TABLESPOONS PACKED LIGHT BROWN SUGAR

1/4 TEASPOON CRUSHED RED PEPPER

MEASURE the oil, fish sauce, tamarind, water, garlic, brown sugar, and crushed red pepper into a 1-gallon zip-top bag and shake or squeeze until blended.

TAMARIND	Tamarind, the earthy and extremely sour pulp of the Indian date tree seed pod, is used in a variety of international cuisines in much the same way we use lemon or lime juice. While it is available as whole pods and bricks of paste, tamarind concentrate is free of seeds and therefore the most user-friendly form. Well-stocked grocery stores—as well as many ethnic markets, including Southeast Asian, Indian, and Mexican—carry tamarind concentrate. Choose a brand that contains nothing but tamarind pulp and water.

SUGGESTED USES: boneless, skinless chicken thighs or pork chops (marinated 2 hours to overnight) or salmon fillets or shrimp (marinated 20 to 45 minutes), grilled

GRILLED SALMON FILLETS

FOR 4 SERVINGS, add 4 skinned, boneless salmon fillets (6 to 8 ounces each) to the Tamarind–Fish Sauce Marinade in the zip-top bag and turn to coat. Seal the bag, letting out all the air. Marinate for at least 20 minutes and up to 45 minutes at room temperature.

Remove the fillets from the marinade, pat dry with paper towels, then grill on an oiled grill grate over direct high heat until medium-rare, 8 to 10 minutes (or until the desired doneness), turning once. The fillets will barely begin to flake when they are medium-rare.

Serve the salmon fillets with grilled bell pepper and onion slices and jasmine rice.

Marinade for Thai Street Vendor Chicken Wings

This recipe is inspired by the fried chicken sold by street vendors in Thailand. It's particularly interesting because the marinade doubles as a batter—it includes rice flour for a super-crisp crust. The result is the most delicious fried chicken ever, if I do say so myself. Traditionally, cilantro root is used in this sort of marinade, but as it's nearly impossible to find in this country, I use cilantro stems. The rice flour can settle out as the marinade sits overnight, so give the chicken a thorough toss right before frying.

TOOLS: mortar and pestle • 1-gallon zip-top bag

YIELD: about 1 cup (enough for 3 to 4 servings)

1/4 TEASPOON CORIANDER SEEDS, TOASTED

1/8 TEASPOON WHITE PEPPERCORNS, TOASTED

2 GARLIC CLOVES, SLICED

1 TABLESPOON MINCED CILANTRO STEMS

1/2 CUP WATER

2 TABLESPOONS FISH SAUCE

1 TABLESPOON SOY SAUCE

1 CUP RICE FLOUR

GENEROUS PINCH OF CAYENNE PEPPER

POUND the coriander and white peppercorns in a mortar and pestle until finely ground. Add the garlic and cilantro stems and pound to a paste. Transfer to a bowl, add the water, fish sauce, soy sauce, rice flour, and cayenne, and whisk until smooth.

THAI STREET VENDOR CHICKEN WINGS

FOR 3 TO 4 SERVINGS, combine the Marinade for Thai Street Vendor Chicken Wings and 2 to 2 1/2 pounds chicken wing flats and drumettes in a 1-gallon zip-top bag and turn to coat. Seal the bag, letting out all the air. Marinate overnight in the refrigerator.

Set the bag of bag aside at room temperature for about half an hour. Turn the bag several times to redistribute the rice flour in the marinade. Shaking off any excess marinade, deep-fry the chicken in batches in 375°F canola oil until golden brown and crisp and just cooked through, 6 to 7 minutes. The chicken will float at the top of the oil and the bubbles will begin to subside when it is just cooked through. Transfer the chicken to a paper towel–lined baking sheet and season to taste with salt.

Serve the chicken wings with your choice of either jasmine or sticky rice. Though no sauce is required, sriracha may be offered on the side.

INDIAN
MARINADES

Like all good Indian cooking, the marinades in this chapter rely on a harmonious balance of garlic, ginger, chiles, cumin, and other warm spices, all perked up with a dash of fresh cilantro and lime juice. Of course, the classic Tandoori Marinade, which—thanks to the yogurt it contains—not only flavors meat but tenderizes it as well, appears here, along with a smattering of other Indian-inspired if not exactly authentic flavors.

Curry Marinade

This bright yellow mixture isn't exactly an authentic Indian recipe, but it's sure to satisfy fans of curry.

TOOL: 1-gallon zip-top bag

YIELD: about 1/2 cup (enough for 2 to 4 servings)

3 TABLESPOONS CANOLA OIL

1 TABLESPOON FRESHLY SQUEEZED LIME JUICE

1 TABLESPOON MINCED FRESH GINGER

3 GARLIC CLOVES, MINCED

1 JALAPEÑO, SEEDED AND MINCED

1 TABLESPOON MINCED FRESH CILANTRO

2 TEASPOONS CURRY POWDER

KOSHER SALT

MEASURE the oil, lime juice, ginger, garlic, jalapeño, cilantro, and curry powder into a 1-gallon zip-top bag and shake or squeeze until blended. Season to taste with salt.

SUGGESTED USES: boneless, skinless chicken thighs, pork chops, or lamb chops (marinated 2 hours to overnight) or shrimp (marinated 20 to 45 minutes), grilled

GRILLED LAMB RIB CHOPS

FOR 2 SERVINGS, add 6 frenched lamb rib chops (about 1 inch thick) to the Curry Marinade in the zip-top bag and turn to coat. Seal the bag, letting out all the air. Marinate for at least 2 hours and up to overnight in the refrigerator.

Set the bag aside at room temperature for about half an hour. Remove the chops from the marinade, pat dry with paper towels, then grill over direct high heat until medium-rare, 10 to 12 minutes (or until the desired doneness), turning once. Moisture will just begin to accumulate on the surface of the chops when they are medium-rare. Tent the chops with foil and let rest for 5 to 10 minutes before serving.

Serve these lamb chops with dal and basmati rice, or any other Indian-style side dishes you like.

Tandoori Marinade

The single most popular Indian restaurant dish seems to be tandoori chicken. It's easy to make on the grill at home, and the same marinade can be used with beef, lamb, and shrimp. While food coloring is often used to give the chicken the familiar red hue, this recipe relies on plenty of paprika for color. Yogurt is a potent tenderizer, so oil the grill grate thoroughly to avoid sticking and tearing of the meat, especially when using this marinade with chicken.

TOOL: 1-gallon zip-top bag

YIELD: about 1/2 cup (enough for 2 to 4 servings)

1/3 CUP PLAIN YOGURT

1 TABLESPOON FRESHLY SQUEEZED LEMON JUICE

2 TEASPOONS MINCED FRESH GINGER

2 GARLIC CLOVES, MINCED

2 TEASPOONS PAPRIKA

3/4 TEASPOON CUMIN SEEDS, TOASTED AND GROUND

1/8 TEASPOON GROUND CARDAMOM

GENEROUS PINCH OF CAYENNE PEPPER

KOSHER SALT

FRESHLY GROUND BLACK PEPPER

MEASURE the yogurt, lemon juice, ginger, garlic, paprika, cumin, cardamom, and cayenne into a 1-gallon zip-top bag and shake or squeeze until blended. Season to taste with salt and black pepper.

SUGGESTED USES: skinless chicken pieces (marinated 2 hours to overnight), grilled; cubes of beef sirloin or lamb leg (marinated 2 hours to overnight) or shrimp (marinated 20 to 45 minutes), skewered and grilled

TANDOORI CHICKEN

FOR 4 SERVINGS, remove the skin from 8 chicken drumsticks and/or thighs and cut 2 slashes nearly to the bone in each one. Add the chicken to the Tandoori Marinade in the zip-top bag and turn to coat. Seal the bag, letting out all the air. Marinate for at least 2 hours and up to overnight in the refrigerator.

Set the bag aside at room temperature for about half an hour. Remove the chicken from the marinade, pat dry with paper towels, then grill, covered, on an oiled grill grate over direct medium heat until just cooked through, 20 to 25 minutes, turning once. The chicken will be firm to the touch, the meat will have noticeably shrunk away from the knuckles, and the juices will run clear when it is just cooked through. Tent the chicken with foil and let rest for 5 to 10 minutes before serving.

Serve the chicken with grilled bell peppers and onions and spiced basmati rice (check out my first book, *Seared to Perfection*, for a recipe) or naan.

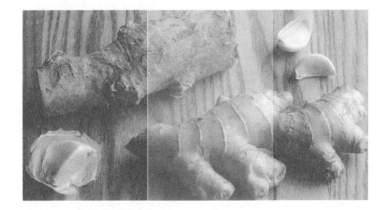

Cilantro-Mint Marinade

If you're a fan of the bright green mint chutney served at Indian restaurants, you're sure to love this marinade. It gives a zippy, fresh flavor to grilled meats and is especially good with lamb.

TOOLS: blender • 1-gallon zip-top bag

YIELD: about 1 cup (enough for 4 servings)

1/2 CUP CANOLA OIL

2 TABLESPOONS FRESHLY SQUEEZED LIME JUICE

1/2 CUP LIGHTLY PACKED FRESH CILANTRO LEAVES

1/2 CUP LIGHTLY PACKED FRESH MINT LEAVES

1 GARLIC CLOVE, SLICED

3 SERRANO CHILES, STEMMED

1/2 TEASPOON CUMIN SEEDS, TOASTED

KOSHER SALT

COMBINE the oil, lime juice, cilantro, mint, garlic, chiles, and cumin in a blender and blend until smooth. Season to taste with salt.

SUGGESTED USES: cubes of boneless, skinless chicken thighs, beef sirloin, or lamb leg (marinated 2 hours to overnight), skewered and grilled

GRILLED LAMB KABOBS

FOR 4 SERVINGS, combine the Cilantro-Mint Marinade and 2 lamb leg steaks (1 to 1 1/4 inches thick), cut into 1 1/4-inch pieces, in a 1-gallon zip-top bag and turn to coat. Seal the bag, letting out all the air. Marinate for at least 2 hours and up to overnight in the refrigerator.

Set the bag aside at room temperature for about half an hour. Remove the lamb from the marinade, pat dry with paper towels, and skewer onto bamboo skewers that have been soaked in water. Grill the skewers over direct high heat until medium-rare, 10 to 14 minutes (or until the desired doneness), turning once. Moisture will just begin to accumulate on the surface of the lamb when it is medium-rare. Tent the skewers with foil and let rest for 5 to 10 minutes before serving.

Nestle the lamb kabobs atop basmati rice pilaf or fold inside warm naan along with some sliced tomatoes and onions.

Tamarind-Ginger Marinade

The idea for this marinade came from the sweet-and-sour tamarind chutney served at so many Indian restaurants.

TOOL: 1-gallon zip-top bag

YIELD: about 1/2 cup (enough for 2 to 4 servings)

1/4 CUP WATER

2 TABLESPOONS CANOLA OIL

2 TABLESPOONS TAMARIND CONCENTRATE (SEE PAGE 240)

1 TEASPOON MINCED FRESH GINGER

1 GARLIC CLOVE, MINCED

2 TABLESPOONS PACKED LIGHT BROWN SUGAR

1 TEASPOON GUAJILLO CHILE POWDER

1/2 TEASPOON CUMIN SEEDS, TOASTED AND GROUND

KOSHER SALT

MEASURE the water, oil, tamarind, ginger, garlic, brown sugar, chile powder, and cumin into a 1-gallon zip-top bag and shake or squeeze until blended. Season to taste with salt.

SUGGESTED USES: boneless, skinless chicken thighs or lamb chops (marinated 2 hours to overnight) or shrimp (marinated 20 to 45 minutes), grilled

GRILLED SHRIMP

FOR 2 SERVINGS, add 1/2 to 3/4 pound peeled, deveined large shrimp (21/25 count) to the Tamarind-Ginger Marinade in the zip-top bag and turn to coat. Seal the bag, letting out all the air. Marinate for at least 20 minutes and up to 45 minutes at room temperature.

Remove the shrimp from the marinade, pat dry with paper towels, then grill on an oiled grill grate over direct high heat until just cooked through, 4 to 5 minutes, turning once. The shrimp will be firm to the touch, opaque and pink, and beginning to curl when they are just cooked through.

Serve the shrimp sprinkled with chopped cilantro and nestled atop basmati rice.

Seekh Kabob–Style Marinade

Seekh kabob is typically made of ground lamb that's formed into a sausage shape on skewers and cooked in a tandoor oven. I love its combination of flavorings and always order it when we go out for Indian food. Because the dish is a bit labor-intensive, I reinterpreted it into marinade form so that I could quickly make it at home whenever the craving strikes. The spice blend garam masala is made of roughly equal parts toasted and ground cardamom, cinnamon, cloves, black peppercorns, cumin, and possibly coriander or nutmeg. You can make your own or purchase it at any well-stocked grocery store.

TOOL: 1-gallon zip-top bag

YIELD: about 1/2 cup (enough for about 2 servings)

2 TABLESPOONS CANOLA OIL

1/4 CUP GRATED YELLOW ONION

1 TEASPOON MINCED FRESH GINGER

2 GARLIC CLOVES, MINCED

1 JALAPEÑO, SEEDED AND MINCED

2 TABLESPOONS MINCED FRESH CILANTRO

1 TEASPOON GARAM MASALA

3/4 TEASPOON CORIANDER SEEDS, TOASTED AND GROUND

1/2 TEASPOON CUMIN SEEDS, TOASTED AND GROUND

GENEROUS PINCH OF CAYENNE PEPPER

KOSHER SALT

FRESHLY GROUND BLACK PEPPER

MEASURE the oil, onion, ginger, garlic, jalapeño, cilantro, garam masala, coriander, cumin, and cayenne into a 1-gallon zip-top bag and shake or squeeze until blended. Season to taste with salt and black pepper.

SUGGESTED USES: cubes of boneless, skinless chicken thighs, beef sirloin, or lamb leg (marinated 2 hours to overnight), skewered and grilled

CHEATER'S SEEKH KABOB

FOR 2 SERVINGS, add 1 lamb leg steak (1 to 1¹/₄ inches thick), cut into 1¹/₄-inch pieces, to the Seekh Kabob–Style Marinade in the zip-top bag and turn to coat. Seal the bag, letting out all the air. Marinate for at least 2 hours and up to overnight in the refrigerator.

Set the bag aside at room temperature for about half an hour. Remove the lamb from the marinade, pat dry with paper towels, and skewer onto bamboo skewers that have been soaked in water. Grill the skewers over direct high heat until medium-rare, 10 to 14 minutes (or until the desired doneness), turning once. Moisture will just begin to accumulate on the surface of the lamb when it is medium-rare. Tent the skewers with foil and let rest for 5 to 10 minutes before serving.

Serve the lamb kabobs over spiced basmati rice (check out my first book, *Seared to Perfection*, for a recipe).

Ginger-Nigella Marinade

Nigella seeds, also known as *kalonji*, taste very much like fresh thyme and bear a strong resemblance to black sesame seeds. They're delicious, so it's surprising that they're not more common. If you've never tasted them before, and even if you have, try this marinade for a unique flavor experience. Look for nigella seeds at Indian markets and specialty spice merchants.

TOOL: 1-gallon zip-top bag

YIELD: about 1/2 cup (enough for 2 to 4 servings)

1/4 CUP CANOLA OIL

2 TABLESPOONS FRESHLY SQUEEZED LIME JUICE

2 TABLESPOONS MINCED FRESH GINGER

2 GARLIC CLOVES, MINCED

2 TEASPOONS NIGELLA SEEDS

1/2 TEASPOON GROUND TURMERIC

KOSHER SALT

FRESHLY GROUND BLACK PEPPER

MEASURE the oil, lime juice, ginger, garlic, nigella, and turmeric into a 1-gallon zip-top bag and shake or squeeze until blended. Season to taste with salt and pepper.

SUGGESTED USES: boneless, skinless chicken thighs, pork chops, or lamb chops (marinated 2 hours to overnight), grilled or broiled

GRILLED CHICKEN THIGHS

FOR 4 SERVINGS, add 8 boneless, skinless chicken thighs (about 4 ounces each) to the Ginger-Nigella Marinade in the zip-top bag and turn to coat. Seal the bag, letting out all the air. Marinate for at least 2 hours and up to overnight in the refrigerator.

Set the bag aside at room temperature for about half an hour. Remove the chicken from the marinade, pat dry with paper towels, then grill, covered, on an oiled grill grate over direct medium heat until just cooked through, 12 to 14 minutes, turning once. The chicken will be firm to the touch and the juices will run clear when it is just cooked through. Tent the chicken with foil and let rest for 5 to 10 minutes before serving.

Serve the chicken thighs with basmati rice and sliced tomatoes and onions.

CENTRAL ASIAN, MIDDLE EASTERN, AND AFRICAN
MARINADES

The marinades in this chapter hail from places as far afield as Uzbekistan, Iran, Morocco, Tunisia, and southern Africa. Recipes such as Chermoula Marinade, Harissa Marinade, and Piri Piri Marinade may seem foreign to American palates, but the flavor combinations are bold and intriguing, and I am hopeful that adventurous cooks and eaters will give them a try. The Shashlik Marinade from my native Uzbekistan is especially near and dear to me because it's a family recipe.

Shashlik Marinade

This is my family's recipe for shashlik, which is Uzbekistan's version of shish kebab. Growing up, it was required fare at every family gathering and celebration. Shashlik is traditionally made with lamb—the fattier, the better—but beef and pork can be prepared in the same manner. The meat is threaded closely together onto enormous sword-like skewers and grilled until it is seared on the surface and succulent within. Though it may seem as though this recipe yields a ton of marinade, the sliced onion makes it bulky, so a large volume must be used for a relatively small quantity of meat.

TOOL: 1-gallon zip-top bag

YIELD: about 4 cups (enough for about 4 servings)

1/4 CUP DISTILLED WHITE VINEGAR

1 TABLESPOON CANOLA OIL

1 LARGE YELLOW ONION, THINLY SLICED

2 BAY LEAVES, CRUMBLED

1 TEASPOON CUMIN SEEDS

1/2 TEASPOON GROUND CUMIN

1/2 TEASPOON CORIANDER SEEDS, OPTIONAL

1/2 TEASPOON BLACK PEPPERCORNS

6 ALLSPICE BERRIES

KOSHER SALT

FRESHLY GROUND BLACK PEPPER

MEASURE the vinegar, oil, onion, bay leaves, whole and ground cumin, coriander, peppercorns, and allspice into a 1-gallon zip-top bag and shake or squeeze until blended. Season to taste with salt and a generous amount of pepper.

SUGGESTED USES: cubes of pork sirloin, beef sirloin, or lamb leg (marinated overnight), skewered and grilled

SHASHLIK

FOR 4 SERVINGS, add 2 lamb leg steaks (1 to 1¼ inches thick), cut into 1¼-inch pieces, to the Shashlik Marinade in the zip-top bag and turn to coat. Seal the bag, letting out all the air. Marinate **overnight** in the refrigerator.

Set the bag aside at room temperature for about half an hour. Remove the lamb from the marinade and pat dry with paper towels, picking off any onion and spices. Skewer the meat onto skewers (you can use soaked bamboo, but my family always uses flat metal skewers) and grill over direct high heat until medium-rare, 10 to 14 minutes (or until the desired doneness), turning once. Moisture will just begin to accumulate on the surface of the lamb when it is medium-rare.

Serve the shashlik with Middle Eastern flatbread or basmati rice and a salad of slivered tomatoes and thinly sliced yellow onions and Kirby cucumbers seasoned with only salt and pepper.

Shawarma Marinade

The shawarma is essentially the Middle East's version of the gyro. The spices are a bit different, but it's a wrap with thinly sliced meat and many of the same toppings.

TOOL: 1-gallon zip-top bag

YIELD: about 1/2 cup (enough for about 4 servings)

2 TABLESPOONS EXTRA-VIRGIN OLIVE OIL

2 TABLESPOONS FRESHLY SQUEEZED LEMON JUICE

1/4 CUP GRATED YELLOW ONION

1 TEASPOON GROUND CUMIN

1 TEASPOON GROUND CORIANDER

1/8 TEASPOON GROUND CINNAMON

GENEROUS PINCH OF CAYENNE PEPPER

KOSHER SALT

FRESHLY GROUND BLACK PEPPER

MEASURE the oil, lemon juice, onion, cumin, coriander, cinnamon, and cayenne into a 1-gallon zip-top bag and shake or squeeze until blended. Season to taste with salt and black pepper.

SUGGESTED USES: boneless, skinless chicken thighs, beef steaks, or lamb leg steaks (marinated 2 hours to overnight), grilled

CHICKEN SHAWARMA

FOR 4 SERVINGS, add 8 boneless, skinless chicken thighs (about 4 ounces each) to the Shawarma Marinade in the zip-top bag and turn to coat. Seal the bag, letting out all the air. Marinate for at least 2 hours and up to overnight in the refrigerator.

Set the bag aside at room temperature for about half an hour. Remove the chicken from the marinade, pat dry with paper towels, then grill, covered, on an oiled grill grate over direct medium heat until just cooked through, 12 to 14 minutes, turning once. The chicken will be firm to the touch and the juices will run clear when it is just cooked through. Tent the chicken with foil and let rest for 5 to 10 minutes before carving and serving.

Serve the chicken thighs, thinly sliced, wrapped in Middle Eastern flatbread with shredded lettuce, sliced tomatoes and onions, and a sauce of Greek yogurt, lemon juice, and garlic.

Persian Kabob Marinade

I once had an Iranian coworker who generously taught me to cook a handful of her country's most popular dishes. She gave me one recipe for chicken kabobs and another for ground beef kabobs. In my hands, the two merged into this one delicious recipe. Yogurt is a potent tenderizer, so oil the grill grate thoroughly to avoid sticking and tearing of the meat, especially when using this marinade with chicken.

TOOLS: mortar and pestle • 1-gallon zip-top bag

YIELD: about 1/2 cup (enough for about 2 servings)

2 TABLESPOONS EXTRA-VIRGIN OLIVE OIL

2 TABLESPOONS PLAIN GREEK YOGURT

1 TABLESPOON FRESHLY SQUEEZED LIME JUICE

1/4 CUP GRATED YELLOW ONION

1 JALAPEÑO, SEEDED AND MINCED

1/8 TEASPOON GROUND TURMERIC

GENEROUS PINCH OF SAFFRON, GROUND WITH A MORTAR AND PESTLE

KOSHER SALT

FRESHLY GROUND BLACK PEPPER

MEASURE the oil, yogurt, lime juice, onion, jalapeño, turmeric, and saffron into a 1-gallon zip-top bag and shake or squeeze until blended. Season to taste with salt and pepper.

SUGGESTED USES: cubes of boneless, skinless chicken thighs, beef steak, or lamb leg (marinated overnight), skewered and grilled

PERSIAN BEEF KABOBS

FOR 2 SERVINGS, add 1 sirloin steak (1 to 1 1/4 inches thick), cut into 1 1/4-inch pieces, to the Persian Kabob Marinade in the zip-top bag and turn to coat. Seal the bag, letting out all the air. Marinate overnight in the refrigerator.

Set the bag aside at room temperature for about half an hour. Remove the beef from the marinade, pat dry with paper towels, and skewer onto metal skewers or soaked bamboo skewers. Grill the skewers on an oiled grill grate over direct high heat until medium-rare, 10 to 14 minutes (or until the desired doneness), turning once. Moisture will just begin to accumulate on the surface of the beef when it is medium-rare.

Serve the beef kabobs with grilled onions and tomatoes and basmati rice cooked with a dab of butter and a pinch of saffron.

Pomegranate Marinade

Pomegranate molasses, a sweet-and-sour syrup made from reduced pomegranate juice, is the main flavoring in this marinade. It's available at Middle Eastern markets and some well-stocked supermarkets. Here I've paired it with a Turkish chile called urfa biber. Urfa biber is uniquely delicious—it has a fruity, roasted flavor—and worth seeking out at specialty spice merchants. If you can't find it, use the more readily available Aleppo pepper.

TOOL: 1-gallon zip-top bag

YIELD: about 1/3 cup (enough for about 2 servings)

1/4 CUP EXTRA-VIRGIN OLIVE OIL

1 TABLESPOON POMEGRANATE MOLASSES

1 TABLESPOON FRESHLY SQUEEZED LEMON JUICE

2 GARLIC CLOVES, MINCED

1/2 TEASPOON DRIED MINT

2 TEASPOONS GROUND URFA BIBER

1/2 TEASPOON GROUND CUMIN

KOSHER SALT

FRESHLY GROUND BLACK PEPPER

MEASURE the oil, pomegranate molasses, lemon juice, garlic, mint, urfa biber, and cumin into a 1-gallon zip-top bag and shake or squeeze until blended. Season to taste with salt and pepper.

SUGGESTED USES: boneless, skinless chicken thighs, beef steaks, or lamb chops (marinated 2 hours to overnight), grilled

GRILLED LAMB RIB CHOPS

FOR 2 SERVINGS, add 6 frenched lamb rib chops (about 1 inch thick) to the Pomegranate Marinade in the zip-top bag and turn to coat. Seal the bag, letting out all the air. Marinate for at least 2 hours and up to overnight in the refrigerator.

Set the bag aside at room temperature for about half an hour. Remove the chops from the marinade, pat dry with paper towels, then grill over direct high heat until medium-rare, 10 to 12 minutes (or until the desired doneness), turning once. Moisture will just begin to accumulate on the surface of the chops when they are medium-rare. Tent the chops with foil and let rest for 5 to 10 minutes before serving.

Serve the lamb chops over basmati rice. If desired, scatter with pomegranate seeds and minced fresh mint.

Chermoula Marinade

Chermoula is a mixture of herbs, spices, and preserved lemon served in Morocco and throughout northern Africa. It can be used as a marinade or a sauce, and it's most often paired with fish. Look for preserved lemons, which are packed in their own juice and copious amounts of salt, at Mediterranean markets and gourmet shops.

TOOLS: food processor • 1-gallon zip-top bag

YIELD: about 1 cup (enough for 5 to 8 servings)

1/3 CUP EXTRA-VIRGIN OLIVE OIL

1 CUP PACKED FRESH CILANTRO LEAVES

3/4 CUP PACKED FRESH FLAT-LEAF PARSLEY LEAVES

1 SMALL PRESERVED LEMON, CUT INTO EIGHTHS (INCLUDING RINDS)

1 TABLESPOON MINCED FRESH GINGER

5 GARLIC CLOVES, SLICED

1 TABLESPOON PAPRIKA

1 1/2 TEASPOONS CORIANDER SEEDS, TOASTED AND GROUND

1 TEASPOON CRUSHED RED PEPPER

1/2 TEASPOON CUMIN SEEDS, TOASTED AND GROUND

1/8 TEASPOON BLACK PEPPERCORNS, TOASTED AND GROUND

GENEROUS PINCH OF SAFFRON

KOSHER SALT

COMBINE the oil, cilantro, parsley, preserved lemon, ginger, garlic, paprika, coriander, red pepper, cumin, black pepper, and saffron in a food processor and process until smooth. Season to taste with salt.

SUGGESTED USES: chicken breasts (marinated 2 hours to overnight) or shrimp or sea scallops (marinated 20 to 45 minutes), grilled; halibut fillets (marinated 20 to 45 minutes), baked

BAKED HALIBUT FILLETS

FOR 8 SERVINGS, combine the Chermoula Marinade and 8 skinned, boneless halibut fillets (6 to 8 ounces each) in a 1-gallon zip-top bag and turn to coat. Seal the bag, letting out all the air. Marinate for at least 20 minutes and up to 45 minutes at room temperature.

Remove the fillets from the marinade and place on a rimmed baking sheet. Bake the fillets in a preheated 450°F oven until just cooked through, 12 to 13 minutes. The fillets will begin to flake when they are just cooked through.

Serve couscous with garbanzo beans alongside these fish fillets.

Moroccan Marinade

Experience the exotic flavors of Morocco and North Africa with this marinade.

TOOL: 1-gallon zip-top bag

YIELD: about 1/2 cup (enough for 2 to 4 servings)

1/4 CUP EXTRA-VIRGIN OLIVE OIL

1 TABLESPOON FRESHLY SQUEEZED LIME JUICE

2 TEASPOONS MINCED FRESH GINGER

4 GARLIC CLOVES, MINCED

2 TABLESPOONS MINCED FRESH CILANTRO

2 TEASPOONS CORIANDER SEEDS, TOASTED AND GROUND

1 1/4 TEASPOONS CUMIN SEEDS, TOASTED AND GROUND

3/4 TEASPOON PAPRIKA

1/2 TEASPOON GROUND CINNAMON

GENEROUS PINCH OF CAYENNE PEPPER

KOSHER SALT

FRESHLY GROUND BLACK PEPPER

MEASURE the oil, lime juice, ginger, garlic, cilantro, coriander, cumin, paprika, cinnamon, and cayenne into a 1-gallon zip-top bag and shake or squeeze until blended. Season to taste with salt and black pepper.

SUGGESTED USES: boneless, skinless chicken thighs or lamb chops (marinated 2 hours to overnight) or white fish fillets (marinated 20 to 45 minutes), grilled

GRILLED CHICKEN THIGHS

FOR 4 SERVINGS, add 8 boneless, skinless chicken thighs (about 4 ounces each) to the Moroccan Marinade in the zip-top bag and turn to coat. Seal the bag, letting out all the air. Marinate for at least 2 hours and up to overnight in the refrigerator.

Set the bag aside at room temperature for about half an hour. Remove the chicken from the marinade, pat dry with paper towels, then grill, covered, on an oiled grill grate over direct medium heat until just cooked through, 12 to 14 minutes, turning once. The chicken will be firm to the touch and the juices will run clear when it is just cooked through. Tent the chicken with foil and let rest for 5 to 10 minutes before serving.

Serve the chicken thighs over couscous with dried fruit.

Harissa Marinade

The Tunisian spiced chile paste known as harissa is often eaten as a condiment, but it makes a tremendous marinade as well. In my version, I use Aleppo pepper, which is available at Middle Eastern markets and gourmet shops, for flavor without too much fire.

TOOL: 1-gallon zip-top bag

YIELD: about 1/2 cup (enough for 2 to 4 servings)

1/4 CUP PLUS 2 TABLESPOONS EXTRA-VIRGIN OLIVE OIL

1 TABLESPOON FRESHLY SQUEEZED LEMON JUICE

3 GARLIC CLOVES, MINCED

1/2 TEASPOON DRIED MINT

1/3 CUP ALEPPO PEPPER

1/2 TEASPOON CUMIN SEEDS, TOASTED AND GROUND

1/2 TEASPOON CORIANDER SEEDS, TOASTED AND GROUND

1/2 TEASPOON CARAWAY SEEDS, TOASTED AND GROUND

KOSHER SALT

FRESHLY GROUND BLACK PEPPER

MEASURE the oil, lemon juice, garlic, mint, Aleppo pepper, cumin, coriander, and caraway into a 1-gallon zip-top bag and shake or squeeze until blended. Season to taste with salt and black pepper.

SUGGESTED USES: boneless, skinless chicken thighs, beef steaks, or lamb chops (marinated 2 hours to overnight), white fish fillets, shrimp, or sea scallops (marinated 20 to 45 minutes), or vegetables (marinated 30 minutes to 1 hour), grilled

GRILLED CHICKEN THIGHS

FOR 4 SERVINGS, add 8 boneless, skinless chicken thighs (about 4 ounces each) to the Harissa Marinade in the zip-top bag and turn to coat. Seal the bag, letting out all the air. Marinate overnight in the refrigerator.

Set the bag aside at room temperature for about half an hour. Remove the chicken from the marinade, pat dry with paper towels, then grill, covered, on an oiled grill grate over direct medium heat until just cooked through, 12 to 14 minutes, turning once. The chicken will be firm to the touch and the juices will run clear when it is just cooked through. Tent the chicken with foil and let rest for 5 to 10 minutes before serving.

Serve couscous with garbanzo beans alongside these chicken thighs.

Piri Piri Marinade

This marinade is based on the sauce of the same name. The fiery condiment, which comes from southern Africa and has Portuguese influences, is traditionally made from African bird's eye chiles. Since these chiles are difficult to find here, and since they are so incendiary, I use the readily available and relatively tame Fresno chiles. If you'd like to pump up the heat, throw in some Thai red chiles—or tone it down by substituting half a bell pepper for half of the chiles. But don't be tempted to leave in the Fresno seeds, as they have a tough, unappealing texture.

TOOLS: food processor • 1-gallon zip-top bag

YIELD: about 3/4 cup (enough for 4 to 6 servings)

3 TABLESPOONS EXTRA-VIRGIN OLIVE OIL

2 TABLESPOONS FRESHLY SQUEEZED LEMON JUICE

3 GARLIC CLOVES, SLICED

6 FRESNO CHILES, STEMMED AND SEEDED

KOSHER SALT

COMBINE the oil, lemon juice, garlic, and chiles in a food processor and process until smooth. Season to taste with salt.

SUGGESTED USES: chicken breasts (marinated 2 hours to overnight) or white fish fillets or shrimp (marinated 20 to 45 minutes), grilled

GRILLED SHRIMP

FOR 4 SERVINGS, combine the Piri Piri Marinade and 1 to 1 1/2 pounds peeled, deveined large shrimp (21/25 count) in a 1-gallon zip-top bag and turn to coat. Seal the bag, letting out all the air. Marinate for at least 20 minutes and up to 45 minutes at room temperature.

Remove the shrimp from the marinade, pat dry with paper towels, then grill on an oiled grill grate over direct high heat until just cooked through, 4 to 5 minutes, turning once. The shrimp will be firm to the touch, opaque and pink, and beginning to curl when they are just cooked through.

Serve the shrimp with rice and peas.

ISLAND
MARINADES

Whether you prefer Hawaii or the Caribbean, these marinades will take you away to the islands, if just for one meal. Spicy chiles, citrus juice, and tropical fruits—including mango, pineapple, passion fruit, and papaya—figure heavily in the recipes. Beware, the fiery Jamaican Jerk Marinade is loaded with habaneros and not for the faint of heart.

Jamaican Jerk Marinade

Scotch bonnets, one of the world's hottest chiles, and plenty of allspice, along with several other herbs and spices, make Jamaican jerk deliciously distinctive and increasingly incendiary.

TOOLS: food processor • 1-gallon zip-top bag

YIELD: about 2/3 cup (enough for 2 to 6 servings)

2 TABLESPOONS CANOLA OIL

2 TABLESPOONS FRESHLY SQUEEZED LIME JUICE

3/4 CUP SLICED SCALLIONS

1 TABLESPOON PLUS 1 TEASPOON MINCED FRESH GINGER

3 GARLIC CLOVES, SLICED

2 OR 3 SCOTCH BONNET OR HABANERO CHILES, STEMMED

2 TABLESPOONS PACKED LIGHT BROWN SUGAR

1 TEASPOON GROUND ALLSPICE

1/2 TEASPOON GROUND CINNAMON

1/4 TEASPOON FRESHLY GRATED NUTMEG

1 TEASPOON LIGHTLY PACKED FRESH THYME

KOSHER SALT

COMBINE the oil, lime juice, scallions, ginger, garlic, chiles, brown sugar, allspice, cinnamon, nutmeg, and thyme in a food processor and process until smooth. Season to taste with salt.

SUGGESTED USES: whole chicken or pork ribs (marinated overnight) or white fish fillets or shrimp (marinated 20 to 45 minutes), grilled

JERK CHICKEN

FOR 4 TO 6 SERVINGS, combine the Jamaican Jerk Marinade and 1 whole chicken (3 1/2 to 4 pounds), butterflied, in a 1-gallon zip-top bag and turn to coat. Seal the bag, letting out all the air. Marinate **overnight** in the refrigerator.

Set the bag aside at room temperature for about half an hour. Remove the chicken from the marinade, pat dry with paper towels, then grill over indirect medium heat until just cooked through, 55 to 65 minutes, turning occasionally. The chicken will be firm to the touch, the meat of the drumsticks will have noticeably shrunk away from the knuckles, the juices will run clear, and a meat thermometer inserted in the thickest part of the breast will register 160°F when it is just cooked through. Tent the chicken with foil and let rest for 15 to 20 minutes before carving and serving (the internal temperature should rise to 165°F).

Serve the chicken with beans and rice and fried plantains.

Cuban Mojo Marinade

Tangy, citrusy mixtures like this one are the marinade of choice for Cuban roast pork. A blend of orange, lemon, and lime juices approximates the sour orange juice that's traditionally used in Cuba.

TOOL: 1-gallon zip-top bag

YIELD: about 1 cup (enough for 8 to 10 servings)

1/3 CUP EXTRA-VIRGIN OLIVE OIL

1/3 CUP FRESHLY SQUEEZED ORANGE JUICE

2 1/2 TABLESPOONS FRESHLY SQUEEZED LEMON JUICE

2 1/2 TABLESPOONS FRESHLY SQUEEZED LIME JUICE

8 GARLIC CLOVES, MINCED

2 1/4 TEASPOONS MINCED FRESH OREGANO

1 1/4 TEASPOONS GROUND CUMIN

GENEROUS PINCH OF CAYENNE PEPPER

KOSHER SALT

FRESHLY GROUND BLACK PEPPER

MEASURE the oil, orange juice, lemon juice, lime juice, garlic, oregano, cumin, and cayenne into a 1-gallon zip-top bag and shake or squeeze until blended. Season to taste with salt and black pepper.

SUGGESTED USES: pork butt, belly, or ribs (marinated overnight), roasted

CUBAN SANDWICHES	Leftover Cuban Mojo roasted pork butt makes delicious Cuban sandwiches. Stuff 1/4-inch slices of the pork roast, thinly sliced ham, Swiss cheese, and pickle chips into split hoagie rolls spread with yellow mustard and hot sauce and cook in a panini press until golden brown and crisp and heated through.

ROASTED PORK BUTT

FOR 8 TO 10 SERVINGS, add 1 boneless pork butt roast (about 4 pounds) to the Cuban Mojo Marinade in the zip-top bag and turn to coat. Seal the bag, letting out all the air. Marinate overnight in the refrigerator.

Set the bag aside at room temperature for about half an hour. Remove the pork from the marinade and place, fat side up, on a rack in a roasting pan. Roast the pork in a pre-heated 300°F oven until well-done, 3 to 4 hours. A meat thermometer inserted in the center will register 160°F when it is well-done. Tent the roast with foil and let rest for 15 to 20 minutes before carving and serving.

Serve the pork roast with black beans and rice.

Hawaiian Marinade

A mixture of tropical fruit juices gives an island flavor to this recipe. Be sure to use pasteurized pineapple juice, as fresh pineapple juice contains an enzyme that can cause marinated foods to become mushy.

TOOLS: fine-mesh sieve • 1-gallon zip-top bag

YIELD: about ¾ cup (enough for 4 to 6 servings)

2 PASSION FRUITS (SEE PAGE 276)

2 ½ TABLESPOONS KETCHUP

2 TABLESPOONS PASTEURIZED PINEAPPLE JUICE

2 TABLESPOONS MANGO JUICE

1 ½ TABLESPOONS SOY SAUCE

1 TABLESPOON CANOLA OIL

1 ½ TEASPOONS SRIRACHA SAUCE

½ TEASPOON MINCED FRESH GINGER

1 GARLIC CLOVE, MINCED

FRESHLY GROUND BLACK PEPPER

HALVE the passion fruits and scoop out the flesh with a spoon. Force the passion fruit flesh through a fine-mesh sieve to remove the seeds. Measure the passion fruit puree, ketchup, pineapple juice, mango juice, soy sauce, oil, sriracha sauce, ginger, and garlic into a 1-gallon zip-top bag and shake or squeeze until blended. Season to taste with pepper.

SUGGESTED USES: chicken pieces, pork chops or ribs, or beef steaks (marinated overnight) or fish fillets (especially mahi-mahi or swordfish), shrimp, or sea scallops (marinated 20 to 45 minutes), grilled

GRILLED SHRIMP

FOR 4 SERVINGS, add 1 to 1 1/2 pounds peeled, deveined large shrimp (21/25 count) to the Hawaiian Marinade in the zip-top bag and turn to coat. Seal the bag, letting out all the air. Marinate for at least 20 minutes and up to 45 minutes at room temperature.

Remove the shrimp from the marinade, pat dry with paper towels, then grill on an oiled grill grate over direct high heat until just cooked through, 4 to 5 minutes, turning once. The shrimp will be firm to the touch, opaque and pink, and beginning to curl when they are just cooked through.

Serve these shrimp with sticky rice and grilled vegetables such as Maui onions and green and red bell peppers.

Marinade for Poke

Poke is a popular Hawaiian snack of marinated diced raw fish; if you like sashimi or tuna or salmon tartare, you will most certainly love it. This is the simplest version of the marinade, which I feel best allows the subtle flavor of the raw fish to shine, but you can add diced Maui onion, tomato, and/or jalapeño. Use only pristine fish from a reputable fishmonger to make poke. Grate the ginger and garlic with a Microplane for the best results.

TOOL: 1-gallon zip-top bag

YIELD: about $1/4$ cup (enough for 4 to 6 servings)

$1/4$ CUP SOY SAUCE

$1/4$ TEASPOON TOASTED SESAME OIL

3 TABLESPOONS SLICED SCALLIONS

$1/8$ TEASPOON GRATED FRESH GINGER

1 GARLIC CLOVE, GRATED

$1/2$ TEASPOON SUGAR

1 TEASPOON TOASTED SESAME SEEDS

MEASURE the soy sauce, sesame oil, scallions, ginger, garlic, sugar, and sesame seeds into a 1-gallon zip-top bag and shake or squeeze until blended.

SPICY MARINADE FOR POKE: Add 1 teaspoon sriracha sauce.

POKE

FOR 4 TO 6 SERVINGS, add 1 pound ahi tuna or salmon, cut into $1/2$-inch cubes, to the Marinade for Poke in the zip-top bag and turn to coat. Seal the bag, letting out all the air. Marinate for at least 45 minutes and up to 1 hour in the refrigerator.

Serve the chilled poke, marinade and all, with diced avocados.

Spicy Mango-Habanero Marinade

A trip to Maui, where every dish from appetizer to entrée to dessert was loaded with mangoes, inspired this marinade. The sweet and sour character of mangoes makes them particularly well suited for use in savory preparations such as this. If habaneros are too hot for your taste, substitute one or two Fresno chiles.

TOOLS: blender • 1-gallon zip-top bag

YIELD: about 1¼ cups (enough for about 6 servings)

3 TABLESPOONS FRESHLY SQUEEZED LIME JUICE

2 TABLESPOONS CANOLA OIL

1 SMALL MANGO, DICED

¼ CUP DICED RED ONION

1 HABANERO CHILE, STEMMED

KOSHER SALT

COMBINE the lime juice, oil, mango, onion, and habanero in a blender and blend until smooth. Season to taste with salt.

SUGGESTED USES: cubes of boneless, skinless chicken thighs or pork sirloin (marinated 2 hours to overnight) or cubes of fish fillets (especially mahi-mahi or swordfish), shrimp, or sea scallops (marinated 20 to 45 minutes), skewered and grilled

GRILLED MAHI-MAHI OR SWORDFISH KABOBS

FOR 6 SERVINGS, combine the Spicy Mango-Habanero Marinade and 6 skinned, boneless mahi-mahi fillets or swordfish steaks (6 to 8 ounces each; the swordfish should be about 1 inch thick), cut into 1¼-inch pieces, in a 1-gallon zip-top bag and turn to coat. Seal the bag, letting out all the air. Marinate for at least 20 minutes and up to 45 minutes at room temperature.

Remove the fish from the marinade, pat dry with paper towels, and skewer, alternating with chunks of red and green bell peppers, Maui onion, and pineapple, onto bamboo skewers that have been soaked in water. Grill the skewers on an oiled grill grate over direct high heat until the fish is just cooked through, 10 to 12 minutes, turning once. The fish will begin to flake when it is just cooked through.

Serve these kabobs with coconut or plain sticky rice.

Mango-Ginger Marinade

After experimenting with my island-style Spicy Mango-Habanero Marinade (page 273), I discovered that I love mango marinades! I was immediately inspired to create more variations on the theme, and this was one of the resulting recipes.

TOOLS: blender • 1-gallon zip-top bag

YIELD: about 3/4 cup (enough for 4 to 6 servings)

1 TABLESPOON CANOLA OIL

1 TABLESPOON FRESHLY SQUEEZED LIME JUICE

1 TABLESPOON SOY SAUCE

1/2 LARGE MANGO, DICED

1 TEASPOON MINCED FRESH GINGER

1 GARLIC CLOVE, SLICED

1 TABLESPOON PACKED LIGHT BROWN SUGAR

GENEROUS PINCH OF CAYENNE PEPPER

KOSHER SALT

COMBINE the oil, lime juice, soy sauce, mango, ginger, garlic, brown sugar, and cayenne in a blender and blend until smooth. Season to taste with salt.

SUGGESTED USES: boneless, skinless chicken thighs or pork chops (marinated 2 hours to overnight) or fish fillets (especially mahi-mahi or swordfish), shrimp, or sea scallops (marinated 20 to 45 minutes), grilled

GRILLED CHICKEN THIGHS

FOR 6 SERVINGS, combine the Mango-Ginger Marinade and 12 boneless, skinless chicken thighs (about 4 ounces each) in a 1-gallon zip-top bag and turn to coat. Seal the bag, letting out all the air. Marinate for at least 2 hours and up to overnight in the refrigerator.

Set the bag aside at room temperature for about half an hour. Remove the chicken from the marinade, pat dry with paper towels, then grill, covered, on an oiled grill grate over direct medium heat until just cooked through, 12 to 14 minutes, turning once. The chicken will be firm to the touch and the juices will run clear when it is just cooked through. Tent the chicken with foil and let rest for 5 to 10 minutes before serving.

Serve these chicken thighs with coconut rice and grilled pineapple slices.

Mango-Cilantro Marinade

This is yet another recipe I whipped up when I was on my mango marinade kick. It is as flavorful as it is colorful.

TOOLS: blender • 1-gallon zip-top bag

YIELD: about 1 cup (enough for 5 to 8 servings)

1 TABLESPOON CANOLA OIL

1 TABLESPOON FRESHLY SQUEEZED LIME JUICE

1/4 CUP LIGHTLY PACKED FRESH CILANTRO LEAVES

1/2 LARGE MANGO, DICED

1 GARLIC CLOVE, SLICED

KOSHER SALT

FRESHLY GROUND BLACK PEPPER

COMBINE the oil, lime juice, cilantro, mango, and garlic in a blender and blend until smooth. Season to taste with salt and pepper.

SUGGESTED USES: boneless, skinless chicken thighs or pork chops (marinated 2 hours to overnight) or fish fillets (especially mahi-mahi or swordfish), shrimp, or sea scallops (marinated 20 to 45 minutes), grilled

GRILLED MAHI-MAHI FILLETS OR SWORDFISH STEAKS

FOR 8 SERVINGS, combine the Mango-Cilantro Marinade and 8 skinned, boneless mahi-mahi fillets or swordfish steaks (6 to 8 ounces each; the swordfish should be about 1 inch thick) in a 1-gallon zip-top bag and turn to coat. Seal the bag, letting out all the air. Marinate for at least 20 minutes and up to 45 minutes at room temperature.

Remove the fillets from the marinade, pat dry with paper towels, then grill on an oiled grill grate over direct high heat until just cooked through, 10 to 12 minutes, turning once. The fillets will begin to flake when they are just cooked through.

Serve these fish fillets with coconut rice or on brioche buns with a salsa of mango, fresh cilantro, red onion, jalapeño, and lime juice.

Passion Fruit Marinade

Though passion fruit is most commonly used for desserts and sweet preparations, its tart and exotic floral flavor makes it perfectly suited for use as the main ingredient in a marinade.

TOOLS: fine-mesh sieve • 1-gallon zip-top bag

YIELD: about 1/2 cup (enough for 2 to 4 servings)

3 PASSION FRUITS (SEE BELOW)

2 TABLESPOONS CANOLA OIL

2 TABLESPOONS GRATED RED ONION

1 GARLIC CLOVE, MINCED

1 SERRANO CHILE, SEEDED AND MINCED

1 TABLESPOON PACKED LIGHT BROWN SUGAR

KOSHER SALT

FRESHLY GROUND BLACK PEPPER

HALVE the passion fruits and scoop out the flesh with a spoon. Force the passion fruit flesh through a fine-mesh sieve to remove the seeds. Measure the passion fruit puree, oil, onion, garlic, serrano, and brown sugar into a 1-gallon zip-top bag and shake or squeeze until blended. Season to taste with salt and pepper.

PASSION FRUIT	Ripe passion fruit should look shrunken and wrinkled or, as I like to say, *shrinkled*. One passion fruit will yield approximately 1 tablespoon (1/2 ounce) of puree. Thawed frozen passion fruit puree, if available, can be used in place of fresh passion fruits.

SUGGESTED USES: chicken breasts, pork chops, or beef (especially flank) steaks (marinated 2 hours to overnight) or fish fillets (especially mahi-mahi or swordfish), shrimp, or sea scallops (marinated 20 to 45 minutes), grilled

GRILLED CHICKEN BREASTS

FOR 4 SERVINGS, add 4 boneless, skinless chicken breasts (about 8 ounces each), pounded to an even thickness of $1/2$ to $3/4$ inch, to the Passion Fruit Marinade in the zip-top bag and turn to coat. Seal the bag, letting out all the air. Marinate for **at least 2 hours and up to overnight** in the refrigerator.

Set the bag aside at room temperature for about half an hour. Remove the chicken from the marinade, pat dry with paper towels, then grill on an oiled grill grate over direct high heat until just cooked through, 10 to 12 minutes, turning once. The chicken will be firm to the touch and the juices will run clear when it is just cooked through. Tent the chicken with foil and let rest for 5 to 10 minutes before serving.

Serve the chicken breasts with coconut rice and grilled pineapple and mango slices.

Papaya-Chile Marinade

This marinade is for those of you who love the musky, tropical flavor of papaya. Papaya contains an enzyme that breaks down protein, so the recipe calls for diced papaya rather than puree or juice and a relatively short marination time to ensure that the meat does not become mushy.

TOOL: 1-gallon zip-top bag

YIELD: about 1 cup (enough for 5 to 8 servings)

3 TABLESPOONS CANOLA OIL

3 TABLESPOONS FRESHLY SQUEEZED LIME JUICE

3 TABLESPOONS SOY SAUCE

1/2 CUP DICED PAPAYA

1 SHALLOT, MINCED

1/2 TEASPOON MINCED FRESH GINGER

1 GARLIC CLOVE, MINCED

1 JALAPEÑO, SEEDED AND MINCED

1 Fresno CHILE, SEEDED AND MINCED

3 TABLESPOONS PACKED LIGHT BROWN SUGAR

GENEROUS PINCH OF CAYENNE PEPPER

FRESHLY GROUND BLACK PEPPER

MEASURE the oil, lime juice, soy sauce, papaya, shallot, ginger, garlic, jalapeño, Fresno chile, brown sugar, and cayenne into a 1-gallon zip-top bag until blended. Season to taste with black pepper.

SUGGESTED USES: chicken breasts, pork chops, or beef steaks (marinated 2 to 6 hours) or fish fillets (especially mahi-mahi or swordfish), shrimp, or sea scallops (marinated 20 to 45 minutes), grilled

GRILLED RIB-EYE OR STRIP STEAKS

FOR 8 SERVINGS, add **8 boneless rib-eye or strip steaks (1 to 1¼ inches thick)** to the Papaya-Chile Marinade in the zip-top bag and turn to coat. Seal the bag, letting out all the air. Marinate for **at least 2 hours and up to 6 hours** in the refrigerator.

Set the bag aside at room temperature for about half an hour. Remove the steaks from the marinade, pat dry with paper towels, then grill over direct high heat until medium-rare, 12 to 14 minutes (or until the desired doneness), turning once. Moisture will just begin to accumulate on the surface of the steaks when they are medium-rare. Tent the steaks with foil and let rest for 5 to 10 minutes before serving.

Serve the steaks with a salsa of diced papaya, red onion, jalapeños, minced fresh cilantro, and freshly squeezed lime juice.

Pineapple-Soy Marinade

This marinade is inspired by one that an extremely popular Tex-Mex restaurant chain uses for its signature fajitas. I actually think that it has more of a Hawaiian flavor profile, so I like to serve the food I marinate it in with sticky rice instead of tortillas and salsa. Be sure to use pasteurized pineapple juice, as fresh pineapple juice contains an enzyme that can cause marinated foods to become mushy.

TOOL: 1-gallon zip-top bag

YIELD: about 1/2 cup (enough for 2 to 6 servings)

1/4 CUP PASTEURIZED PINEAPPLE JUICE

2 TABLESPOONS SOY SAUCE

1 TABLESPOON CANOLA OIL

2 GARLIC CLOVES, MINCED

GENEROUS PINCH OF CRUSHED RED PEPPER

MEASURE the pineapple juice, soy sauce, oil, garlic, and crushed red pepper into a 1-gallon zip-top bag and shake or squeeze until blended.

SUGGESTED USES: chicken breasts, pork chops, or beef steaks (marinated 2 hours to overnight) or fish fillets or shrimp (marinated 20 to 45 minutes), grilled

GRILLED FLANK STEAKS

FOR 4 TO 6 SERVINGS, add 2 flank steaks (1 to 1 1/2 pounds each) to the Pineapple-Soy Marinade in the zip-top bag and turn to coat. Seal the bag, letting out all the air. Marinate for at least 2 hours and up to overnight in the refrigerator.

Set the bag aside at room temperature for about half an hour. Remove the steaks from the marinade, pat dry with paper towels, then grill over direct high heat until medium-rare, 10 to 12 minutes (or until the desired doneness), turning once. Moisture will just begin to accumulate on the surface of the steaks when they are medium-rare. Tent the steaks with foil and let rest for 5 to 10 minutes before carving and serving.

Serve the steaks, thinly sliced, with sticky rice and steamed or stir-fried vegetables.

DESSERT AND SWEET
MARINADES

When fruit is soaked in a flavorful liquid, we say that the fruit is macerated rather than marinated. The flavorful liquid is most often a syrup made with sugar, honey, or other sweetener and flavorings such as herbs, spices, and liqueurs. As recipes like Cayenne-Lime Syrup, Spiced Red Wine Syrup, and Caramel-Vanilla Syrup demonstrate, macerated fruit can be enjoyed raw or cooked—especially on the grill.

Mint Syrup

Fruit soaked in this syrup makes a light and refreshing finish to any meal.

TOOLS: saucepan • blender • 1-gallon zip-top bag

YIELD: about 1/3 cup (enough for about 8 servings)

1/4 CUP SUGAR

1/4 CUP WATER

1/4 CUP LIGHTLY PACKED FRESH MINT LEAVES

COMBINE the sugar and water in a small saucepan and heat until the sugar dissolves. Let cool to room temperature. Combine the syrup and mint in a blender and blend until smooth.

MACERATED MELON AND BERRIES

FOR 6 TO 8 SERVINGS, combine the Mint Syrup and 3 pounds (total weight) watermelon, cantaloupe, and honeydew, cut into 1-inch cubes, and assorted berries in a 1-gallon zip-top bag and turn to coat. Seal the bag, letting out all the air. Macerate for at least 30 minutes and up to 45 minutes at room temperature.

Serve the fruit, syrup and all, as a fruit salad or dessert.

Lemon Balm–Mint Syrup

Here's a fresh-flavored syrup to make if you have lemon balm in your garden.

TOOLS: saucepan • blender • 1-gallon zip-top bag

YIELD: about 1/3 cup (enough for about 8 servings)

1/4 CUP SUGAR

1/4 CUP WATER

1/4 CUP LIGHTLY PACKED FRESH LEMON BALM LEAVES

1 TABLESPOON LIGHTLY PACKED FRESH MINT LEAVES

COMBINE the sugar and water in a small saucepan and heat until the sugar dissolves. Let cool to room temperature. Combine the syrup, lemon balm, and mint in a blender and blend until smooth.

MACERATED MELON AND BERRIES

FOR 6 TO 8 SERVINGS, combine the Lemon Balm–Mint Syrup and 3 pounds (total weight) watermelon, cantaloupe, and honeydew, cut into 1-inch cubes, and assorted berries in a 1-gallon zip-top bag and turn to coat. Seal the bag, letting out all the air. Macerate for at least 30 minutes and up to 45 minutes at room temperature.

Serve the fruit, syrup and all, as a fruit salad or dessert.

Basil Syrup

Basil works wonders with sweet as well as savory flavors, as this syrup proves.

TOOLS: saucepan • blender • 1-gallon zip-top bag

YIELD: about 1/3 cup (enough for about 8 servings)

1/4 CUP SUGAR

1/4 CUP WATER

1/4 CUP LIGHTLY PACKED FRESH BASIL LEAVES

COMBINE the sugar and water in a small saucepan and heat until the sugar dissolves. Let cool to room temperature. Combine the syrup and basil in a blender and blend until smooth.

MACERATED MELON AND BERRIES

FOR 6 TO 8 SERVINGS, combine the Basil Syrup and 3 pounds (total weight) watermelon, cantaloupe, and honeydew, cut into 1-inch cubes, and assorted berries in a 1-gallon zip-top bag and turn to coat. Seal the bag, letting out all the air. Macerate for at least 30 minutes and up to 45 minutes at room temperature.

Serve the fruit, syrup and all, as a fruit salad or dessert.

Cinnamon Syrup

This syrup tastes sort of like Red Hots candy—if you're a true cinnamon fan, you'll love it. I also like it with peeled and sliced oranges or tangerines.

TOOLS: saucepan • 1-gallon zip-top bag

YIELD: about $1/3$ cup (enough for about 8 servings)

1/4 CUP SUGAR

1/4 CUP WATER

1/4 TEASPOON GROUND CINNAMON

COMBINE the sugar, water, and cinnamon in a small saucepan and bring to a boil. Remove from the heat and let cool to room temperature.

GRILLED FRUIT

FOR 6 TO 8 SERVINGS, combine the Cinnamon Syrup and 3 pounds (total weight) quartered ripe but still firm apricots, peaches, nectarines, and/or plums, or pineapple cut into $1/2$- to $3/4$-inch-thick slices, in a 1-gallon zip-top bag and turn to coat. Seal the bag, letting out all the air. Macerate for at least 30 minutes and up to 45 minutes at room temperature.

Remove the fruit from the syrup. Grill the fruit on an oiled grill grate over direct high heat until just heated through, 3 to 4 minutes, turning once.

Serve the fruit atop vanilla ice cream.

Cayenne-Lime Syrup

The popular Mexican street food of mango spears sprinkled with cayenne, lime juice, and salt inspired this spicy, zesty syrup.

TOOLS: saucepan • 1-gallon zip-top bag

YIELD: about 1/2 cup (enough for about 10 servings)

1/4 CUP SUGAR

1/4 CUP WATER

2 TEASPOONS GRATED LIME ZEST

GENEROUS PINCH OF CAYENNE PEPPER

1 TABLESPOON FRESHLY SQUEEZED LIME JUICE

KOSHER SALT

COMBINE the sugar, water, lime zest, and cayenne in a small saucepan and bring to a boil. Remove from the heat and let cool to room temperature. Stir in the lime juice and season to taste with salt.

MACERATED TROPICAL FRUIT

FOR 6 TO 8 SERVINGS, combine the Cayenne-Lime Syrup and 3 pounds (total weight) pineapple and/or mango, cut into wedges, in a 1-gallon zip-top bag and turn to coat. Seal the bag, letting out all the air. Macerate for at least 30 minutes and up to 45 minutes at room temperature.

Serve the fruit, syrup and all, as a snack.

Lavender Syrup

Lavender, in combination with honey and lemon, is one of my favorite ways to add interest to fruit.

TOOLS: saucepan • fine-mesh sieve • 1-gallon zip-top bag

YIELD: about 2/3 cup (enough for about 16 servings)

1/4 CUP HONEY

1/4 CUP WATER

1 TABLESPOON DRIED LAVENDER FLOWERS (SEE BELOW)

1/4 CUP FRESHLY SQUEEZED LEMON JUICE

COMBINE the honey, water, and lavender in a small saucepan and bring to a boil. Remove from the heat and let cool to room temperature. Strain through a fine-mesh sieve and stir in the lemon juice.

LAVENDER	When using lavender in your cooking, make absolutely certain that it's unsprayed and suitable for human consumption. Edible, culinary-grade lavender—which is sometimes a component of herbes de Provence (see page 188)—is available in the spice section of most gourmet shops.

MACERATED FRUIT

FOR 6 TO 8 SERVINGS, combine the Lavender Syrup and 3 pounds (total weight) watermelon, cantaloupe, honeydew, and pineapple, cut into 1-inch cubes, and raspberries, halved strawberries, and stemmed grapes in a 1-gallon zip-top bag and turn to coat. Seal the bag, letting out all the air. Macerate for at least 30 minutes and up to 45 minutes at room temperature.

Serve the fruit, syrup and all, as a fruit salad or dessert.

Ginger Syrup

Macerate almost any fruit you can think of—from berries and melons to tangerines, mango, or kiwi—in this syrup. The ginger flavor is very bold, so feel free to adjust the amount as you like.

TOOLS: saucepan • 1-gallon zip-top bag

YIELD: about 1/2 cup (enough for about 10 servings)

1/4 CUP HONEY

1/4 CUP WATER

1 TEASPOON MINCED FRESH GINGER

COMBINE the honey, water, and ginger in a small saucepan and bring to a boil. Remove from the heat and let cool to room temperature.

GRILLED FRUIT

FOR 6 TO 8 SERVINGS, combine the Ginger Syrup and 3 pounds (total weight) quartered ripe but still firm apricots, peaches, nectarines, and/or plums, or pineapple cut into 1/2- to 3/4-inch-thick slices, in a 1-gallon zip-top bag and turn to coat. Seal the bag, letting out all the air. Macerate for at least 30 minutes and up to 45 minutes at room temperature.

Remove the fruit from the syrup. Grill the fruit on an oiled grill grate over direct high heat until just heated through, 3 to 4 minutes, turning once.

Serve the fruit atop vanilla ice cream.

Balsamic-Peppercorn Syrup

Strawberries drizzled with balsamic vinegar and sprinkled with black pepper is a popular Italian dessert, but the truth is that it's worth eating only if the vinegar is of the finest quality—in other words, extremely expensive. This version is delicious even with supermarket-quality balsamic vinegar.

TOOLS: saucepan • 1-gallon zip-top bag

YIELD: about $1/3$ cup (enough for about 8 servings)

$1/4$ CUP PACKED LIGHT BROWN SUGAR

$1/4$ CUP BALSAMIC VINEGAR

$1/8$ TEASPOON FRESHLY CRACKED BLACK PEPPERCORNS

COMBINE the brown sugar, balsamic vinegar, and pepper in a small saucepan and heat until the sugar dissolves. Let cool to room temperature.

MACERATED STRAWBERRIES

FOR 6 TO 8 SERVINGS, combine the Balsamic-Peppercorn Syrup and 3 pounds quartered strawberries in a 1-gallon zip-top bag and turn to coat. Seal the bag, letting out all the air. Macerate for at least 30 minutes and up to 45 minutes at room temperature.

Serve the strawberries, syrup and all, over vanilla ice cream or panna cotta.

Spiced Red Wine Syrup

A jewel-toned wine syrup perfumed with spices and citrus seems fancy but is exceedingly easy to make.

TOOLS: saucepan • 1-gallon zip-top bag

YIELD: about $1/3$ cup (enough for about 8 servings)

$1/2$ VANILLA BEAN (SEE PAGE 295)

$1/4$ CUP SUGAR

$1/4$ CUP PINOT NOIR OR OTHER DRY RED WINE

2 STRIPS ORANGE ZEST

2 STRIPS LEMON ZEST

2 WHOLE CLOVES

1 CINNAMON STICK

WITH a paring knife, cut the vanilla bean in half lengthwise. With the tip of the knife, scrape out the seeds, reserving the pod for another use (see page 295). Combine the vanilla seeds, sugar, wine, orange and lemon zest, cloves, and cinnamon in a small saucepan and bring to a boil. Remove from the heat and let cool to room temperature.

MACERATED ORANGES AND TANGERINES

FOR 6 TO 8 SERVINGS, combine the Spiced Red Wine Syrup and 3 pounds peeled and sliced oranges and tangerines in a 1-gallon zip-top bag and turn to coat. Seal the bag, letting out all the air. Macerate for at least 30 minutes and up to 45 minutes at room temperature.

Serve the fruit, syrup and all, as a dessert.

Jasmine Tea Syrup

Berries and tropical fruit are lovely when infused with delicate, floral jasmine tea. Loose-leaf Dragon Pearl jasmine tea is available wherever fine teas are sold. This syrup also works well with cubes of pineapple, mango, or kiwi.

TOOLS: saucepan • fine-mesh sieve • 1-gallon zip-top bag

YIELD: about 1/3 cup (enough for about 8 servings)

1/4 CUP SUGAR

1/4 CUP WATER

2 TABLESPOONS DRAGON PEARL JASMINE TEA LEAVES

COMBINE the sugar and water in a small saucepan and bring to a boil. Remove from the heat, add the tea, and let stand until the tea is steeped to the desired strength, 8 to 10 minutes. Strain through a fine-mesh sieve and let cool.

MACERATED BERRIES AND LITCHIS

FOR 6 TO 8 SERVINGS, combine the Jasmine Tea Syrup and 3 pounds (total weight) berries and pitted litchis in a 1-gallon zip-top bag and turn to coat. Seal the bag, letting out all the air. Macerate for at least 30 minutes and up to 45 minutes at room temperature.

Serve the fruit, syrup and all, as a fruit salad or dessert.

Ispahan Syrup

Ispahan is a variety of rose and the name of a series of rose-flavored raspberry and litchi desserts created by the great French pastry chef Pierre Hermé. The floral sweets made such an impression on me when I first tasted them in Paris years ago that I have been gathering rose petals from my garden and using them in my cooking ever since. Use only unsprayed, organic rose petals.

TOOLS: saucepan • fine-mesh sieve • 1-gallon zip-top bag

YIELD: about 1/2 cup (enough for about 8 servings)

1/3 CUP SUGAR

1/3 CUP WATER

2 OUNCES FRAGRANT ROSE PETALS

1/2 TEASPOON ROSE WATER, OPTIONAL

COMBINE the sugar and water in a small saucepan and heat until the sugar dissolves. Add the rose petals and bring to a bare simmer, stirring constantly. As soon as the petals wilt completely into the syrup, remove from the heat and let cool to room temperature. Strain through a fine-mesh sieve and stir in the rose water, if desired.

MACERATED RASPBERRIES AND LITCHIS

FOR 6 TO 8 SERVINGS, combine the Ispahan Syrup and 3 pounds (total weight) raspberries and pitted litchis in a 1-gallon zip-top bag and turn to coat. Seal the bag, letting out all the air. Macerate for at least 30 minutes and up to 45 minutes at room temperature.

Serve the fruit, syrup and all, as a fruit salad or dessert.

Orange Blossom Syrup

In the winter, when citrus is in season, select a colorful variety of oranges (navel and blood oranges and Cara Caras) and tangerines to slice and soak in this floral syrup. Toss mixed berries with it in the summertime. Orange blossom water is available at Mediterranean and Middle Eastern markets.

TOOLS: saucepan • 1-gallon zip-top bag

YIELD: about 1/3 cup (enough for about 8 servings)

1/4 CUP SUGAR

2 STRIPS ORANGE ZEST

1/4 CUP FRESHLY SQUEEZED ORANGE JUICE

1/2 TEASPOON ORANGE BLOSSOM WATER

COMBINE the sugar, orange zest, and orange juice in a small saucepan and bring to a boil. Remove from the heat and let cool to room temperature. Stir in the orange blossom water.

MACERATED ORANGES AND TANGERINES OR BERRIES

FOR 6 TO 8 SERVINGS, combine the Orange Blossom Syrup and 3 pounds peeled and sliced oranges and tangerines or berries in a 1-gallon zip-top bag and turn to coat. Seal the bag, letting out all the air. Macerate for at least 30 minutes and up to 45 minutes at room temperature.

Serve the fruit, syrup and all, as a dessert. Citrus slices can be shingled on a large platter and sprinkled with fresh mint leaves and chopped pistachios.

Caramel-Vanilla Syrup

No one can resist fruit soaked with caramel and vanilla.

TOOLS: saucepan • 1-gallon zip-top bag

YIELD: about 1/4 cup (enough for about 6 servings)

1/4 CUP SUGAR

1/4 CUP PLUS 3 TABLESPOONS WATER

1 VANILLA BEAN (SEE PAGE 295)

COMBINE the sugar and 3 tablespoons of the water in a small, heavy saucepan. Bring to a boil, brush down the sides of the pan with water, and boil until the sugar is fragrant and a deep amber color, 5 to 6 minutes. Remove the pan from the heat and carefully add the remaining 1/4 cup water, stirring to dissolve the caramel. With a paring knife, cut the vanilla bean in half lengthwise. With the tip of the knife, scrape out the seeds, reserving the pod for another use (see page 295). Add the vanilla seeds to the caramel syrup and let cool to room temperature.

CARAMEL-VANILLA-BRANDY SYRUP: Stir in 1 tablespoon brandy once the syrup has cooled.

CARAMEL-VANILLA-BOURBON SYRUP: Stir in 1 tablespoon bourbon once the syrup has cooled.

GRILLED FRUIT

FOR 4 TO 6 SERVINGS, combine the Caramel-Vanilla Syrup and 2 pounds quartered ripe but still firm apricots, peaches, nectarines, and/or plums, or pineapple cut into 1/2- to 3/4-inch-thick slices, in a 1-gallon zip-top bag and turn to coat. Seal the bag, letting out all the air. Macerate for at least 30 minutes and up to 45 minutes at room temperature.

Remove the fruit from the syrup. Grill the fruit on an oiled grill grate over direct high heat until just heated through, 3 to 4 minutes, turning once.

Serve the fruit atop vanilla ice cream.

VANILLA BEANS

Pure vanilla extract is lovely, but vanilla beans provide a depth of flavor that even the best-quality extract cannot match. When I make marinades and syrups, I use just the seeds scraped from a freshly split bean. I save the pod to use when making vanilla ice cream or crème brûlée or crème anglaise, or I simply leave it buried it in a canister of granulated sugar for a week or two to make vanilla sugar, which can be used in place of plain sugar in baked goods.

Vanilla beans should be fragrant and pliable, not dry or brittle. They are available at most well-stocked grocery stores.

Caramel-Orange Syrup

Orange and caramel are a combination made in heaven. I especially like to soak slices of navel and blood oranges in this syrup for a more-orangey-than-orange flavor.

TOOLS: saucepan • 1-gallon zip-top bag

YIELD: about $1/4$ cup (enough for about 6 servings)

$1/4$ CUP SUGAR

$1/4$ CUP PLUS 3 TABLESPOONS WATER

1 TABLESPOON GRATED ORANGE ZEST

COMBINE the sugar and 3 tablespoons of the water in a small, heavy saucepan. Bring to a boil, brush down the sides of the pan with water, and boil until the sugar is fragrant and a deep amber color, 5 to 6 minutes. Remove the pan from the heat and carefully add the remaining $1/4$ cup water, stirring to dissolve the caramel. Add the orange zest and let cool to room temperature.

CARAMEL-LEMON SYRUP: Substitute lemon zest for the orange zest.

MACERATED ORANGES AND TANGERINES OR BERRIES

FOR 4 TO 6 SERVINGS, combine the Caramel-Orange Syrup and 2 pounds peeled and sliced oranges and tangerines or berries in a 1-gallon zip-top bag and turn to coat. Seal the bag, letting out all the air. Macerate for at least 30 minutes and up to 45 minutes at room temperature.

Serve the fruit, syrup and all, as a dessert.

Hungry Cravings

For more cooking inspiration and information and the latest news on my culinary adventures, please visit my blog at hungrycravings.com. There you will find lots more recipes as well as tutorials demonstrating techniques used for recipes in this book:

HOW TO DICE AND CHOP ONIONS:

hungrycravings.com/2008/11/cutting-onions-dice-chop.html

HOW TO SLICE AND JULIENNE ONIONS:

hungrycravings.com/2008/09/cutting-onions-slice-versus-julienne.html

HOW TO MINCE SHALLOTS:

hungrycravings.com/2008/12/shallot-minced.html

HOW TO ROAST BELL PEPPERS AND CHILES:

hungrycravings.com/2009/01/roasted-peppers-chiles.html

A VARIETY OF SALSA RECIPES:

hungrycravingssubjects.blogspot.com/2009/01/salsa.html

Acknowledgments

Thank you to Dan Rosenberg, Adam Salomone, and Bruce Shaw for recognizing the need for a book on marinades and allowing me to write it. Thank you to Virginia Downes for entrusting the photography to me and always offering direct and honest criticism. Also thank you to Pat Jalbert-Levine for so capably shepherding this and also my previous two books to completion and being such a pleasure to work with all the while. And sincere and heartfelt thanks to the entire crew at The Harvard Common Press for your tireless work editing, designing, and truly bringing out the best in all of my books.

Thank you to Roy Finamore for being such a thoughtful and patient editor. It's eye-opening the way you organize my thoughts so clearly and fill in the gaps that I leave. Your contributions to this book and the last have been invaluable.

Thank you to copy editor Karen Wise for being a fellow nitpicker and never overlooking any detail, no matter how large or small. Your input truly helped me realize my vision for this book.

Thank you to Deborah Kerner for creating a book design that is as beautiful as it is functional.

Thank you to my husband for supporting me in everything I do, even when it means you get a dozen random samples instead of a proper dinner.

Thank you to my brother Andrew for joining in on brainstorming session after brainstorming session in the quest to reach 200 recipes.

Thank you to my parents for raising me on shashlik and teaching me about the magic of marinades from an early age. And particular thanks to my mother for requiring daily—and sometimes twice-daily—progress reports and for strictly enforcing my four o'clock afternoon break time with a daily phone call.

Measurement Equivalents

OVEN TEMPERATURE CONVERSIONS

°F	GAS MARK	°C
250	½	120
275	1	140
300	2	150
325	3	165
350	4	180
375	5	190
400	6	200
425	7	220
450	8	230
475	9	240
500	10	260
550	BROIL	290

WEIGHT CONVERSIONS

U.S. / U.K.	METRIC
½ OZ	14 G
1 OZ	28 G
1 ½ OZ	43 G
2 OZ	57 G
2 ½ OZ	71 G
3 OZ	85 G
3 ½ OZ	100 G
4 OZ	113 G
5 OZ	142 G
6 OZ	170 G
7 OZ	200 G
8 OZ	227 G
9 OZ	255 G
10 OZ	284 G
11 OZ	312 G
12 OZ	340 G
13 OZ	368 G
14 OZ	400 G
15 OZ	425 G
1 LB	454 G

LIQUID CONVERSIONS

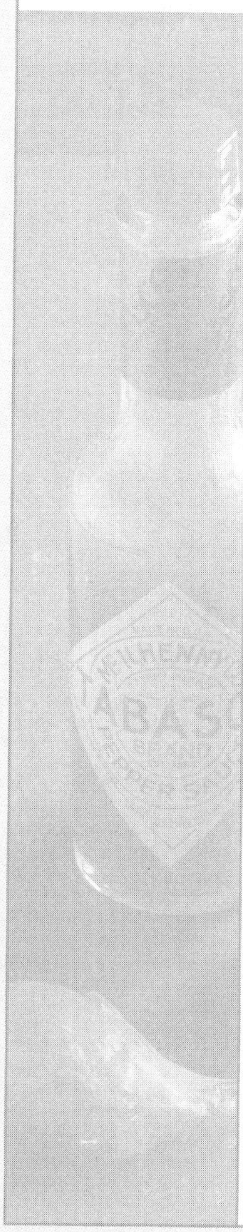

U.S.	METRIC
1 TSP	5 ML
1 TBS	15 ML
2 TBS	30 ML
3 TBS	45 ML
¼ CUP	60 ML
⅓ CUP	75 ML
⅓ CUP + 1 TBS	90 ML
⅓ CUP + 2 TBS	100 ML
½ CUP	120 ML
⅔ CUP	150 ML
¾ CUP	180 ML
¾ CUP + 2 TBS	200 ML
1 CUP	240 ML
1 CUP + 2 TBS	275 ML
1 ¼ CUPS	300 ML
1 ⅓ CUPS	325 ML
1 ½ CUPS	350 ML
1 ⅔ CUPS	375 ML
1 ¾ CUPS	400 ML
1 ¾ CUPS + 2 TBS	450 ML
2 CUPS (1 PINT)	475 ML
2 ½ CUPS	600 ML
3 CUPS	720 ML
4 CUPS (1 QUART)	945 ML
	(1,000 ML IS 1 LITER)

Index of Marinade Recipes

(See page 314 for Index of Suggested Use Recipes.)

Index of Suggested Use Recipes

Note: Each of the marinade recipes in this book also includes a complete additional recipe that shows how to use the marinade with a specific meat, fish, or vegetable. Those meats, fishes, and vegetables are covered in this Index of Suggested Recipes. For the Index of Marinade Recipes, see page 302.

About the Author

Lucy Vaserfirer is a chef, culinary educator, blogger, and the author of *Flavored Butters: How to Make Them, Shape Them, and Use Them as Spreads, Toppings, and Sauces* and *Seared to Perfection: The Simple Art of Sealing in Flavor*. Her blog, Hungry Cravings, demystifies complicated cooking and baking techniques and offers delicious, foolproof recipes. Lucy teaches at Clark College in Washington and Mount Hood Community College in Oregon and has taught both home and professional cooks and bakers for years. A Le Cordon Bleu graduate, she lives with her husband in Vancouver, Washington.